BOXING DAY

THE FIGHT THAT CHANGED THE WORLD

— ABOUT THE AUTHOR —

Jeff Wells is a Melbourne-born and trained journalist, but has spent much of his career overseas. In 1985, after a five-year stint as a news reporter with *The New York Post*, he returned to Australia and began a distinguished career as a sportswriter. He has written for *The National Times, The Australian,* and *The Sydney Morning Herald,* and is now a syndicated columnist for Sydney's *Daily Telegraph.* He lives in Sydney.

BOXING DAY

THE FIGHT THAT CHANGED THE WORLD

JEFF WELLS

Editor's Note

Some words appear in this book, mostly in quotes from written sources or in the names of certain events or organisations, as they were commonly spelt at the time. Many of these words are Americanised forms of English/Australian spelling: for example, 'color'.

Kosciusko is also spelt as per the standard spelling of the day, and not the technically correct 'Kosciuszko'.

Harper*Sports*

An imprint of HarperCollins*Publishers*

First published in Australia in 1998
by HarperCollins*Publishers* Pty Limited
ACN 009 913 517
A member of the HarperCollins*Publishers* (Australia) Pty Limited Group
http://www.harpercollins.com.au

Copyright © 1998 Jeff Wells

HarperCollins*Publishers*
25 Ryde Road, Pymble, Sydney, NSW 2073, Australia
31 View Road, Glenfield, Auckland 10, New Zealand
77-85 Fulham Palace Road, London W6 8JB, United Kingdom
Hazelton Lanes, 55 Avenue Road, Suite 2900, Toronto, Ontario M5R 3L2
and 1995 Markham Road, Scarborough, Ontario M1B 5M8, Canada
10 East 53rd Street, New York NY 10032, USA

National Library of Australia Cataloguing-in-Publication data:

Wells, Jeff, 1942–
    Boxing Day: the fight that changed the world.
    ISBN 0 7322 6480 4.
    1. Johnson, Jack, 1878-1946. 2. Burns, Tommy, 1881-1955.
    3. McIntosh, Hugh D. (Hugh Donald), 1876-1942. 4. London,
    Jack, 1876-1916 - Political and social views. 5. Boxing
    matches - New South Wales - Sydney. 6. Boxers (Sports) -
    Canada. 7. Afro-American boxers - United States. 8.
    Racism. 9. Discrimination in sports. I. Title.
796.83099441

Front cover photo of Jack Johnson reproduced with permission of
Mirror Australian Telegraph Publications
Front cover photo of Jack Johnson and Tommy Burns reproduced
with permission of Image Library, State Library of NSW
Back cover Norman Lindsay illustration reproduced with permission of Jane Glad
Printed in Australia by Griffin Press Pty Ltd on 79gsm Bulky Paperback

9 8 7 6 5 4 3 2 1
01 00 99 98

—ACKNOWLEDGMENTS—

For help in researching this book, I would like to thank the State Library of NSW, the *Daily Telegraph* library, the *Vancouver Sun* library, the National Film and Sound Archive, and boxing publisher and historian Sugar Ray Wheatley.

DEDICATION

To Jessica, Joel and Mary.

THE FIGHTS

7 September 1892
James J. Corbett KO 21 John L. Sullivan
Wins first gloved heavyweight title

17 March 1897
Bob Fitzsimmons KO 14 James J. Corbett
Wins heavyweight title

9 June 1899
James J. Jeffries KO 11 Bob Fitzsimmons
Wins heavyweight title

26 August 1904
James J. Jeffries KO 2 Jack Munroe
*Jeffries retains title but retires and nominates
Marvin Hart and Jack Root to fight for vacant title*

28 March 1905:
Marvin Hart W 20 Jack Johnson
*Non-title fight. Johnson comprehensively outboxes
Hart but loses on points*

3 July 1905
Marvin Hart KO 12 Jack Root
Wins heavyweight 'title'

20 December 1905
'Philadelphia' Jack O'Brien KO 13
  Bob Fitzsimmons
*Non-title fight, but O'Brien claims heavyweight title
on the strength of his win over the former champion*

23 February 1906
Tommy Burns W 20 Marvin Hart
        Burns also claims heavyweight title

28 November 1906
Tommy Burns D 20 'Philadelphia' Jack O'Brien
        Title claimants draw

8 May 1907
Tommy Burns W 20 'Philadelphia' Jack O'Brien
        Burns becomes undisputed champion

4 July 1907
Tommy Burns KO 1 'Boshter' Bill Squires
        *Burns KO's Australian challenger in just
47 seconds*

24 August 1908
Tommy Burns KO 13 'Boshter' Bill Squires
        *Burns puts paid to Squires' title aspirations
for good*

26 December 1908
Tommy Burns v. Jack Johnson ...

CONTENTS

INTRODUCTION

THIS IS THE STORY OF four men who, on Boxing Day, 1908, gathered at a timber stadium thrown up on a plot of market garden in Sydney, Australia, for a fight that would change the world.

One of these men was perceived as a big, dumb, flash Texan 'nigger' who wrapped his penis in gauze bandages so that it would bulge out of his tights and attract white women. Another, a Canadian, was seen as a diminutive, white 'Napoleonic' warrior who brought unimagined nobility and style to his bloody sport. The third, a gun-toting Australian spiv and one-time pie salesman who would go on to enrich himself beyond his wildest dreams by stealing the fight from under the noses of the world's great boxing entrepreneurs, was understandably regarded as something of an upstart. Then there was the great American 'socialist' and 'humanitarian' who saw a terrible injustice done and sent a clarion call around the world for it to be rectified.

But, in reality, the truth about each man was very different.

Jack Johnson was no dumb nigger. Yes, he was colourful — the Muhammad Ali of his day — and full of jive, but he was also funny, musical, generous and intelligent. He would eventually go down as one of the all-time great scientific boxers, against whom a massive injustice had been systematically carried out by whites.

Tommy Burns was one hell of a fighter, but he was no Napoleon, for all the airs he assumed when he found a country willing to fall at the feet of a world champion. He was as much a hardheaded wheeler-dealer as he was an iron-skulled pug. Eventually history would discard him, and fail to recognise that while Johnson had the fighting skills on that fateful day it was Burns who was the father of big-money boxing we know today.

Promoter Hugh D. 'Huge Deal' McIntosh was certainly not averse to a little violence in the cause of conciliation, but that was to be expected from somebody who had lived on his wits since the age of seven, scrabbling for ore in silver mines, and selling pies at bareknuckle fights and brothels. For him the fight game was merely a stepping stone to becoming one of the lavish impresarios of the Australian theatre. Burns may have known how to cash in with his fists, but McIntosh helped pioneer the idea of filming sporting events and so made an enormous fortune. Eventually he died broke, but only after a fabulous life built on fearless risks, amazing luck, and street cunning.

Jack London was the world's most famous contemporary writer and a master of adventure yarns — many of them based on his own reckless deeds — but he was also recognised as one of the first great socialist writers, a voice for the downtrodden. Even though his presence at ringside was a stroke of luck for McIntosh it was a tragedy for Johnson, for it was London who would instigate the search for the 'Great White Hope'.

There were other important characters in the drama of this cathartic day. There was Bill Squires, the great Australian hope and basher from the bush without whom the plot for such an event could not have developed in such an unlikely outpost; Lola Toy, Johnson's white Australian love interest, who featured in a bizarre court case to clear her name; Jewel, Burns' beautiful wife, who became the darling of Australian society; 'The Amateur', the eminent boxing writer who was supposed to uphold the great Australian 'fair go' for black sportsmen, but who became little more than a paid flack for the Burns caravan; Teddy Roosevelt's Great White Fleet, which had rumbled into the Pacific to advertise American power; and above all, the tens of thousands of Australian sports fans who financed the deal when McIntosh's fiscal planning went wildly astray.

I became interested in Burns–Johnson as the 90th anniversary of the fight approached, not just as a boxing writer but as an Australian puzzled as to why this momentous event had not become engraved on my nation's sporting consciousness. To this day, it remains some kind of ancient oddity.

Australia is a small nation which has found an identity in the deeds of its sporting men and women, and has long prided itself as being the 'greatest little sporting country in the world'. It plays more sport than any other country, has had countless sporting triumphs, and has produced some of the world's greatest sporting heroes — Sir Donald Bradman, Dawn Fraser, and Herb Elliott, to name just a few. In 1956, Melbourne became the only southern hemisphere city to host an Olympic Games. It was regarded as the blueprint for the modern 'friendly Games' in which the athletes mingle in a celebration of sport at the closing ceremony. However, nothing in Australian sport — or perhaps any field — has ever matched the worldwide sociological significance of Burns–Johnson.

I have titled this book *Boxing Day*, but it could just as easily have been called *The Blackest Day*. It was the 'blackest' day because it was both a day of celebration for the black races of the world and a day of humiliation for those who would keep them down.

Burns and Johnson had been presented as the champions of their races, and the fight itself was largely conceived as a battle between good and evil. It took place in an obscure port at the bottom of the world and yet, as the telegraph hummed, the western world hung on every blow. After it was over it was not possible for white and black to ever think of themselves, or look at each other, in the same way again.

The historical significance of the fight was enough in itself to begin researching this book. Johnson's provocative character, and his remarkable life after becoming world champion, have been well-portrayed in the book, play and film, *The Great White Hope*. But little has been written about Australia's role in his journey to greatness, and why it was in Australia, of all places, a dot on the great steamer routes, that the egregious 'colour line' — the shameful battlement behind which supposedly great knucklemen like John L. Sullivan had hidden while proclaiming themselves 'champions' of the world — was torn down.

A couple of things held my fascination. One was the sports-page language of the day — gonzo stuff indeed; larrikin argot spiced with literary references. Then there were the stories on the news pages of those old microfilmed sheets. They served to illustrate how little things change no matter how far we think we have progressed.

There was, of course, trouble in the Balkans in 1908, and control of the Pacific was an issue, with the American fleet headed to Australia; without their visit there certainly wouldn't have been a Burns–Johnson fight in Sydney. But above all of that, however, was the race issue. The victory of Johnson, one of the so-called 'inferior' peoples, could not be divorced from racial paranoia in Australia about the 'yellow peril' of Asia to the north.

Looking back, the white-Australian perception of Asians and black people in 1908 is almost comical in its extremism. Yet in 1998 Australia is again in the grip of an ugly race debate. Pauline Hanson and the One Nation Party have proved, with their simplistic but inflammatory rhetoric about Asian immigration and government benefits to Aboriginal-Australians, that the same spectres still haunt a small but significant percentage of the Australian population.

Today, another great sporting event looms. The Sydney 2000 Olympics will turn the eyes of the world on the harbour city and the nation of Australia which, in 1908, had witnessed a black man annex sport's greatest prize in a way which would change the world forever. Ninety years later, Australia is still struggling with its own identity to the point that it has no clear idea of how it should present itself to the world in September 2000. At least in 1908 the issues were out in the open and, as the aftermath of this boxing match revealed, there was no shortage of strong opinion and little censorship of ideas.

As Australia frets over the issue of becoming a republic — the idea of the representative of the House of Windsor opening the Sydney 2000 Olympics is anathema to a culture shaped by polyglotic post-war immigration — the question must be asked: Is there any remaining relevance to our British past? To some that past is a genocidal abomination. To others there is only one fallback position in the race debate, and that is an ethic formed on the playing fields of great English public schools of the nineteenth century. It is called 'fair play' or 'cricket', or as it has evolved in a less-mannered way in Australia, a 'fair go'.

If there is one national trait that appeals above all others when the semantics of issues like racism are stripped away, and their human consequences are bared, this one, grounded in the culture and tradition of sport, is it. As you will see in the reaction to Johnson's victory it may be Britain's greatest legacy to multicultural Australia.

Burns–Johnson evoked a fusillade of debate: Fair Go v. Crook Go. Flash v. Modest. Black v. White. White v. Yellow. Man v. Wimp. Anglophile v. Anglophobe. Christian v. Barbarian. Woman v. Man. It was 1908 and it was only a boxing match. But it was a boxing match which laid bare the souls of nations so that they could never feel the same way again.

– J.W., *Sydney, November 1998*

PART ONE

BILL

1

I N 1906 THE STRIPLING NATION of Australia thought it had the next world heavyweight boxing champion. His name was William Squires, and in the argot of the times he was nicknamed 'Boshter Bill' for his barge-and-bash style.

Squires was not artful in the American style of infighting which had, under the gloved Marquess of Queensberry rules, become more sophisticated — Gentleman Jim Corbett was said to have been one of the first of the new great 'scientific' boxers — yet he bowled over his opponents with such combustion and such regularity that the sportsmen of the nation figured that no fighter in the world could stand in his way. This was an educated guess, and not just local hype, as Australia, albeit an antipodean outpost, was a regular steamer stop for many of the best boxers and athletes of Europe and America.

In the history of Australian boxing the first recorded bareknuckle epic was a 50-rounder between two convicts, John Parton and Charles Sefton, in 1814. The sport flourished during the gold rushes of the 1850s, with an 1854 fight between James Kelly and Jonathan Smith at the Fiery Creek diggings postulated as a world record after six hours of desultory action. But by the 1870s the powers of conservatism seemed to be winning an ongoing struggle against the prize ring, as the colonies, which would form the nation of Australia in 1901, began to take on some pretences of civilisation.

In 1877, former English champion Jem Mace arrived with the new gloves and gospel of Queensberry, but it wasn't until 1884, after the death of a man named Alec Agar, that bareknuckles were virtually retired. Behind Randwick Racecourse with 150 people watching, Agar had taken on a black American named James Lawson and was so badly beaten that he died from his injuries in a hansom cab on the way to hospital. Lawson was jailed for a year. He would not be the first black American to cauterise Australian society.

One of Mace's main converts was the Australian champion Larry Foley, whose Sydney gymnasium would become the great seat of learning for Australian boxing. Foley was born in 1851 and as a lad was encouraged to spar by a Catholic priest. Fully grown he stood only 175 cm and weighed only 67 kg yet he took on all comers and was never beaten in the prize ring. He also became the champion of the 'Green' against the 'Orange' in the wars between the Irish gangs in The Rocks area of Sydney Harbour.

Jem Mace declared that Foley, with his spearing jab and loaded right hand, was the best fighter in the world at his weight. When he retired from the ring he was to become one of the world's greatest teachers, helping shape the careers of three extraordinary fighters — Bob Fitzsimmons, Peter Jackson, and Young Griffo.

'Ruby Robert' Fitzsimmons was a skinny, gristly, balding Cornishman who developed his strength working as a blacksmith in New Zealand, where he moved with his family when he was nine. After being spotted by Mace, Fitzsimmons moved to Sydney to train with Foley, and turned professional. Such was the strength of the fight game in Australia that he took his lumps in a number of fights before moving to America to seek his fortune. In New Orleans in 1891 he knocked down the original Jack Dempsey 13 times in 13 rounds to win the world middleweight championship.

In 1897, in Carson City, Nevada, Fitzsimmons delivered one of the celebrated blows of history, the 'solar plexus punch', to dethrone Corbett as world heavyweight champion. For 13 rounds Corbett, who had become the first official gloved world heavyweight champion by defeating 'The Boston Strongboy', John L. Sullivan, in 21 rounds in 1892, had carved up Fitzsimmons like a raw steak with his superior boxing.

But in the 14th, with Corbett's hands held high, Ruby Robert switched his attack to the exposed body of the champion for the first time. He hit Corbett under the heart with a right and dug a left into his solar plexus, leaving Corbett, who was draped on the canvas like a deflated spinnaker, to be counted out.

Fitzsimmons held the title until 1899 when, like a greyhound up against a bull-mastiff, he defended it against 'giant' American boilermaker, Jim Jeffries. Ruby Robert was thrashed in 11 rounds, but he had already become an immortal part of Australia's boxing pedigree.

So was Peter Jackson, the beloved West Indian, who, at age 19, was brought to Australia by his sailor father who had deserted ship and made a small fortune on the goldfields. A gentle, dignified man, Peter was a champion swimmer and rower before Foley taught him to box.

After winning the Australian heavyweight title he went to America to challenge Sullivan but the great man drew the 'colour line' against him. Sullivan, who was fond of spouting that he could lick any sonofabitch in the saloon, or the world for that matter, said there was no way that he would sully his 'title' by fighting a 'nigger'.

In 1891, in California, Jackson fought a hallowed 61-round draw with Corbett, but later neither Corbett, nor his successor Fitzsimmons, would give Jackson a crack at the title. Like Sullivan they too drew the 'colour line'. Jackson may have been the finest black fighter in the world, and one of the greatest ever of any colour, but no champion would fight him. Jim Jeffries fought him in 1898, the year before he became world champion, but by then Jackson was 37, and easy meat, going down after three rounds. He died from tuberculosis in Queensland three years later, in 1901. After that Jeffries, too, would draw the colour line. But in the quest for a black world champion the memory of Peter Jackson was never far from the action.

Young Griffo, born Albert Griffiths, was a brawling newsboy from The Rocks who developed two extraordinary qualities as a young man. One was his thirst. He appeared to be perpetually shickered, even on fight nights. The other was an amazing ability to avoid being hit in the ring. He is remembered as Australia's 'unofficial' world champion.

He had 114 professional fights before his first loss, to world lightweight champion Jack McAuliffe in 1894, a fight which ringsiders thought Griffo had dominated. In 1890, in Sydney, he beat New Zealander Billy Murphy who had claimed the world featherweight title. But that title was also claimed by black Canadian George Dixon, and Griffo fought him three times for three draws. So the official title evaded him. Great American lightweight of the 1920s Benny Leonard said of Griffo, 'It's just possible that he was the best fighter who ever lived. He was also the funniest, the dumbest, the drunkest.'

It was no wonder, then, that Australia, in its first decade as a nation, was besotted with boxing. It had runners, swimmers, cricketers, footballers, rowers, and cyclists who could compete with the world's best, but the prospect of a world heavyweight champion was stupendous.

Bill Squires had dizzied the nation. The forces of righteousness, which wanted to ban boxing, were battling for survival. The flying fists of Boshter Bill had set in train a course of events that would climax in the most important moment in Australian sporting history, and one of the immortal events in the history of world sport.

2

BILL SQUIRES WAS BORN ON a sheep station near the New South Wales bush town of Narrabri in 1879. His father, 'One Eye' Bill Squires, was a fair bareknuckle man in his time in an area where, it was said, one only had to mention a fight to get one.

Young Bill was a shearer, timber-cutter, railway navvy, cook (with a speciality in Johnny cakes and damper), cricketer, footballer and bareknuckle fighter unbeaten in ten blues before he came to Newcastle to learn the finer points of pugilism from bantamweight champion Paddy King. Defence was never the strong point of the sinewy 179-cm Squires, but when his opponents were on the deck he didn't need a lot of it.

He started fighting in the hard-scrabble Newcastle area in 1902, and by 1904 had 12 early knockouts, a 15-round points win, and a six-round draw from his first 14 fights. He won three more fights on fouls, then lost his first decision, to Arthur Cripps, on a foul.

He was a classic case of a fighter who — not unlike a lot of politicians and racehorses — looks unstoppable until he moves to the elite level. But he was impressive enough in twice knocking out adopted black West Indian and former Australian heavyweight champion Peter Felix, who was in his late thirties, to sufficiently convince Melbourne gambling boss John Wren — who had parlayed the profits of an illegal totalisator into a string of private racecourses — to manage him and promise him a shot at the world title.

From then onwards, Australia became obsessed with the Squires quest and the plot seemed to change almost weekly as propositions skimmed across the international wires.

The heavyweight title was in a state of flux. Jim Jeffries had defended his title seven times in five years, his last fight being a second-round KO of Jack Munroe in San Francisco in 1904. After that, Jeffries figured he had no worthy challenger, and simply retired. But, with an arrogance which went unchallenged, he reserved the right to decide his successor, and fancied a 28-year-old Kentuckian, Marvin Hart.

He matched Hart with former light-heavyweight champion Jack Root. Hart knocked out Root in July 1905 to claim the title, but in his first defence in Los Angeles in February 1906, he lost it, on a 20-round points decision to a little-known Canadian, Noah Brusso, who fought under the name of Tommy Burns.

But all the same, Jeffries, retired to a California alfalfa farm and stacking on weight, remained the 'people's champion'. Such was Jeffries' stature that the world figured that any time he wanted to return to the ring he was entitled to the return of his crown. In Australia so little regard was given to Burns' interregnum that he wasn't even considered the automatic opponent for Squires' world-title challenge.

The one certainty in Australia was that whoever stood in front of Boshter Bill would fall. It could be Burns, or Jeffries, or even the brash 'Philadelphia' Jack O'Brien, who wasn't shy about pushing his own claims on the strength of a win over the former champion Fitzsimmons in a December 1905 non-title fight in San Francisco.

In September 1906, all the talk in Australia was of a Squires–O'Brien match for the title — despite Burns having won it by succession — after John Wren cabled the American an offer. Wren was proposing to bring O'Brien to Melbourne even though the Victorian Government was threatening legislation to ban boxing. If the heat was too strong Wren would simply take the fight interstate.

O'Brien at first appeared to be interested but then, it was reported, a cable arrived which shattered the Australian fans. It read: 'Match off ... refuse to visit a country where sport is a crime and athletes outlaws'. Some boxing writers, however, had doubts that such a cable existed — it could have been a fabrication by the politically savvy Wren to embarrass the anti-boxing lobby.

Soon a different explanation emerged. The London papers were running a story that O'Brien had found himself a nice little earner in a fight for £10000 (or $50000 in American currency), much more than Wren could offer, with the famous wrestler George 'The Russian Lion' Hackenschmidt. Hackenschmidt, it appeared, had been taking boxing lessons from English heavyweight Gunner Moir.

This deservedly drew criticism in Australia, because it would have been an unheard of purse for such a fight. Furthermore, during a visit to Sydney Hackenschmidt had sparred with the old master Larry Foley and had been made to look foolish. Hallowed Foley maxims like 'the eye, the hand, and the foot should be in line', 'always keep your mouth closed', 'timing is the art which enables the maximum of effect in a blow', and 'countering is the great thing in boxing' had apparently gone straight over the big grappler's head, while Foley's punches had gone straight into his nose.

But O'Brien scrapped that plan after getting an offer to fight Burns for the title in Los Angeles on 28 November 1906. The fight, with a purse of $12000, was to be refereed by Jeffries, with O'Brien the starting favourite, and was advertised as the most exciting heavyweight contest since Corbett–Fitzsimmons.

It would also be fought under the intense glare of lights which were now being used in the filming of major fights. The first such lights made the spectators look as ghoulish as resurrected corpses, and the blood of the fighters flowed as black as ink.

There was a kerfuffle before the fight when O'Brien objected to an inflated belt, or girdle, which Burns was wearing around his stomach — allegedly to protect an injury. Burns, who was to have a history of sporting such suspicious prostheses, refused to remove it. O'Brien refused to fight. The promoter began tearing at his hair. O'Brien began tearing at Burns' trunks to demonstrate that the upholstery was pure padding. Burns, who had often criticised the gamesmanship of O'Brien, in turn grabbed O'Brien's trunks. The crowd began to laugh, but Jeffries was not amused. He stepped in and ordered Burns back to the dressing-room to ditch the thing.

This did little to improve Burns' temper and O'Brien soon found out that his favourite tactics of circling and jabbing and fighting at a distance were not going to work. Little Tommy, who was only 170-cm tall, bore in and, ripping O'Brien's arms away, pounded to the body before Jeffries could prise them apart.

Burns seemed the stronger, and the taller O'Brien hardly looked the same man who had easily dealt with big names like Al Kaufmann and Bob Fitzsimmons. By the fifth round O'Brien was dancing and dodging to survive while Burns taunted him with cries of: 'Why don't you stand and fight?'

For the rest of the fight Burns rushed and O'Brien evaded. O'Brien had no appetite for the new infighting; he preferred playing the Fancy Dan at a distance. A clean break allowed him to throw a punch and then move in and grab Burns with impunity. Burns' backers were howling that Jeffries was pulling Burns away before he had a chance to do any damage on the inside.

O'Brien successfully landed some long-range punches near the end of the fight as Burns tired from the chase. When the final bell rang Jeffries instantly raised the hands of both men in a draw, even though Burns had done much more of the fighting and would have been a clear points-winner under today's conditions.

However, before the bout both fighters and Jeffries had come to an agreement that there would be no 'hairline decision' if it was close — and there had been no knockdown in 20 rounds. Jeffries, who looked strong enough to beat both of them at the same time, was not prepared to give a decision to either.

The big question in Australia, of course, was what this stalemate meant to the ascendancy of Squires. Burns and O'Brien were both still claiming the title.

The same day as that fight, *The Referee*, an influential Sydney sporting paper, ran the headline 'Our American Budget', a roundup from its so-called 'Special Commissioner in America', the Hearst newspapers writer W.W. Naughton. It featured a photograph of a big, sullen-looking black man, and was captioned: 'Jack Johnson, heavy-weight colored champion of the world, coming to Australia in January'.

Naughton noted that contender Al Kaufmann had backed away from a fight with this 'tall colored man'. Ironically, a week earlier the same paper had run a story from *The Kansas City Star* about the new prominence of 'Ikey' (Jewish) fighters. They were fair fighters, and no quitters, it was conceded. In fact, the *Star* declared that Kaufmann and Sam Berger, along with Burns and O'Brien, should be thrashing out the undecided issue of the world heavyweight title.

There had been little mention of Jack Johnson in any of this title talk, but now Naughton was reporting that the Texan was commanding more attention from the press. Johnson was telling the world that he was ready for Jeffries, should he return, but meanwhile was prepared to clean up any 'loose heavies in sight' — provided they would 'submit to the process'.

Kaufmann, however, didn't fancy 'the process'. He much preferred a chance to fight Berger. He also said, 'My folks did not like the idea of me being matched with a coloured man.'

'Poor Johnson,' wrote Naughton. 'I have no doubt he is becoming quite used to being left out in the cold … he has performed like an in-and-outer, has Mr Johnson, but, with all his inexplicable showing, some of us cannot help thinking that he has it in him to make any of the new crop of candidates hustle, and for that matter, is equal to the task of making Jeffries extend himself.

'What I would like to see is a contest between Johnson and Jack O'Brien. I have often scored the negro for a vagabond, but I am willing to buy just one more pool on him, as the Americans say.'

In Australia, the American papers were scoured for news of this Johnson, who had, indeed, been signed by Sydney promoter James Brennan for fights at his National Amphitheatre, 'to meet the best men available in Australia'. The immediate question, of course, was whether that included the unstoppable Boshter Bill.

The big-circulation *New York Police Gazette* had surveyed the field for likely candidates for a challenge to Jeffries, who had gone public with the idea that he might come back for just one more fight. It was most unkind to Philadelphia Jack: 'While [his] eligibility might be apparent to himself and his own personal following, the fact remains that as an opponent for the mighty Jeffries he is, in the opinion of the general public, a huge joke.'

And, it opined, the same could be said of Kaufmann, Berger, and Burns, the Canadian being much too light.

'The one possibility is the negro Jack Johnson and consideration must be given to the color line and Jeff's antipathy to fighting a black man for the championship.'

Johnson was telling the world that he was prepared to fight the recognised contenders one-by-one and winner-take-all. If he was beaten by any of them he would 'allow Jeffries to go on his way in peace'. That a man with the colour line set against him like the Great Wall of China should 'allow' the great man Jeffries to do anything seemed to some the height of preposterous arrogance.

In fact, a list of Johnson's mediocre performances was trotted out to suggest that Jeffries really had little to fear. Included was Johnson's loss to Marvin Hart in San Francisco in March 1905.

Hart was considered 'something of a joke in pugilism', and it was said that if Johnson had been any good at all he would have put Hart away. Most Australian papers just looked at the result alone — Hart d. Johnson — and figured the 'dinge' was not much chop. Bitter lessons were to be learned later in Australia about Johnson's laconic fighting style, and his record, which should have had a greater number of clean knockouts to complement his skill, power, and endurance.

Meanwhile, reported *The New York Evening Mail*, the 'big smoke' Johnson appeared to be retaining his good humour. He had been noted, in Philadelphia, 'togged out simply gorgeous', calling men 'honey', and enjoying the prestige of having put the frighteners on the heavyweight division.

None of this American discussion, which had somehow failed to factor the antipodean champion into the title equation, could deflate the Australian euphoria over Squires, who kept on hammering the locals. In October 1906, he drew 15 000 to John Wren's Ascot Racecourse in Melbourne, where in pouring rain, he knocked out Peter Kling in three bloody rounds. Then on 3 December 1906, he creamed battler Bill Smith in the first round before a record crowd at Melbourne's Cyclorama. The best of the Aussies, it was bellowed, were falling before Squires like corn before the sickle.

The opinion of W.W. Naughton was sought. What were the prospects of Boshter Bill in America? Well, mused Naughton, Bill at least figured in the hunt to find the real champion. But he recalled a personal conversation with Jeffries after the big man had hung up the gloves for the bucolic delights of Burbank. Said Jeffries to Naughton: 'If some foreigner came to this country and, after licking our best men, was about to walk off with the championship, I'd say to him, "Hold, sonny, it's you and I for it before you can call yourself the champion of the world."'

So, said Naughton, Bill might have to do a little mopping up of Yankees before he took care of the giant boilermaker. No problem, thought the Squires push. But this Johnson talk was getting to be a nuisance. *The Referee* had published a letter from an American manager, Sig Hart, saying that O'Brien had probably been scared off by Squires but that this Johnson would certainly beat any man in Australia.

'He is clever, can hit hard, and can stand the gaff,' wrote Hart. Johnson was the best big man in the world. Johnson, he said, was even better than Peter Jackson.

This was a bit too much for W. F. Corbett, Australia's most eminent boxing scribe, who wrote for *The Referee* under the pseudonym 'The Amateur'. He was moved to editorialise.

'This is rot,' he wrote.

3

IN DECEMBER 1906, SQUIRES DREW a crowd of 10 000 to Wren's Richmond Racecourse in his title defence against Mike Williams, champion of England and South Africa, and supposedly his toughest opponent yet.

The wind blew down the canopy over the ring and the men fought in the sun. There were no problems with sunburn, however, as Squires blew away Williams in 46 seconds. Squires came in at a taut 80 kg, with Williams two kilograms heavier, and not looking overmatched.

One reporter rhapsodised: 'Both in point of development of thew and sinew [Squires] looked [a] perfect Hercules ... when the eye travelled over their gigantic upper-works it seemed almost impossible to improve upon them.'

Only one fighter, however, knew much about putting the muscle to work. The grinning Squires first hit Williams in the gut then bombarded him with head punches without receiving a blow in return. It was the quickest knockout of a heavyweight ever seen in Melbourne and the Squires bandwagon was now a juggernaut. Williams himself jumped aboard when he said, through a broken nose: 'Well, Bill you beat me fair and square, and you're a better man than I am. You don't know how hard you can hit. I'm sure you'll beat them all.'

Then, in *The Referee* of 2 January 1907, came the mother of all announcements. 'Boshter Bill' — whose motto was 'I just 'its 'em' — would face the immortal James Jeffries for the world heavyweight title.

W.W. Naughton had confirmed as bona fide an American offer for Squires to fight Jeffries for a purse of $30 000 — or £6000 pounds in Australian money. (In all purse discussions the American dollar was five to the English and Australian pound.)

Sixty per cent of this mammoth purse would go to the winner, 40 per cent to the loser. The fight would be held at the goldfields at Rhyolite, Nevada, in April. A steamer ticket would be cabled to Bill and he would be boarding the S.S. *Sonoma* on 28 January. A $10 000 guarantee had been lodged by promoters with the Farmers and Merchants Bank. It was 'dollars to doughnuts' that the knockout of Williams had done the job.

But what of Jeffries' condition? Gleefully, The Amateur reported: 'Jim Jeffries retired some time ago to the comparative quiet of farm life because there were no more kings to conquer. He settled down on a huge ranch, and mowed and hoed and ploughed from early morn to dewy eve, and at night slept the sleep that comes to all who follow the simple life, till his crops grew, and his livestock increased and multiplied.

'Then Jim didn't work so hard, because there was no necessity, and, though he tramped the woods (up hill and down dale) in quest of game every now and again, his load of "too, too solid" grew alarmingly, till some months since, 'twas published from one end of the Murkan [American] continent to the other that the shaggy-bodied retired champion tipped the beam at something little short of 20 stone [127 kg].'

Jeffries had promised to come back when needed and it had to be accepted that he was as good as his word.

Squires arrived at *The Referee*'s Sydney office and, with typical country-boy modesty, was quoted as saying, 'Fancy a mug like me getting a chance to meet the champion of the world, and for a £6000 purse too.'

The euphoria over Squires–Jeffries lasted precisely one week, the time it took for Naughton's next 'American Budget' to be published. A copy of a 'preliminary agreement', dated 28 December 1906, for Squires to fight Jeffries for the world championship, was displayed on *The Referee*'s front page. The purse was confirmed at $30 000 — 60 per cent to the winner, 40 per cent to the loser — and would be furnished by the Rhyolite Association. It was fight to the 'finish' (to a knockout), with five-ounce gloves under Queensberry rules. Unfortunately, Naughton was forced to explain, it was also unlikely to happen.

It seemed that Jeffries had heard of an offer of a $45 000 purse by big American promoter Tex Rickard to come out of retirement and fight Jack Johnson. Why Johnson? Well, it looked like Burns and O'Brien would be rematched and Johnson was the only other credible candidate. There was also a lurking suspicion that Johnson was a class above Burns and O'Brien.

O'Brien had refused point-blank to fight the black man. But when Johnson asked Burns about a match, Burns said, 'If I defeat O'Brien, and the Los Angeles Club will give us a purse, I'll meet you.'

When Burns sniffed the big goldfields money around for Jeffries, however, he went running to the big man wanting to jump the queue. And Jeffries, it was reported, had said, 'I'll box you if you get away with O'Brien. Now run away and be a good fellow.'

Well, so much for Bill getting an immediate shot at Jeffries and the world title which rightfully belonged to him — even if he had given it up. But, even so, there soon came an announcement that Squires would cross the equator to fight anyone for a purse of £4000.

By now Jeffries had been flushed out to the point of making this statement: 'I have made up my mind to return to the ring. The big purses that are being offered in Nevada have caused me to come forth from my retirement. I need the money, and I will fight any white man living. When Tommy Burns said I promised him a match he told the truth. I have no objection to boxing Squires if he comes to this country. I want it to go on record, however, to the effect that under no circumstances can I be prevailed upon to meet Johnson or any other colored man. It doesn't matter what I have done in the past. So far as I am concerned Johnson is entirely out of the question.'

Jeffries said he needed until April, training carefully, to get in shape. The whole thing, however, started to sound like a lot of hot air when Rickard announced that he had no intention of putting up the huge purse, now said to be $50 000, for Jeffries or any other heavyweight.

The fight he was really after was a rematch between Joe Gans and Battling Nelson for the lightweight title. Gans, the great black fighter, had beaten Nelson, the Dane, on a disqualification after 42 rounds at Goldfield, Nevada, in September 1906. That had been Rickard's first promotion. He had displayed the $30 000 purse in the window of his Goldfield gambling saloon and shamelessly publicised it as a black–white affair. (Eventually, he would go down as one of the great promoters in history — the man who put together Jack Dempsey's fights at Madison Square Garden in the 1920s.)

The whole thing was so confusing. Australia badly wanted things to happen for Boshter Bill in a hurry — if only the Americans would give him a fair go, if only they would put Jeffries in front of him, he would go straight to the top and bring home the world's greatest sporting prize.

W.W. Naughton, regarded as some kind of Yankee 'grand panjandrum' by rivals of *The Referee*, had built up Australia's hopes to the point of hysteria. Now they had frittered away and he had egg all over his anonymous face.

Actually, with a big question mark over Jeffries, there really wasn't much awaiting Squires in America, Naughton said. He put it down to the 'bad word' circulating America about Squires' fight in Melbourne with Peter Kling. Reports just reaching America, with the usual time delay, had portrayed it as a ragged piece of business. Some of the Melbourne papers had even described it as 'a slovenly affair and entirely devoid of classy ringmanship'. American writers were now branding a contest between Jeffries and Squires as a fiasco. Squires would just have to get over there and prove himself against other contenders.

Jack Johnson, meanwhile, riled by the racial stand by Jeffries — who before he was champion, only fought blacks when he knew he could beat them easily — had left America in disgust. He had sailed for Australia on the *Sonoma*, out of San Francisco, on 27 December 1906.

--------------------- 4 ---------------------

IN FACT, BECAUSE OF THE communication gap of the day, Jack Johnson was arriving in Sydney for the first time in January 1907 at around the same time he was being reported as leaving San Francisco.

Promoter James Brennan and The Amateur took an early-morning launch out on to the harbour to greet the *Sonoma*, only to learn that Johnson had already been taken ashore, with his manager Alex Maclean, and was holding forth at the National Sporting Club.

The first report by The Amateur who, at the time, had no interest in putting down Johnson, was glowing. He wrote: 'A little chat discovered Johnson a bright, brainy fellow, able to talk intelligently, and as one who knew his subjects well, of American fighting and fighters, and the country's resources generally.

'Our visitor is tall and straight as the proverbial rush, and, to my idea, built as a boxer should be — fully developed about the shoulders, narrowing down to the hips, and comparatively light underpinned. The punching power is there apparently and also the lithesomeness and the agility necessary to evade hostile attentions.'

Johnson stood 184-cm tall and weighed 95 kg getting off the boat — but his fighting weight, he said, was 87 kg. He was 28 years old and said he had been fighting in public — meaning 'recorded' bouts — for seven years, for 64 wins and one loss; an outrageous decision, he claimed, given by the referee to Marvin Hart.

Johnson's early life is a bit of a mystery because most people relied on his 1927 autobiography, *Jack Johnson — In the Ring and Out*, published the year after he retired, for information. Later, when researchers who realised the importance of Johnson had a closer look they concluded that the book, like a lot of Johnson's straight-faced tales to the press during his career, was a bit of a leg-pull, written like a dime adventure novel to make a quick buck.

What is known for certain is that John Arthur Johnson was born in Galveston, Texas, on 31 March 1878, the third of five children, and the eldest son of former slave Henry Johnson and his wife Tiny. In the book, he revealed very little about his family, except to say that his father was a pious man, a school caretaker and preacher. Johnson preferred to get straight into the 'adventures' which, he said, had dominated his life.

But it was later established that Henry Johnson was a cripple who had struggled manfully to raise his family, the first generation of free blacks, and own his own small home in the poorer black section of the gulf port, which was the biggest town in Texas with a population of around 25 000.

There were stories that Henry Johnson had been a bareknuckle fighter, and that he had fought for Robert E. Lee in the Civil War, but they were never confirmed. The most that could be said for him was that he held down a job as a school janitor, and that even though he was illiterate, all of his children had learned to read and write. The most famous story about Tiny Johnson is that she refused to tolerate her young son Jack's whining about beatings at school — his supposed inherent 'yellow streak' — and had turned him into a winner in playground stoushes.

Most of Johnson's boyhood adventures are the product of a fertile imagination fed by a creed of rebellion against white oppression. He claimed that the first of these escapades, at the age of 12, was to run away from home in search of his greatest hero, Steve Brodie, the man who claimed he had jumped off New York's Brooklyn Bridge in 1886 and survived. Many people felt Brodie had faked the incident, using a dummy, but all the same he had built a stage career around the yarn.

Johnson wrote that he attempted running the gauntlet of brutal railroad bulls to grab a boxcar headed north, but had no luck. Eventually, he claimed, he hid on a steamship and was thrown off it at Key West, at the tip of the Florida Keys. He took a job as a sponge fisherman to survive, and when alone in a small boat, with only sponge nets for protection, he got into a serious — and life-threatening — confrontation with a seven-metre shark.

'By some miracle I managed to escape the jaws of the monster until companions came to my rescue,' he wrote. This far into the yarn most adults might have tossed the book away. But Johnson's life had been so extraordinary that nothing could be discounted — save by those historians who figured he was still hanging around Galveston at the time.

Johnson claimed he stowed away on a boat headed for New York, was caught, and made to peel potatoes in the galley. He was beaten so badly by the cook that passengers took pity on him and raised his fare. It was, he said, the first time he wanted to beat up a man himself. For 20 years, revenge on that cook was rarely far from his thoughts.

On the streets of New York people took the mickey out of him by pointing out any number of Steve Brodies. Hungry and footsore, he wound up in The Bowery and was taken under the wing of the so-called 'mayor' and leader of the toughs and losers, Chuck O'Connor. It was O'Connor who introduced him to the real Steve Brodie, who became his great friend.

The plot then skips to Boston where little Jack is working in the stables of some society people. But he breaks his leg while exercising a horse and, after a stay in hospital, finds his way back home to Galveston. There, at the age of 13, he is sent to work on the brawling, gambling docks.

It was on the waterfront that he started fighting, and copping hidings from bigger lads. But he was not one to shy from a fight and when he started winning a few brawls he had himself a bit of a reputation. It was then, he said without explication, that he took up boxing, to learn some science. He must have paid attention, for in Jack Johnson, there would be a no more scientific fighter in his time.

One day his sister Lucy saw him being ragged by an older boy, a 'giant of a fellow', and prodded him into a fight. After taking some early punishment his newfound science prevailed. Next he whipped the reigning bully of the docks in a quarrel over a quarter bet on a dice game.

Somehow, while working and fighting on the docks, Johnson had also managed to finish grade school. In fact he was able to startle many people during his boxing career by quoting from the classics. He may have been fond of gilding the lily about his *Boys' Own* adventures but he was a highly intelligent man; the way in which his speech and manner were later lampooned by hack journalists and cartoonists during his visits to Australia was nothing short of disgraceful.

At 15, after beating up the dockland bully, he was sent by his father to Dallas, where he worked in a carriage-painting shop for an amateur boxer named Walter Lewis, who encouraged him to spar. It was then, he said, that he began to think about a career in boxing.

He went back to Galveston and had his first fight in a ring in an open field. Still not 16 years old, he went 16 rounds with an experienced fighter named John Lee in front of a crowd. But he gained even more credibility from a fight with another local thug named Dave Pierson, over another dice game.

Johnson dropped into the game after being sent to a tailor to pick up his father's overcoat. The cops raided the game and he and Pierson were arrested. Pierson then put the word around that Johnson was a stool pigeon. Johnson responded by calling Pierson a liar. They were brought face to face and it was on — no gloves.

'I fought grimly and as viciously as I have ever fought in my life,' he wrote. 'I gave him a tremendous beating.'

It was a telling remark, for Johnson rarely fought grimly or viciously in the ring after he turned professional, preferring to relax, and chat, and beat his men with skill.

But the reputation of 'Li'l Arthur' as he was then known — a nickname which the New York writer and cartoonist Tad Dargan was to immortalise in the American newspapers — was now made in Galveston. When a pro named Bob Thompson came to town, offering $25 to any man who could stay four rounds with him, young Li'l Arthur was that man.

But, Johnson said, such was the battering he received in staying four rounds he couldn't emerge for two weeks. It was the hardest-earned money of his life.

After that, he claimed he hopped a freight train in the Galveston yards and took off on the hobo life, learning to live off scraps and dodge train crews. He spent time in small-town jails as a vagrant until he reached Springfield, Illinois, where an athletic club was looking for fighters for a 'battle royal'.

This was one of the stories most told about Johnson when he first arrived in Australia: how, near starvation, he entered the fray and knocked out four men to win. It was likely that Johnson had been in more than one battle royal but he was understandably loath to talk about them, for they were a heinous form of exploitation and humiliation of blacks by whites. Half a dozen blacks would be put in a ring, with no rules, and the last man standing would be paid in a shower of coins. Johnson no doubt survived attacks by several men ganging up on him, while the whites jeered and made bets. It was his ability to fend off punches which later defined his style. Sometimes the fighters were treated like circus animals, made to fight naked, or blindfolded, or in masks. Sometimes even the crippled and handicapped fought for the amusement of white 'sportsmen'.

It is also likely that it was in these battle royals that Johnson learned to taunt his opponents and so unnerve them. He said that the promoter of the Springfield battle, Johnny Connors, was impressed enough by his performances to take him to Chicago, where he was put in the ring with a popular black fighter named Klondike Haynes. Johnson lost the six-rounder but figured he had won half the rounds and a lot of friends. Afterwards, he went to the Springfield races and blew his purse money.

At 17, Johnson figured it was time to start training properly, and learn from older fighters. One of them, in Chicago, was Dan Creedon — one of a string of Australian fighters who had boarded steamers for San Francisco in the 1890s seeking bigger purses and (if the Australian fight commentators were to be believed) ended up teaching the wild-swinging Americans the finer points of the Jem Mace school.

On the way to New York, Johnson stopped in Pittsburgh and whipped a much bigger white man in five rounds. He was paid with a hatful of dollars. In New York he found work as a sparring partner for established fighters, but Johnson couldn't find fights — he was just too young — and returned home to Galveston. However, the terrible hurricane of 1900, which wiped out 6000 people and flattened his father's house, virtually ended any home life for Johnson in Galveston, and made him even more restless.

He had plenty of small local fights, but in his autobiography couldn't remember his record too well. Some fights were out of sequence; others historians chose to ignore. He was rematched with Klondike Haynes and claimed a win, although most records have it as a 20-round draw.

In Australian records his first fight was listed as a three-round loss to the Jewish fighter Joe Choynski in Galveston on

25 February 1901. Two one-legged black boys fought the preliminary at Harmony Hall.

Johnson claimed that the fight was stopped by the police as a violation of Texas anti-boxing laws — any semblance of a 'scientific exhibition' having been abandoned — and that he and Choynski were both thrown in jail for three weeks. There are famous pictures of them stuck in a cell together.

In jail, said Johnson, he refined his technique in spars with Choynski arranged by the warders. Johnson had neglected to mention in his autobiography that he had been stretched out by a Choynski right cross when the Texas Rangers burst into the ring to stop it. But it was no surprise that Choynski — who fought his own campaign against anti-Semitic prejudice — beat the slim Johnson: he was one of the great heavyweights of the era. (In 1897, in one of his most famous bouts, he lost after 27 bloody rounds with Gentleman Jim Corbett on a grain barge anchored off San Francisco.)

When they finally ended up in court, the Texas judicial system, and even the Governor, seemed determined to punish Johnson and Choynski heavily, but two grand juries refused to prosecute and both men were released on $1000 bonds.

Embittered, Johnson moved on to Memphis, then Denver, where he claimed a win over a pug named Mexican Pete Everett at the Cripple Creek diggings. Johnson revealed in his book that at that point he had a 'wife' who left him the day after the fight. Her name was Mary Austin, a light-skinned black woman, but there was no record of the marriage. That, however, was Johnson's way — he had a loose appreciation of the legalities of relationships; there could be several 'Mrs Johnsons' running loose in one town at any time.

Johnson was now living in a rented shack and cooking for a bunch of fighters who were trying to organise a tent show — including, according to Johnson but not researchers, the Irishman Tom Sharkey, who had lost on points in an epic 25-rounder to Jim Jeffries in New York in 1899.

After that scene broke up Johnson reunited with Austin and wound up in California where he knocked out Joe Kennedy, one of Jim Jeffries' sparring partners, in four rounds, and big Jim's brother Jack in five rounds. That fight drew a good crowd in Los Angeles and Jack Jeffries, who had a beautiful build but none of his brother's ability, was made favourite over Johnson, who was described as 'a long, lean, bullet-headed, flat-chested coon' and was dressed in outrageous pink tights.

Johnson toyed with Jack Jeffries then knocked him out with a right uppercut. It was little wonder, then, that Jim Jeffries had an aversion to this man, and when white sportswriters began to refer to Johnson as a 'wild beast' it became more difficult for him to find white opponents.

Out of the ring, Johnson had become a gaudy, but stylish dresser, with sharp suits, canes, and golf caps. He sipped wine through a straw, had a good line of patter, and was likened to ragtime musician Jelly Roll Morton. Indeed, some suggested that his fighting had the same sort of rhythms as Morton's piano playing, but he was the sort of 'sport' whose strutting angered whites. He had also developed a longtime habit of running up bills and jumping on trains to avoid debt collectors.

It was around this time that he hooked up with a beautiful black prostitute from Philadelphia named Clara Kerr. He was particularly infatuated with her but she ran off with one of millionaire Cornelius Vanderbilt's horse trainers named William Bryant. Johnson claimed this was the first time he had been driven to the bottle and 'other forms of dissipation'. (A few years later when he was happily 'married' again he learned that Kerr was in jail in New Jersey for the murder of her brother. He claimed he paid a lawyer who got Kerr acquitted, and then helped set her up in a hotel. When the FBI later started hunting down Johnson it gathered evidence that Kerr was a prostitute and that Johnson had lived off her earnings. But they couldn't make it stick. The worst that could be said of Johnson was that he was attracted to hookers. He could not, however, be accused of pimping.)

Later in 1902, Johnson claimed he beat George Gardiner in 20 rounds for the world light-heavyweight title, although the records don't recognise a champion in that division until Jack Root beat Kid McCoy in Denver in 1903. Root then lost his title to Gardiner, who in turn lost it to Bob Fitzsimmons, who turned it over to Philadelphia Jack O'Brien in 1905.

Johnson's records were certainly muddled but he did recall that two of his hardest fights ever were 20- and 15-round draws in California with black fighter Hank Griffin that year, while he was being managed by a gun-toting saloon owner named Frank Carrillo.

He also beat another good black heavyweight named Frank Childs over 12 rounds, but appeared to carry him through the distance. This was symptomatic of the problems of black heavyweights of the time — they were expected to conform to stereotypes of laziness and lack of killer instinct. But black fighters had to eat. They didn't want to frighten away white opponents by beating fellow blacks too viciously, and often mollycoddled white fighters to earn a decision. That way they kept on getting further bouts.

Johnson had seven fights, on the east and west coasts, in 1903, and four in 1904, without a defeat. In early 1903 he beat Denver Ed Martin, a big, fast fighter, on a decision over 20 rounds in Los Angeles for the so-called 'Negro Heavyweight Championship'. The belt had been created by west coast sportswriters who knew that while Jeffries reigned there was no chance of a black, especially a good one like Johnson, winning the real title.

Johnson left California with the black West Indian world welterweight champion Joe Walcott — for whom he had been a sparring partner — and arrived back on the east coast with a posh English accent copied from his friend, and a new ring name —

J. Arthur Johnson. He also began telling reporters that he wanted Jeffries' title.

However, after beating Jack Munroe for a second time in August 1904, Jeffries took no more fights and finally, in mid-1905, retired, throwing the heavyweight division into confusion. It didn't offer much hope for the acknowledged best black fighter in the world.

In 1905, Johnson had a strange year: 13 fights for one loss on points (Hart); one loss on a foul; one win on a foul; three knockouts; two wins on points; and four no-decisions. The loss to Hart hurt Johnson deeply.

Most commentators agree that Johnson, who laughed at some of Hart's clumsier efforts, comprehensively outboxed his man. But once more he lacked the aggression to go all out for the knockout. That allowed promoter/referee Greggains to award the fight to Hart for showing more 'heart'.

Johnson was like a man caught in a time warp — he was the fighter of the future trapped in a present where boxing skills were not rewarded with points added up over the rounds. He quoted Tad Dargan as saying that in the excitement the referee 'pointed to the wrong man'. But, while he may have been robbed, he should have seen it coming. He sucker-punched himself when he had the chance to stand up and make a claim for a title shot almost undeniable.

As a consequence, Johnson was consigned to a meaningless series of fights on the east coast — most of them six rounds or less. He had abandoned the west coast in a rage, but in the east the fight game had been almost emasculated by reformers.

All through America, money for boxing seemed to have temporarily dried up. The sting had gone out of Johnson. He appeared to be interested only in putting on a show, until he met white fighter Sandy Ferguson. Johnson took out his anti-white rage on Ferguson, decimating him, until Ferguson blatantly sank a punch into his groin and lost on a foul.

These were dog years for Johnson. He managed himself and was hopeless at it. Broke and unable to find a major opponent for a big purse, he fought black Joe Jeanette five times in what were little more than exhibitions. Black heavyweights like Johnson, Jeanette, Sam Langford, and Harry Wills seemed to be fighting each other over and over again — Langford fought Wills 23 times! — but Jack had no stomach for hurting his own people, and the opinion grew among white sportswriters that he didn't have the moxie.

In April 1906, however, he did get serious enough to settle the question of who was the black boss man by battering the much-lighter Langford through 15 rounds. However, that didn't stop another smear campaign against Johnson — that Langford was so good that Jack avoided him for the rest of his career.

By now, Johnson had started affairs with white women. The colour line had changed him. He was taking it out on white men in the ring and taking out white women in public. Then he accepted the offer from James Brennan and headed off to Australia. He knew that Australia welcomed fighters and that the sport drew good crowds. The Australian heavyweights looked easy pickings.

By the time the boat reached New Zealand the word on Bill Squires was raging. Johnson cabled John Wren. He wanted Squires.

—————————— 5 ——————————

THROUGHOUT HIS EXTRAORDINARY LIFE, TROUBLE had little difficulty locating Jack Johnson. In Sydney he suddenly found himself in the middle of a slanging match with Squires.

Soon after he arrived he was shown — had it 'poked under his nose' was the Sydney version — a telegram from Wren. It said that Boshter Bill would not be hanging around to deal with the black man, but would be heading straight for America, bent on dealing with others more immediate to his plans.

Johnson, who had been holding court, regaling an audience with stories about the fight game in the 'home of the wood ham', interrupted the bull session to read the telegram and reacted angrily.

'Say,' he said, 'here's a nice thing. I've journeyed thousands of miles to hear that your champion, who advertised himself ready to meet anybody in the world, is going to sidestep me directly [the moment] I set foot on Australian soil. Is this the guy that pretended such great anxiety to shape up to Jeffries?

'Let him go to America. I'll bet his cake'll be dough when he gets there. They want 'em hallmarked in that country. Native-born make-believes have little chance of foisting themselves on the sports of the States and I don't see how a stranger and a foreigner, as they'll call Squires, is going to do better.'

When word of this outburst reached Melbourne, Squires took great exception to being called a 'guy', as if it was slander. In a rare burst of pique he unburdened himself to the Melbourne *Age*: 'The unusual experience of arriving bang in the midst of people who are accustomed to treat all visitors, irrespective of colour, with respect, appears to have turned the head of Mr Jack Johnson, coloured champion boxer of the world. For, according to the interesting message published by you from Sydney, Mr Johnson hardly recovered his breath after climbing up the slope from the Quay than he used all his available wind in a thunderous blast of denunciation of me for daring to think of going to America without first asking his permission, and accuses me of "sidestepping" him.

'Furthermore, he calls me a "guy", and all this before he has either seen or spoken to me. Pretty breezy sort of behaviour this, and quite unnecessarily rude, in my opinion. If Mr Johnson had used ordinary discretion before he exploded, and asked a few commonplace questions, he would have learned that I have been negotiating for a match in America for a considerable time … I am a professional boxer solely and simply for the financial advantage accruing to the business, and I think that there is more money to be made in America for a considerable time, and there are those around him now who could have assured him that his arrival in Australia was not taken into consideration at all in those negotiations.'

Perhaps, said Squires, he and Johnson could exchange 'buffets' in America at a later date, because he certainly didn't intend to draw the colour line against Johnson. As his affairs were now in the hands of Wren there could be a fight if Johnson could come up with an offer as good as anything Wren might be able to arrange for him in America.

Meanwhile, in Sydney, more than 100 'sportsmen' gathered at James Brennan's National Amphitheatre for a beery reception for Johnson. The question of whether Squires should fight or dodge the American was the subject of hot debate.

Johnson modestly avowed that he was ready to meet Australia's best, but Larry Foley warned him that he would be foolish to underestimate Squires as the local man was among the world's best.

Before the occasion, The Amateur had written that any comparison between Johnson and Peter Jackson was 'rot'. But now the prince of boxing scribes rose and advised the crowd that the great W.W. Naughton had recommended the black man as of a 'high-class brand', and that this opinion was supported by good judges throughout America. In fact, it was said that Johnson was as good as Peter Jackson — there could be no higher recommendation. (This was the first incarnation of The Amateur in Johnson's life. The second would be quite different.)

The Amateur went on to say that Squires should stay in Australia and fight Johnson as Burns and O'Brien had been rematched and, in the meantime, would be on the road showing pictures of their last battle. Besides, he reasoned, American heavyweights were disinclined to fight more than once every six months.

If Squires went to America, continued The Amateur, he might have to wait a year for a significant fight, and frankly, Squires had yet to go in against a 'known thorough good one'. It was that age-old argument about proving yourself against class being more important than looking good against stiffs.

The Amateur concluded that this was an era of relatively poor heavyweights and that Johnson was the perfect chance for Squires to prove his mettle. The editor of a rival paper, *The Sportsman*, then got up and said Johnson should first prove himself against the coloured veteran Peter Felix and then no Australian would draw the colour line against him. This received loud applause.

'Sportsman' W.P. Crick suggested that if Squires did sidestep Johnson, then Wren would be to blame. Rabbiting on, he began singing the praises of the great Peter Jackson, who may have been black but had a 'white heart'. Ah yes, he said, they don't make fighters or horses like they used to.

A 'Mr Diamond' said he had received a letter from Joe Choynski — Jack's old cellmate — stating that while Johnson was black he was 'a thorough white man'. He said Choynski had written that old men like himself and Bob Fitzsimmons were waiting for Squires in America and that it would only take them six rounds to teach Squires something about the game. This caused Foley to jump to his feet and brand Choynski a 'squib', which created something of a hullabaloo and, by all reports, the occasion degenerated into loose drinking.

Obviously stung by the barrage from Sydney, Wren countered with an offer to Johnson to fight Squires, if he could match a stake of £1000. The fight would be in Melbourne and if, as was likely, Squires won, there could be a rematch in Sydney for the same amount. It was an offer, said Wren, which a 'good plucky sportsman' like Brennan — as the backer of Johnson —

should not refuse. 'Squires has boxed a number of contests and got comparatively little out of them,' he said. 'Now he is champion he deserves adequate reward when he enters the ring.'

Maclean asserted that his man was in town to make money and that the sooner arrangements were finalised the better. Squires could fight Johnson winner-take-all or the usual 60 per cent to the winner and 40 per cent to the loser. He could also choose the style of the fight — a clean break from a clinch or hit with one hand free in a clinch.

'This is a big thing,' he said. 'It means prominence for one man while the other goes right down under ... if your man beats Johnson we'll shake hands with him.'

Brennan said he would be on the way to Melbourne to see Wren and the highest bidder should get the fight, even though he figured Sydney would be ideal as he might be able to squeeze 20 000 people into the Sydney Sports Ground. But such was the mistrust between the Sydney and Melbourne fight scenes that Brennan said he would have no Melbourne referee — he wanted somebody impartial.

So, as far as Sydney was concerned, a dream match was almost guaranteed. That was until a report appeared in the Melbourne press quoting Wren quite differently — that following legal advice concerning Squires' contract, there was not the 'slightest probability of a match' with the coloured champion.

Melbourne had gone to water. But, more than that, after all the huff and puff about fair play, history was left to judge whether the colour line had been drawn against Jack Johnson again.

Squires himself had set a date for the fight of 16 February. With negotiations being handled through the newspapers, Squires lodged a deposit for the fight with the Melbourne *Herald*, but withdrew it two weeks before the fight when Johnson's money, partly due to restricted banking hours, failed to materialise.

The Johnson camp claimed the Squires deposit was all a bluff. 'There was a nice handy piece of string to that deposit,' said

Maclean, 'and it would have been pulled pretty smartly on some flimsy pretext, no matter when we made a move to place our money alongside.'

Even the date of the fight seemed improbable. How could Squires fight in Melbourne on that afternoon and be guaranteed to catch his steamer out of Sydney on the 18th unless he hired a private train? It all seemed like a transparent game. Here was a chance for Squires to win £2000, winner-take-all, plus a cut of the film rights, and it appeared that he too was dodging the black man. One Melbourne gambler had even been seen around the betting traps trying to get down good money to say that the great fight would never come off.

After withdrawing his money, Squires announced that he had quit training until his voyage to America; thus, there could be no fight with the coloured man. He was still aiming for a fight — but with Jeffries.

The news on Jeffries was that Tex Rickard would continue to try to lure him out of retirement with an offer of $50 000 to fight Burns and O'Brien on the same night. That didn't make the prospects for Jeffries–Squires very healthy, as the Australian would not be enough of a drawcard to satisfy the ex-champ's inflated price tag. But it didn't stop the talk in Australia. It was still Boshter Bill all the way.

In Sydney, Wren was being blamed for producing, out of the blue, the contract which prevented Squires from fighting Johnson. While in Melbourne, Squires was being given credit for breaking away from Wren to lodge his own money with the Melbourne *Herald*, even though it was not so obvious where the money had come from.

Meanwhile, Johnson had been in training for the 'Colored Championship of the World' against the spent Peter Felix. Part of his routine to earn a 'quid' were three-round spars at the Queens Hall after screenings of the film of the Burns–O'Brien fight.

At his camp at the Sir Joseph Banks Hotel, a grand Italianate building in the working-class suburb of Botany in southern Sydney, Johnson was happy to fool with anybody who wanted to step into the ring and had the critics applauding his displays of 'shadow-sparring', a new idea to Australian boxing. Johnson's footwork was flashy as he chased his invisible opponents around a 12-ft circle, but old-timers wondered if it was as toughening as pounding a mail bag filled with kapok, the way they did it in Larry Foley's day. Peter Jackson never did things Johnson's way and he was, of course, in Australian minds the greatest of all time. Jackson liked to train 20 three-minute rounds with the bags and yet he had 'the softness and the glide of a panther'.

Foley visited the Johnson camp and found some local 'actors and writers' there for the daily performance. He was then goaded into getting in the ring with Johnson. It was a chance for the critics to see old methods against new, and some figured that for his middle-age and smaller size, Foley acquitted himself well. No doubt Jack was giving old Larry an easy time of it, but followers of the Jem Mace school considered some of Johnson's methods heresy. Mace fighters had the weight on the back foot. The front foot was for stepping in and out. Johnson, like any modern fighter, had the weight on his front foot, with his back foot balanced on the toes. He also spread his feet and crouched, contradicting the Mace theory that a fighter should always make use of his height.

Johnson, said one observer, was a fine fellow, and an excellent boxer, but the old-timers would have been all over him. It was expected that Felix would extend him in this 'coloured' title, which had first been bestowed on Boston's 'Chocolate' Godfrey. There was also a rumour circulating that the loudly dressed black American was refining his footwork with a local white lady of some wealth. Johnson seemed to be carrying on from where he left off back in Philadelphia.

6

So, IN FEBRUARY 1907, BOSHTER Bill Squires, with his manager — one of Wren's men, Barney Reynolds — was preparing to board a steamer for America. The world, and the great heavyweights of the era, would surely be at his feet.

For once the church was on the side of a fighter. Squires had been painted in the press as a modest type who 'never had much to say', and was low on braggadocio. To the Reverend James Leask, of St John's Church in Portarlington, this somehow translated into Boshter Bill remaining 'aloof from the world's temptations'. A regular Sir Galahad this lad.

Digging deep into the scriptures, the reverend gentleman managed to unearth a sentiment of St Paul, who had once compared himself to a great boxer of his time: 'To the Apostle the boxer was no mere mountain of brute force, no mere mass of animalism, but a man trained and disciplined to a magnificent self-control, a man, in short, pledged to a constant battle with his own passions.' Squires, with his moral equilibrium, was 'a fair working model of Lenten self-discipline'.

In Sydney, Jack Johnson was not showing his usual self-discipline against fellow black fighters. Having lost the chance of an important fight against Squires he impatiently took out his frustration on the hapless Felix, knocking him out in the first round for the farcical Colored Championship of the World at the Gaiety Athletic Hall. The packed crowd was taken by the way Johnson flashed that luminescent smile. Then he flashed one good body punch and Felix hit the floor. He got up quickly but went down again from a punch that nobody seemed to see. He rose again briefly but a right hook sent him crashing for the last time.

Some critics were impressed, calling Johnson high-class. The Amateur said that may have been correct, but Felix had never looked worse.

Meanwhile, at a sumptuous farewell dinner for Squires, Wren used the occasion to attack the 'rabid' section of the community seeking to bring in anti-gaming legislation. He also had a dig at those not so-understanding members of the clergy, the so-called 'pink-headed parsons', who were down on boxing. Squires, he said, would do more to advertise Australia abroad than any of them. And to show that Bill was not afraid of Johnson, he was prepared to put up £2000 for a fight with him within 12 months — no doubt when Squires returned victorious to his native shores.

Wren also announced that there was a stake of £500, the largest in Australian history, for Johnson to fight Bill Lang at his Richmond Racecourse in Melbourne on 4 March. Wren was no doubt buoyed in his efforts to keep boxing and gambling afloat by reports in the press of new statistics on sporting fatalities in America for the previous year. The figures were: automobiling 110, shooting and hunting 72, football 14, baseball 8, horseracing 7, cycling 5, rowing 4, boxing 2, wrestling 2, gymnastics 1, polo 1, and golf 1. Boxing was in fine Lenten shape, indeed, if it was almost as safe as golf.

The Melbourne *Herald*, to the chagrin of the wowsers, chose to make much of the Lang–Johnson fight, hailing it as a match between a representative of the Commonwealth and the Colored Champion of the World. Lang, it said, was being seriously considered — although not quite as much as Squires — as worthy of a shot at Burns, champion of *all* the world. It ran big photographs of both men in fighting poses. Johnson was lighter in the legs but looked much heavier in the shoulders. Nevertheless, Lang was described as 'a man of herculean proportions and remarkable strength'.

Bill Lang was, in fact, an inexperienced fighter and just as well-known as an Australian Rules footballer for Richmond. He was a well-proportioned athlete at 186 cm and 86 kg — to

Johnson's listed 184 cm and 87 kg — but he was only 23 and having only his 10th fight.

He was born Bill Langfranchi, of Swiss extraction, and had been a blacksmith and an opalminer in western New South Wales, where he was a terror in local amateur contests, flattening his opponents one after another. He had nowhere near the overblown reputation of Squires but would one day go a lot closer than Squires or any other Australian to a world heavyweight belt.

'You see, it is like this,' he told the *Herald*. 'Johnson's reputation doesn't scare me. He may have frightened Jeffries out of the business, but he has no terrors for me. His record, no doubt, bears the imprint of a champion's hand, but every time I look it over I become more confident of my ability to put him "out" ... I will give him all of his wonderful science in, for it's the punch that wins the battle ... his record doesn't prove him to be a hard puncher.'

Lang was obviously unaware of Johnson's habit of carrying many of his opponents. He figured the black man's only chance was to win on points. He had survived a few wild spars with the great Squires and could honestly say that he had never been knocked down or even seriously hurt by a punch.

Johnson, as usual, had applied himself to the task of making a dollar on the side as soon as he got to Melbourne, and on the weekend before the battle was boxing exhibitions at the Cyclorama with local heavyweights — mostly confounding them with his jab — and showing films of Burns–O'Brien. Described by the *Herald* as 'a tall, well-built, upstanding man', he quickly ingratiated himself with the local hacks.

'You ought to be proud of your city,' he told the *Herald*'s reporter. 'My word! It is a fine city, and no mistake. It puts me in mind of Washington.

'They tell me this fellow Lang is a good sound fighter, and that you dug him up right here in Melbourne?' he continued in the polite print version. 'Well I hope he will give me a good go, for I am never more pleased than when I know the public is thoroughly satisfied with a contest in which I am engaged. He is nearly as good as Squires, they say. Well, that will do me.

'He should give me a chance of showing my form, for I had no opportunity, as you know, of displaying it in Sydney in my match with Felix.'

Johnson had seen reports in the local press that he was not much of a hitter.

'Don't mind what you hear,' he said, 'for I can hit all right when I want to. I am big enough aren't I? I am rarely ambitious to knock my man out, for I have great confidence in my staying powers, and I relish a good sound fight as much as the onlookers. I defeated the great majority of my antagonists on points.'

Johnson said his most sensational performance had been to knock out Jim Jeffries' brother Jack in five rounds in Los Angeles.

'Jeffries has previously fought a number of men of my own colour but when I settled his brother, whom Jim thought so highly of, the champion straight away drew the colour line. I repeatedly challenged Jeff and posted a $2000 forfeit. Promoters came forward with a purse of $50 000 but the big fellow could not be lured into the ring against me, and having been unable to "connect" with O'Brien or Burns, I was compelled to seek fresh fields.'

Johnson said he was nearing 29, drank only moderately, and didn't smoke: there was nothing more harmful to an athlete than tobacco. He also said he had not trained 'seriously' for two years, and merely confined himself to a little road work: bag-punching, skipping, and light sparring. For breakfast he would eat four soft-boiled eggs and fruit washed down with weak tea. For lunch he ate boiled vegetables and meat, with a preference for roast beef. For dinner it was boiled fish, calf's foot jelly, sweet cakes, and a bottle of English ale. Then, he said, he followed the Bill Squires habit of an early night and a sound sleep. Jack was certainly saying nothing to stamp his reputation as a carouser.

On the night of the fight the rain pelted down on a crowd estimated at between 15 000 and 20 000 at a Richmond Racecourse lit by arc lamps. A preliminary between two welterweights started late and went the full 20 rounds and it was 10 pm before Johnson stepped into the ring, only to be kept waiting ten minutes by the local football hero.

There was intense curiosity about Johnson and the crowd yelled for the umbrellas to come down, soaking all and sundry. To the press, Johnson cut a comical figure in his hooded robe, described by the *Herald*'s man, with fine fashion sense, as 'duchesse' and made of 'chintz or cretonne, besprinkled with damask roses and lilac sprays, with frills round the hem'.

'We don't want to see Mrs Johnson!' joked a wag in the crowd.

According to reports, Johnson rolled his 'goo goo' eyes at the ragging from the crowd and flashed a smile that would 'hold about 6 lb of sugar'. He could have been 'a hoodoo man from the Congo or Little Red Riding Hood's grandmother'.

Johnson shuffled and bounced impatiently and the crowd, now ankle-deep in water, began to sing 'Auld Lang Syne' as a messenger came from Lang's room saying it was too wet to fight. The crowd ritually counted Lang out and launched into a chorus of 'Waiting at the Church'.

Lang eventually entered the ring but Johnson had to endure a further ten minutes of windbag speeches. Frustrated, he leant over the ropes and, true to the way the Australian press were lampooning his speech, was reported as saying, 'Dere all squabblin' over sumpin. Ahm gettin' a misery waitin's here: it's too bad.'

When he got his gloves he added: 'Ah! Dese are good mitts: maybe we'll warm each oder wid 'em when all the rest is done fightin' wid der tongues.'

When Johnson was finally allowed to take off his robe it didn't bode well for Lang.

The *Herald* commented: 'Stripped he made a beautiful physical specimen, saving only for a falling away in the legs. Great muscles, magnificent in contour, are packed on his shoulders, chest, back, and arms. Under his copper-colored skin they looked hard and solid as bronze. He wears his hair cropped so closely that he appears almost bald, and he has a wide constant smile, which displays a gleaming mass of gold fillings. The smile made the crowd very angry before the fight was over.'

The fight? It could hardly be called that. Johnson summed it up with a comment that would later be used against him when charged with unseemly arrogance.

'Oh! Dis is a joke,' he was quoted as he ambled back to his corner at the end of the second round.

The crowd was shocked by how much bigger Johnson looked, even though the two men were almost equal in height and weight. Somehow Johnson, light in the legs but big up top, managed to look a stone heavier. Lang was stiff and nervous and made the lead for the first two rounds, with the 'indolent' Johnson content to foil him. He twitched his head away from Lang's punches or parried them with his right hand.

In the third round, Lang began to swing hard, but Johnson, to the annoyance of all, just smiled and chopped at Bill's head with jabs and uppercuts, bringing blood down his face in 'little red rills'.

In the sixth round, Johnson trapped Lang in a corner and flashed his wares, with a series of lightning uppercuts. It seemed he had had enough of slopping around in the water.

In the seventh, he dropped Lang with a left to the body. Lang got up but the fight was becoming a farce as he struggled to keep his balance and Johnson kept knocking him down. Or, as one cynic put it, Lang 'sought the boards', flopping around like a porpoise in the shallows to avoid intolerable punishment. Johnson did a 'cakewalk' back to his corner after the round, which had the crowd hooting. He disdained the stool and stood in the corner soaking up the abuse with the rain.

The crowd should have been jeering over the lack of a contest. Lang was totally outclassed and when he crumpled in the ninth, from a left to the jaw, his corner threw in the towel. As the disconsolate mob trudged away there was one question on their minds: How would Bill Squires fare against this black showpony?

The *Herald* correspondent figured he knew: 'The general impression Johnson made on the spectators was that he is strong, clever, powerful, far too good for any of our present heavyweights, with the exception of Champion Squires who, on last night's showing, would probably have outed him.'

The man from the local sporting journal, *The Sporting Judge*, concurred: 'That the American is extremely clever there is no doubt. He makes good use of his long left, but the right doesn't seem to be over-dangerous. Most of his blows are of a jabby nature. As to the probable result of a match between Johnson and Bill Squires, opinions are divided.

'Some think Johnson would prove far too clever and big for the Australian. I am of the opinion Squires would at least hold his own with the black, who appears to be a trifle slow on his feet. Fighting Squires, Jack would have to shift more than Lang made him on Monday, for should he stand and meet Squires after a lead as he did against Lang, it would suit our crack right down to the ground, for he is probably the best infighter Australia has ever seen, and Johnson showed no marked ability at the latter game. Should they ever come together, I think fighter Squires will beat boxer Johnson.'

Poor Jack Johnson. He had travelled all the way to Australia to be told that he would stand little chance against an unproven local boy who had dodged him. What chance then did he stand as he headed back home to take on the champion of the world?

AFTER EXPENSES, JOHNSON AND MACLEAN had about £400 to divide up and they saw fist-to-nose rather than eye-to-eye. Johnson, after being sidestepped by Squires, had hung around looking for some more crumbs but there were few in the offing. There was talk of him fighting two men on the one night but nothing came of it.

'It is time Johnson went,' commented *The Bulletin*. 'His inability to live up to his magniloquent talk grows wearisome.'

Maclean figured Johnson owed him £112 according to an agreement they had made before leaving America, and as he was having trouble convincing Johnson to part with it — it was said that Jack's 'entertainment' expenses were running high — he turned up at Johnson's Sydney hotel with a sheriff's officer.

The three of them stepped into the street. The sheriff's officer proffered Johnson a writ, claiming the said amount, and Johnson, after reading it, proffered a right which broke Maclean's nose. Johnson was arrested on the spot and taken to the lock-up, but was quickly bailed out by James Brennan.

The next day in Police Court, evidence was given by Johnson that Maclean had called him a 'vile' name:

MR LEVIEN (for Johnson): *Your Worship, it appears that there was a legal difficulty between Johnson and Maclean, and the two got to high words. They had not, I suppose, been drinking cloves and peppermint, and Maclean called Johnson a big black ——, and, of course, got knocked down. That's all there was. Johnson, like all pugilists, is a most quiet man.*

MAGISTRATE SMITHERS: If a man calls another man those names he is likely to get something for it.

The magistrate took a lenient view of the matter and fined Johnson £5. The Amateur, however, was much sterner in his appraisal: 'A pugilist should be even more forbearing than an ordinary citizen,' he tut-tutted. 'He should sacrifice a lot — even let the taunts and gibes of some insulting person go to the extent of making him almost appear a coward before attempting to use his fists; and he would be applauded by every right thinking person in the community.'

The Amateur didn't know it but, in Australia, the matter of Johnson, and taunts, would eventually have startling repercussions. But they patched up Maclean's nose and Jack and Alex patched up their deal and suddenly — after a farewell dinner, complete with Tivoli showgirls, was held for Johnson by the Colored Progressive Association — they were gone, with Australia doubting that it would see them again. Johnson had been an entertaining fellow and some were even saying that they had never seen a heavyweight like him. But now he was just a bit player as Squires prepared to strut the world stage.

Meanwhile, Squires and Reynolds, after a few weeks' delay while the S.S. *Ventura* had some repairs, were leaving much better-heeled, with a £1500 stake from John Wren to back them and instructions to plonk down £1000 of that amount to fight any man in America. Jeffries, however, seemed to be fading more and more from the picture, with not even goldfields money enough to entice him away from his farming, refereeing and travels.

But despite this, *The Referee* envisaged the following scenario: Squires would whip Philadelphia Jack O'Brien for the 'long end' (75 per cent) of a $25 000 purse, meaning $18 750. Then he would clobber Tommy Burns for the long end of a $30 000 purse: $22 500. Then he would hook up with Jeffries (without the same degree of certainty) for the 'short end' (25 per cent) of a $40 000 purse: $10 000. Yes, Our Bill would soon be set for life, with $51 250 in his kick and, most likely, the world champion's sash around his waist.

For Australia it meant a few months' wait for the news of how Boshter was ripping and tearing over in America on his way to bringing home the big bacon. W.W. Naughton, however, was inclined towards caution. The big Nevada money seemed to be drying up and the Yanks were not buying Boshter Bill — £1000 stake notwithstanding. He was just an 'unknown South Sea Islander' to them, accused of slipping away from Australia to avoid Johnson.

'Maybe the slur isn't altogether undeserved,' wrote Naughton. But, he said, Squires was probably no worse than any of the other heavies around. And, as nobody seemed to want to tangle with Johnson, he should get worthwhile fights.

The man claiming the title, Tommy Burns, was trying to talk up a fight with Jeffries but some of the press were calling him a 'four-flusher' and a 'bunk champ' after he had demanded, unsuccessfully, a guaranteed 75 per cent of a purse of $20 000 (or more) to fight the Cincinnati Dutchman, Mike Schreck. Meanwhile, said Naughton, Burns was making a buck on the 'vaudeville' circuit sparring with the black heavyweight Klondike Haynes. In May, Burns would go in against O'Brien again and that should settle the question of the true champion, as long as Jeffries remained out of the equation.

Naughton was, however, the first reporter to greet Squires when he arrived in San Francisco. He got a 4 am call to get on a Customs launch to get the scoop, but quarantine officers were delaying matters, trying to size up the Australian sensation.

'They think he isn't big enough for Jeffries and they won't let him land,' one of them joked.

Naughton and Squires sat down to a breakfast of buckwheat and sausage, allowing the writer to run his eye over Squires like a trader buying a horse. He was nowhere near the size of Jeffries, nor was he even as big as Jim Corbett. But he looked like he would strip bigger than he seemed.

'His big strong hands impressed me,' wrote Naughton, 'and I noticed the way his coat tightened across the back and shoulders. I saw that he was well-underpinned, and that he had deep-set eyes and a determined face.' But, he remarked, Squires was painfully shy. Not like American fighters, who were as cheeky as highwaymen, and loved to hog the spotlight. Squires hadn't even landed and couldn't wait to get away to the country.

Naughton told him the news that a fight with Burns, at Colma, California, was being proposed for late May.

'Let me see,' murmured Squires, who knew that he had put on weight during the voyage. 'That will give me only about six weeks. Too soon. A great deal depends upon my first fight and I must have at least two clear months to train and get used to the climate.'

Squires was swamped by a mob of reporters and caricaturists and forced to stretch his stupendous modesty to the limit before he could escape to the rose-coloured village of San Rafael at the foot of Mt Tamalpais to set up training. But first there was a curious, but friendly, crowd to meet him at the dock, and he was taken to *The San Francisco Examiner* to be photographed in fighting poses.

Later in the day Philadelphia Jack O'Brien turned up to meet him and size him up.

'Did you notice how O'Brien's eyes ate Bill up,' commented Barney Reynolds. 'It was awfully funny to me. O'Brien stared, and stared, and stared. His eyes roamed up and down Bill's frame, and they sometimes met and crossed over and came down opposite sides. He was so intent on studying Bill that he lost the thread of what he was saying, and stuttered and stammered.'

Squires brightened up when he got to the gorgeous slopes and orchards of San Rafael. It wasn't Narrabri but it sure looked fine to a country boy, and there was a fully equipped gym at his disposal. A few days later, he deposited his £1000 with Naughton at *The San Francisco Examiner* as either a wager or a guarantee to meet the winner of the Burns–O'Brien fight the following month. He was still haplessly clinging to the idea that Jeffries might storm out of retirement in indignation if a 'foreigner' annexed the title from one of the locals.

After another photographic session with the press and the comments from some wiseheads that the Australian looked the goods, Naughton finally made up his mind and declared, 'I think he is as well-balanced a bit of fighting machinery as I have ever set eyes on, and unless I'm greatly mistaken he'll make his mark among the local heavies.'

Back home, *The Referee's* readers were lapping it up, but Naughton, having seen too many big reputations loom up like mountains only to evaporate like soap bubbles, equivocated: 'There is just one thing I am wondering about, and I guess I'll have to see friend Bill deep in the actual turmoil of a scrap before I'll be able to glean any information on the point.'

And well may he have added such a rider.

Later, when he attended Squires' first training session, Naughton could see that the visitor was no artist on the punching bag, no scientist like the Americans at 'whanging the sphere'. He stood flat-footed, aiming cruel clouts. But he skipped rope niftily and impressed with his dumbbell work, and shadow-boxed well out of his crouch. He was inspired to write: 'My, what a whole-souled slugging match this fellow and Tommy Burns would put up.'

Tommy Burns met Philadelphia Jack O'Brien in Los Angeles on 8 May 1907, to finally settle the matter of the world championship. It was one of the strangest set-ups in boxing history. It started out as a fix and ended up as a doublecross. It was a sign of exactly how hard-headed Burns could be in getting his way. As Naughton wrote, this was 'about as astonishing a mess of crookedness as the game of the ring has known'.

A Los Angeles promoter named Tom McCarey had engaged the fighters but claimed he had doubts about O'Brien turning up. The Australian press had been right to have some doubts about the genuineness of O'Brien because he wanted Tommy to take a dive. Burns had agreed to it for the sake of getting O'Brien into the ring.

The first sign O'Brien had that he might be doublecrossed was just before the fight when Australian referee Charlie Eyton called all-bets-off. That left O'Brien standing in the ring, facing a confident Burns, with no way of pulling out and nowhere to hide.

McCarey explained later: 'There was never any intention of palming off something crooked on the public. We could see that O'Brien would not keep his engagement to box Burns unless Tommy agreed to lay down to him.'

He chuckled about how Burns had leaped from his stool at the opening gong while a bewildered O'Brien sat there until Eyton went over, grabbed him by the arm, and pulled him into the middle.

After that, O'Brien ran and Burns chased for 20 rounds with hardly an effective blow being struck. Burns landed a couple of rights in the third and O'Brien commented, 'I see you're doublecrossing me tonight.'

Burns replied, 'That's right. You have to fight on the square this time.'

'I'm not ashamed of the part I played,' Burns told the press after easily winning the fight. 'I always felt that I was O'Brien's master, but I was afraid I wouldn't get a chance to prove it. He is a better advertiser than I am and he has posed in the limelight for years, while I had to play second fiddle to him in a way ... I fooled him, and I'm proud of it. Now I'm in the limelight where I belong and he is known as an inferior fighter and a faker to boot.'

The one thing that bugged him was that he had bet himself to win $8000, with O'Brien at 10/6 favourite and himself at 2/1. But it had been McCarey's idea to call all-bets-off.

For O'Brien's part he admitted that the fight had been a fix. Sure he had a nice suntan for the occasion but anyone could see that he was overweight and not in shape; he would not have taken the fight in that condition without some kind of deal.

But, he said, the dive was not his idea. McCarey came to him with it. McCarey and Burns had cooked up a plan to get Nevada promoters to put up a $25 000 offer for the fight, so that they could all cash in. But Nevada never got back to them. Then, said Philadelphia Jack, McCarey came up with the idea that he and Burns could toss a coin to see who would remain upright; or alternatively, he could pay Burns $3500 out of his cut to faint in the 11th round. O'Brien saw the advantages in the latter. Then they changed their minds and decided that Burns should last the full 20 rounds, but take a hammering and lose the decision.

'That's all there is in the conspiracy end of it,' shrugged O'Brien. 'As to calling the bets off, I believe they simply became suspicious of something. Maybe they found Burns was doing a little business on his own book, or perhaps they thought I might bet the other way, and give them the doublecross.'

O'Brien said McCarey was pulling legs if there was any suggestion of protecting the public. When McCarey first came to him the promoter had said: 'Jack, the long-haired fellows [reformers] are going to kill the game soon, anyhow, and we are fools if we don't get the money while we can.'

Naughton figured it was a disgrace on everybody involved. But, of course, four weeks later Burns would have to go up against the Australian headcracker Squires, and nobody doubted that boxing would be the winner on that day, for Boshter Bill would be raining punches on Burns in a manner which would leave no doubts in the minds of anybody that this was sporting combat in its finest, fairest, and yet most ferocious traditions. The stage was set for the Australian to not only win the crown but to save boxing.

Burns wasn't interested in a purse percentage, even though the national holiday promised a big crowd at Colma. He had demanded a guaranteed $8000 from promoter Jim Coffroth, plus a $5000 wager to cover the money Squires had lodged with *The San Francisco Examiner*. Burns also insisted on naming his own referee from Chicago, but Squires' manager objected, saying that the man was too old to handle what promised to be a fistic firestorm. Then Jim Jeffries' name came up and it was agreed that he was the only man for the job, despite whatever xenophobic views he may have held.

What a strange situation. Jeffries had promised to come out of retirement only if a 'foreigner' dethroned an American, but Burns wasn't a 'real' American — he just posed as one. Some critics also wondered whether or not Jeffries' comeback plans would influence his decision. If he saw a big pay cheque in reclaiming the title from the intruder he might crown Squires.

Burns kept wavering over the terms, with Jack Johnson standing by in case he got cold feet engaging the mighty Australian, who seemed to have settled into the climate well. When the details were finally released, Burns and Johnson had a shouting match, with both threatening to settle their differences in a backroom. They were cooled down, but Naughton felt that Johnson had compromised his chance of ever getting Burns into the ring.

Bill Squires had finally got his world-title shot. The crowd looked at his muscles and made him a 10/9 favourite in a contest set for 45 rounds.

Back in Australia, sports editors perused the first cable from Colma in disbelief. It read: 'Burns wins, one round.' Urgent cables were sent back to California for confirmation.

Soon another one arrived: 'Burns knocked Squires out in one round. The contest was over in 47 seconds.' That was a little unfair as, actually, it had taken two minutes and eight seconds to burst Boshter's bubble. This was followed by another: 'Squires proved the biggest failure as a championship candidate that ever entered the ring here.'

Sadly, after all that patriotic chin music in Australia, Boshter Bill proved to be what some of the American sportswriters had suspected all along. A lemon. A quince. Slower than cold molasses. He came out looking as stiff and awkward as a yokel in his first fight behind the barn. Burns feinted, Squires fell for it, and Burns dropped him like a log with a big right. The punch landed on his temple and raised a lump the size of a pigeon egg. Rattled, he got up and tried to launch an attack but was floored again 'like a blind puppy running into a brick wall'.

When Squires got up for the second time he wobbled around trying to clinch with Burns, but Burns was standing away, out of reach. Burns sighted the sitting duck, walked in and flattened Squires again with another right. Say g'day, Boshter Bill. It was a fiasco! Jeffries, earning the easiest $1000 of his career, counted him out.

Australia was in shock and mourning. Never had a man been elevated so high, and branded such a champion, only to fall so far and so soon. There was no doubt in America that Squires was a bad joke, a juicy fruit, but back home some other explanation was demanded.

Surely it must have been a fluke. Maybe he had been doped. A first-round knockout could happen to anybody if he hadn't warmed up and ran into the wrong punch. Australia simply could not accept it. Even still, Barney Reynolds, who wept after the fight, cabled John Wren to bring Squires home immediately, fearing he might not attract a good-enough fight to pay his training expenses. A rumour began sweeping the bars of Sydney that Squires had been killed.

The Amateur immediately back-pedalled, saying that Squires had never been properly taught, and was a nervous starter, and couldn't really be rated up there with great Australians like Peter Jackson, Frank Slavin or Joe Goddard.

The first reaction of Wren, who had broken even — Squires' purse of $5000 merely covered the lost bet — was that the Australian charge had been too impetuous. He cabled to Boshter: 'Australians sincerely sorry. Deeply deplore your bad luck.' He then sent off an offer to Burns to come to Australia to meet Squires in Melbourne in Melbourne Cup Week for £500 and the gate.

Wren later issued a strange statement saying that there was a school of opinion that the blow which had brought Squires undone had been a 'tentative clout' — something Boshter Bill might just have easily landed on Burns, and something the Canadian might not have even intended. Also, Squires may have rushed in saturated with patriotism and left himself open.

'Squires' intense anxiety to uphold the athletic credit of Australia is, I believe, really responsible for his defeat,' declared Wren. 'For I cannot think that any man of his own weight could possibly be his physical superior to such a degree as to be able to deal with him so summarily.'

Wren may have been a good judge of mug punters and fast horses, but every man has a weakness and his must have been fighters, for Squires stayed on in America, despite Reynolds' attempts to bring him home. He made contact with Naughton and said that he was looking for another fight.

Squires told Naughton that if he had only survived the first round, and had that time to rest and clear his head, he would have beaten Burns. He was getting more used to the climate and would undoubtedly do better the next time. Likely future opponents were Americans 'Twin' Jack Sullivan and 'Fireman' Jim Flynn.

On 28 September 1907, in San Francisco, Squires did do better. He was knocked out by Sullivan in 19 rounds. On 20 December 1907, at the Bakersfield Opera House in California, he flopped again and was knocked out by Flynn in six rounds. Boshter Bill was now a false alarm. Naughton wasted no sympathy on him, saying he looked 'as awkward as a drunken longshoreman' and 'sick and old' at the end.

It seemed that brave Boshter Bill was possessed of the dreaded crystal mandible. One good rap on the chin and he was history. This was one chapter in Australian sporting history the sooner closed the better.

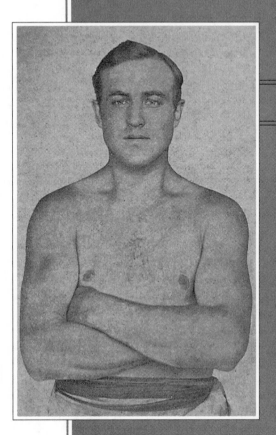

PART TWO

TOMMY

---------------- 1 ----------------

B Y THE END OF 1907, Tommy Burns was in England and the world was trying to figure out what kind of heavyweight champion it had on its hands, for there had been none remotely like him in the past. This little man from Canada had turned the concept of the big, brash, barrel-chested pug in the John L. Sullivan mould on its cauliflower ear. He looked like Napoleon. He even marketed himself as 'The Emperor' and 'The Little General'.

This was a man who later in life would turn to the pulpit. He was, to all appearances, modest, boyish and abstemious. He had a 'little American wife' named Jewel (who wore much-discussed and most-stylish hats and liked to hold demure tea parties) and to the astonishment of some of the more cynical sporting hacks appeared to be 'absolutely devoted to her', as if this was breaking some kind of hallowed tradition of pugdom. She accompanied him everywhere, except to the fights. It was said that she fainted at the sight of violence.

Even Tommy, in his civilian clothes, looked like he might faint at the sight of a flying fist. As the shortest heavyweight champion in history, he stood only 170-cm tall and usually weighed only 79 kg — only a light-heavyweight by today's standards. But he was well-composed and solid, and had a long reach for his height.

So this garden gnome was now the toughest sonofabitch on the planet? Had the great Sullivan spotted him in a saloon he might have laughed enough to spill his beer. However, had he challenged Burns, the Boston Strongboy would soon have been rolling in the sawdust. A lot of big men in the history of the ring have suffered from underestimating sawn-off opponents. Count some of Mike Tyson's victims among them. It is not always easy to punch down at such a man, or keep a good one from shelling your belly.

Burns was fast, strong and clever. He could feint like a magician and draw a man on to his punch. He had fine footwork and had mastered the new American art of infighting, weakening any man who wanted to rest in a clinch. Still, many critics found it hard to conceive of him as a serious threat to the hulking Jeffries. Even as his absence grew longer and his girth larger, true devotees of Jeffries believed that he didn't really need to fight Burns, or anybody else, to win the crown. All he had do was turn up.

It was impossible for Burns to ignore this drivel pouring out of the American blats and he reacted to it in the smartest possible way by actively courting a press which, despite its doubts about his brawling ability, was quite prepared to admit that he was a right little gentleman. Secondly, if in the ring he had an uncanny ability to draw a man into a trap, outside the ring he had a knack for drawing a dollar into his pocket. Real or interim champion, he was going to be a rich champion. Burns sucker-punched as many promoters as he did pugs. He was the fight game's boxer-businessman *par excellence*.

Tommy Burns was born Noah Brusso in Hanover, in the Canadian province of Ontario, on 7 June 1881, and was said to be of French-Canadian stock, though after his death it was revealed that his parents were German. He was thus the first heavyweight champion not of English, Irish or American descent.

He excelled at many sports but his favourite pursuit was the wild and violent game of lacrosse, which was invented by the Algonquin Indians as a close-combat exercise, but scaled down from all-in mayhem by Jesuit priests in Quebec in the early eighteenth century. Brusso was quick and tough enough against full-grown men to be in the town team of nearby Chesley when he was only 12, and loved the sport so much that even when he was heavyweight champion of the world he would occasionally don a false set of whiskers to get into a pick-up game without being recognised. This also reduced the temptation for strangers to try the soundness of his chin with a stick.

Like so many fighters before him he got into the sweet science by happenstance. An itinerant labourer as a teenager, he went to watch some fights at the Detroit Athletic Club. A fighter on the card didn't show, and young Brusso, figuring it to be no more rugged than a village lacrosse barney, volunteered his services and won in five rounds.

He started as a welterweight and the first two official fights on his record, in 1900, were five-round knockouts of a man named Fred Thornton. He had nine KOs, inside 10 rounds, in his first 10 fights. His first loss was on points, over ten rounds, to Mike Schreck in 1902. His first sniff of a big cheque was the fight with Marvin Hart, which won him — at least in his eyes — the world title in February 1906.

Burns, as he was now known, had been fighting at just 78 kg when promoter Tom McCarey offered him the Hart fight in Los Angeles.

'He's a big, tough fellow,' Burns complained.

'I'll give you $15 000 to fight him,' said McCarey.

'Send for him,' said Burns. He won in 20 rounds, and got a taste of just how rich he could get in the fight game.

Now, Burns was sending for anybody but Jack Johnson. The coon would have to come to him, begging, if the colour line was to be withdrawn. Burns' unflinching demand of $30 000 was so high as to be considered a cruel joke. There would be no fight because nobody could afford to stage it.

In December 1907, in his first fight after pummelling Squires, Burns had beaten the English champion Gunner Moir on a 10-round knockout, after coddling him for nine, at London's National Sporting Club, which was crammed with parliamentarians, sporting celebrities, authors and actors.

A fortnight before the fight Burns had sneaked into a vaudeville hall where Moir was featuring. He took one look at the cut of the pride of all Britain and raced out and got a £400 bet on himself. (England has often been a good place for a foreigner to bet when a British heavyweight is carrying the weight of the public's money.)

W.W. Naughton wrote that Burns toyed with the white Moir 'as an alligator toys with a negro baby'. But after the fight, Burns was criticised for making an unseemly spectacle of himself by hissing for his purse money before he left the ring.

Later, he would apologise: 'I am not madly in love with the game ... we are out for the money, you know. My mother has asked me a hundred times to quit the ring and believe me if I could get the money by an easier method you would not find me inside the ropes much. Oh yes, I have an eye to the main chance and the man is a fool who has not.'

Burns then asked for £300 a week to play the English music halls.

After the Moir fight, Jewel was quoted as saying that Tommy would fight Johnson when he returned to the United States after accommodating another English horizontalist, Jack Palmer, in February, and a musclebound character named Jem Roche, who was parading as champion of all Ireland, in March. Jack Johnson and his latest manager, the Australian Sam Fitzpatrick, were on a show tour in Canada when Burns dutifully carried out what his wife had promised, crushing Palmer in four rounds and Roche in one.

'It is generally believed now that Tommy will come home and take his medicine, but he is frank enough to say that there is no hurry about it,' commented W.W. Naughton.

As Johnson would find out as he formulated his own plans for an English stopover to catch up with Burns, there certainly wasn't a rush. And not everybody agreed with Naughton. The colour line seemed still squarely in place. In fact a black second-rater named John Willie announced in America that he was drawing his own colour line — he would no longer fight whites. White fighters always wanted the money, win or lose, he said.

Meanwhile, on the Australian side of the 'herring pond' where news was slow in arriving, the heavyweight picture was the most confusing it had been since the days of John L. Sullivan. The Boston Strongboy was never recognised as a true world champion by the Australian press — even if he had sobered up, got down from 109 kg to 94 kg, and beaten his fellow 'Murkan', Jake Kilrain, over 75 rounds in 1889.

It was the last great bareknuckle fight but it was merely for a phony belt put up by the pink-paged scandal sheet, *The Police Gazette*. Sullivan had refused to fight Peter Jackson, and while on an acting tour of Australia, had similarly refused to fight Australian champion Joe Goddard. It was an insult not soon forgotten.

Australia's love for Jackson meant that it could not tolerate the colour line, but Gentleman Jim Corbett — who had sampled Jackson's mettle in 1891 — had fastidiously maintained it after beating a boozed-out 34-year-old Sullivan with his new 'scientific boxing' in New Orleans in 1892.

Then, in 1897, 'Pompadour Jim' lost his title to Ruby Robert Fitzsimmons, who pulled his left-handed switch and put the dreaded solar plexus punch into the Gent's breadbasket.

Australia — along with England and New Zealand — could claim a part of Fitz. But any perceptive Australian fight fan knew that Fitzsimmons wasn't much more than an old spindle-shanked, bone-and-sinew middleweight when he beat Corbett. So how good could Corbett have possibly been?

When Jim Jeffries came along in 1899, with a 17-kg weight advantage, and disposed of Fitzsimmons in 11 rounds, the world figured that the crown had finally landed in strong, safe hands.

But like Sullivan, Corbett, and Fitzsimmons, Jeffries also drew the colour line. When he eventually relinquished the title, claiming there was nobody worthy to beat, Jack Johnson was disqualified as a legitimate opponent because of the colour of his skin.

So the title had passed to Marvin Hart and then to Burns. But was the Canadian any good? His fight record before Hart looked like a palooka handbook. He had lost to the only fighters of any reputation he had met — Mike Schreck, Philadelphia Jack O'Brien and Twin Jack Sullivan — before winning the title.

His first few appearances as the new king — one-round knockouts over a couple of warm bodies in Jim O'Brien and Jim Walker on the same night in San Diego in March 1906 — didn't exactly help his credibility. But then he began to improve rapidly. He knocked out Fireman Jim Flynn in 15 rounds in Los Angeles in October 1906. Then, the next month, he drew with O'Brien over 20 rounds.

But it wasn't until he dominated O'Brien over 20 rounds in Los Angeles in May 1907 in the farcical reverse fix, that he, Australia, and the world finally believed that the belt was rightfully his. Squires, of course, didn't even last a round against him. So, with only Jack Johnson to be seriously discouraged, and everybody else definitely encouraged, Burns headed for England. Britain had nobody to brag about, and Burns was still a curiosity there. It was the perfect opportunity for the champ to build up his bank account, and he protected it ruthlessly.

There was little reason for Australia to think that it would benefit in any way from Burns' presence in England, or from the heavweight division at all. Squires appeared to be a shot-duck after his three straight knockout losses in America. His trainer, Jimmy Russell, was sending back messages saying that Bill's body was racked by rheumatism and his mind riddled with self-doubt. He had gone off to a logging camp to try to sort both out.

Bill Lang hadn't been able to handle Johnson, so he was not in title reckoning. Then came a report from Toronto — which later proved a dud — that 'Mistah Johnson' had to be rescued after getting into the ring with the Canadian amateur champion, a 'giant Scotchman' named Day. Was the great black hope losing it too?

―――――――――― 2 ――――――――――

WELL, IF JOHNSON'S REPUTATION AS a fighter was in doubt his reputation as a lover wasn't. In late March 1908, the scandal of 'Jack Johnson and a Sydney Lady', as one headline had it, or the 'Massa Johnson case', as other papers reported it, erupted in Australia.

In June 1907, *The Referee* had reprinted an item from a California paper that Johnson had 'modestly stated' that he was to marry a rich Australian white woman named Miss Lola Toy who would soon join him in San Francisco.

'I met her in Australia and after my courtship she consented to accept me,' the paper quoted Johnson. 'I now have something to fight for aside from the honours. I want to make a name for myself that my future wife will not be ashamed of.'

Meaning, said *The Referee*, that here was a white woman who was willing to marry a 'negro professional pugilist'.

Into the NSW Banco Court, to confront the Chief Justice and a jury of four, marched Miss Alma Adelaide Lillian 'Lola' Toy, aged 22, claiming damages of £2000 — a veritable world-title purse — for libel. *The Referee*, she pleaded, had been false and malicious to even reprint such an allegation.

Even back in 1908 it seemed a little far-fetched that a suggestion of marriage to a black man amounted to libel. Black people, it had been proved, were actually *human*. But the case went ahead anyway, like some sort of *Cluedo* game. Who had done what to whom in what room? Was it Mistah Johnson in the ballroom with his . . .

Miss Toy, described as 'well-dressed', had been escorted into court by her brother, a professional violinist, and described herself as an 'accompanist' to him, thus adding a touch of respectability to her cause.

She testified that in February 1907 at the Sir Joseph Banks Hotel in Botany, she had met 'a blackfellow who said his name was Johnson'. This person had taken a gold pin from the dress of her mother, a hotel licensee of Watsons Bay.

Miss Toy went to Botany to recover the pin. She didn't know Johnson and had no 'familiarity' with him. She had been photographed with him once, but that was all there was to it. There had been no 'friendly intercourse' between them at any stage. Since *The Referee*'s item she had been subjected to comments in the street, had received some unpleasant items in the mail, and had suffered vicious taunting from other women.

Miss Toy was then subjected to 'vigorous' cross-examination, no punches pulled, by barrister P.H. Reid, for *The Referee*.

Well, yes, she conceded, she might have spoken to Johnson in the street; she even might have said 'good evening'. However, she certainly did not telephone Johnson and ask him to come out to her mother's Grand Pacific Hotel and punch out a relative, named Ashworth, who had been causing trouble in the bar and generally acting like a cad.

But upon further cross-examination she admitted that, yes, she had stayed at the Sir Joseph Banks one night while Johnson was in residence. There was a dance on there that night but she didn't dance with Jack. Well, she had got up to ask him but he had declined. In fact she did not think he could dance.

MR REID: Oh, well, in that respect he is like very many white men. [Laughter.]

MR GANNON (for Lola): Well, you are not too good at step-dancing, Mr Reid. [Laughter.]

And, said Lola, she was most certainly not out on the verandah keeping the mosquitoes off Johnson with a fan, as the defence was suggesting.

MR REID (handing her a photo): Are you not standing next to Johnson?

MISS TOY: Yes, but I never saw this before.

MR REID: Aren't you holding Johnson's walking-stick?

MISS TOY: There is nothing in holding anybody's stick.

Did the jury expect to believe, asked Reid, that she didn't know Johnson's arm was around her, with his hand on her shoulder?

MISS TOY: I didn't take particular notice of his hand.

MR REID: And such a hand. It must have weighed a hundredweight.

Had she not driven around town with Johnson in a sulky? Well, yes, but only once. And, no, Johnson had not taken to calling her 'baby'.

In arguing the defence, Reid pleaded that it was not in itself libel to say that a white woman intended to marry a coloured man or a pugilist. The judge took that one on the gloves and ruled that that was a matter for the jury to decide.

Johnson's American trainer Stephen Hyland testified that he had first seen Miss Toy at a showing of the film of the Burns–O'Brien fight. Miss Toy had been seen at the Sir Joseph Banks with Johnson on the verandah, going up to his room, and in the garden. It was starting to look shaky for Lola. In big Jack's room?

She had also been in the pavilion to watch him train, said

Hyland. And, of course, on those occasions Johnson was stripped to 'the buff'. One night, Hyland testified, he had even heard her say: 'No, Jack, not that. You can have all my rings. And you can come into town and marry me in the morning.' Hyland had got so fed up with Lola being on the phone and in Johnson's room — thus disrupting training — that he threatened to quit.

Another witness was a constable who spoke of the ructions at the Grand Pacific, and how Lola told him she had called 'gentleman' Johnson, who was also a 'well-made man', to come over and punch out Ashworth. And how Johnson had been seen leaving the place. And how Lola's mother had been in trouble with the law, convicted of perjury. And how Lola's mother had said, after seeing Jack train: 'He's a beautiful man. You ought to see him stripped.'

It seemed that if Lola had set out to redeem her good name she had failed miserably, even if she had offered in court to have herself examined by the finest surgeons in Sydney to refute the implications of the defence.

If this had been a fight it should have been stopped. But she got back in the witness box and denied all the defence evidence. Then, in the coup de grâce, she fainted as she left the witness box and had to be helped out of the court.

Who can ever truly pick the scorecards? The jury believed her enough to award her damages of £500. Jack Johnson, it seemed, just wasn't the right man to be around.

3

THOUSANDS OF MILES AWAY IN England, Burns was setting new standards as a boxer/businessman. For the Roche fight at Dublin's Theatre Royal, he had demanded custom-made four-oz gloves for his 'featherweight' hands. He received 80 per cent of the £1500 purse and £500 from the first two sets of films developed. For all that, the fight only lasted one minute and 28 seconds.

But there was interest in the Dublin farce for all red-blooded Australians, for who should pop up at ringside but Boshter Bill Squires. A modest chap, our Bill, but never short of a proposition. Fresh from a trip to Paris, he was itching for a fight with the champ.

Obligingly, Burns (now described by W.W. Naughton as 'puffed to the bursting point with his own importance') offered to do Squires *and* Englishman Tiger Smith on the same night. He also offered to fight Jack Johnson in England in a 16-ft square ring in which he would hammer the big man's ribs. But this feeler only attracted an offer of $5000 for Burns, and much less for Johnson, and was not taken seriously by Burns' bank manager. (There had been an offer of a $35000 purse floated by California promoter Jim Coffroth, of which Burns would get $25000, but nobody had seen the colour of Coffroth's money.)

Johnson, meanwhile, was demanding to know why Burns wouldn't return to America to fight him. He personally wouldn't hesitate to come to England if Tommy's talk was serious. In fact, Johnson would do just about anything to get the wily Canadian into any kind of ring.

'When we get into it [the ring] he can lock it up and throw away the key,' he said.

But even as Johnson prepared to start chasing Burns around the globe, there was never a serious chance of a fight in England. Johnson had gone to Australia and been stood up by Squires. Now the Australians were meddling in his life again. In April the first words had leaked into the Sydney press that a local 'Sydney Exhibition syndicate' had contacted Burns with an offer. That was all that was known. It was a mystery syndicate and it was a mystery who Burns would fight.

Then, on 30 April, to the amazement of the folks back home, Boshter Bill turned up in Dublin again and knocked out Jem Roche in four rounds. What a revelation! Could this be the first sign of his resurrection? Squires' admirers figured that he might have become

— a bit like Roche — too musclebound after he left Australia; after all, you could strop a razor once too often and take the edge off it. Burns, by comparison, kept himself nice and supple.

Squires was neither supple nor subtle but had somehow come good again. Suddenly he had become a legitimate opponent for Burns. A return match in England was announced.

But the word on Burns coming to Australia was growing stronger. *The Referee* announced on 13 May that the syndicate of 'well-known gentlemen' had received an answer from Burns. The world champion, it seemed, was willing to cross the herring pond, along with Jewel and her hats, for a guaranteed £3000 plus expenses to fight 'whites only'. It looked like the American fleet would be in Sydney and Melbourne in August with big bucks to spend on any big fight involving their man Burns, and a smart promoter might clean up.

But who was there to fight? Nobody could meet Burns' asking price for a Johnson fight and after all, he was already set to fight Squires in England and would most likely finish off the Australian's pretensions for good.

Another wire came back to Sydney saying 'Burns off'. *The Referee* puzzled over this. Was the Burns trip off, or was Burns–Squires off? Was Tommy now starting his customary game of hardball over money?

On 27 May, *The Referee* was bursting with news. Burns–Squires was on — not in London, but in Paris on 13 June. The French capital had suddenly become Tommy and Jewel's type of town. It had three boxing halls going and was paying much bigger purses than England. Even the Moulin Rouge was putting on fight nights. What's more France, always the stylesetter, encouraged ladies to attend and they were flocking to the fights in droves. It was only when large hats obstructed the view that they were discouraged. But for all their enthusiasm, the French crowd was not exactly knowledgeable — they had a 'playful' habit of breaking up the ring if dissatisfied with the performance or the decision!

Meanwhile, a £2000 guarantee for Burns had been lodged by the syndicate with *The Referee*. The Amateur, who had been intimately involved in negotiations, was suddenly moved to rapturous, lionising prose about little Tommy, somehow forgetting Jim Jeffries' place in boxing history along the way. It was hype worthy of Don King.

'He [Burns] really is the only genuine fighting champion of the world this planet has known for many a year,' he gushed. Before Burns, they were just quinces and lemons. Among them were 'John L.' (Sullivan), 'Pompadour Jim' (Corbett), 'Rufus-Headed Robert' (Fitzsimmons) and the 'shaggy-bodied ex-boilermaker' (Jeffries). Tommy's fodder — Squires, Moir, Palmer, Roche — were now top-notchers of the highest ilk.

Some supposed greats of the past, The Amateur waffled, had even disgraced themselves by becoming ham actors and vaudevillians. Gentleman Jim, it was true, had been one of the worst actors in the history of entertainment, but The Amateur seemed to forget that Burns was one of the first fighters to cash in on film rights; he didn't have to exercise his thespian talents because he could make a good buck showing films and punching bags on stage.

'Tommy Burns is quite a different boxing champion to the brand referred to; he is a champion gloved-fist fighter who has never dreamt of going on the stage, nor having men dug out of rural towns and boomed as champions, to be knocked over like so many ninepins.'

And Burns was not afraid of Johnson, The Amateur maintained, even if he wasn't leaving an easy opening for him.

'The black man must be treated with respect and that just about sums the situation up,' he wrote. 'On form Burns should be picked to beat Johnson. Marvin Hart outpointed Jack and Burns subsequently outpointed Hart.'

(Johnson was continuing to pay for the travesty of the Hart decision, the day his often languid style caught up with him.)

The Amateur was even prepared to defend the avarice of Tommy Burns. In his first seven years (1900 to 1907), he said, Burns had made only $70 000 in the ring. He had added at least another $20 000 on his England trip, on top of $1500 a week in 'theatrical engagements' — but nothing as degrading, however, as vaudeville. But what of Tommy's outrageous demand of $30 000 to fight Johnson? Did that not seem just a trifle greedy?

Burns associate Billy Neill tried to legitimise the champ's hefty price tag: 'Burns is out for money. He doesn't claim he is a champion. He's a fighter and he wants to get what he is worth. This fellow Johnson is a negro, and ought to be glad to get a chance to fight with Burns. I understand that Tex Rickard, over at Rawhide, will offer $35 000 for the fight. Well, Johnson ought to be glad to get $5000 for his end. Anyhow, he can take it or leave it.'

Meanwhile, The Amateur had received a letter from the *auteur* of boxing himself. Burns said he had been offered $30 000 to fight Johnson in England — news to all — but knew he could get the same fighting him in America. It was an American fight or none.

Burns moaned: 'I have been considered a joke all through my career, and I suppose that when I have trimmed Johnson I shall not get any more credit than I did after beating Hart and O'Brien, who, as you know, were 5/1 and 2½/1 favourites respectively over me. Even Billy Squires was a 10/7 favourite over me. He was touted as the best man Australia had produced since the days of Peter Jackson, but when I beat him they called him a lemon and a quince. I hope Johnson will be a 100/1 favourite over me as I like to fight when the wise ones think I haven't a chance.

'In all my fights in the last two years nobody has ever got a line on for me, for I simply make it a point to win and no more. I am fighting for Tommy Burns and not for the public.'

It could have been Johnson talking.

These were queasy days for the mystery syndicate. Burns was supposed to be coming but he was babbling about all kinds of big offers elsewhere. What if Squires, by some tremendous fluke, beat him in Paris? John Wren had the rights to Squires. And what if Burns beat Squires so badly that nobody, not even Australians, would want to see a third hammering? Who would there be for Tommy to fight Down Under? The wires were now quoting Burns as saying that Johnson had the 'yellow streak' — or in Australia, a 'tail' — that was typical of the inferior black race. It didn't sound like Burns considered the black as a serious contender in the near future at any price, not even $30 000.

By early June, as Squires was preparing to step in with Burns in Paris, word had leaked that the principal in the syndicate was one Hugh D. McIntosh, known around the sporting traps as 'Huge Deal', an entrepreneur who had previously promoted cycling and made a lot of money selling pies at racetracks.

The Burns visit was, trumpeted McIntosh, the biggest venture in Australia's sporting history. He figured there was money in it, and even if he only 'broke even' it would be worth the chance, just to boost the nation's sporting prestige. Opponents of 'unquestioned calibre' would be provided for the great champion. The Amateur himself, who had recently been so praiseworthy of Burns, was considered a fine choice to handle the champ's affairs in Australia.

At a small ceremony in McIntosh's office, The Amateur opined that the syndicate had shown a great deal of pluck, but behind all the bluster and backslapping, McIntosh was frantically firing off cables to locate Burns in the hope of getting him to call off the Squires fight in Paris so that McIntosh could reschedule the contest in Australia.

However, McIntosh had no chance of talking Burns out of whatever purse he was getting in Paris. It all rested with Squires; he was Huge Deal's only hole card, as there were no other fighters ready to show up in Australia to fight Burns. Even Bill Lang was saying that he wasn't keen to fight Burns after being paid a measly £150 to take his licks from Johnson.

Squires simply had to put up a good-enough showing to make the prospect of a third Burns–Squires fight less than ludicrous. Otherwise, the greatest hype merchant in history could not have saved McIntosh, and on form Squires looked like a patsy. Burns was signed to fight in Sydney on 20 August, so McIntosh had only six weeks to make it all work.

Bill Squires faced Tommy Burns for the second time at Neuilly, Paris, on 13 June 1908, not long after Jack Johnson had arrived in England looking to goad the champion into a fight. The result of the fight, held on the eve of the Grand Prix de Paris races before a large crowd (including a contingent of Squires' Irish fans) at the Bowling Palace, was no real surprise: Burns KO'd Squires after eight rounds.

Squires had lost again, but it was the perfect result for McIntosh. The papers began to fill with accounts of Boshter's brave performance, and the drums started banging immediately. Not only had Squires acquitted himself well, but it seemed that he had pushed Burns to the edge of oblivion.

Burns had started well, and in the second round Squires was down from a body punch, but got up quickly. He was down again just before time was called in the third. In the fourth Squires came good to cries of 'Bravo Squeer!' from the French fans, and near the end of the fifth landed a 'fearful left-hander on the neck' which had Tommy reeling. In the sixth both men seemed to take it easy. At the beginning of the seventh Burns was down. Boshter Bill had decked the world champion, albeit for only a couple of seconds.

Burns came back strongly, and at the beginning of the eighth landed a huge body blow, his own equivalent of a 'solar plexus punch', dropping Squires like a bag of chaff. Boshter didn't get up, the fight was over.

McIntosh however, was up and running. Squires was improving, at least in the eyes of Australia, every time he met Burns. It was announced that Burns had signed to fight both Squires *and* Lang. The world champion was on his way across the herring pond, saloon-class, with Jewel and her hats.

What a close call it had been. That punch from Squires in the fifth round in Paris is long-forgotten, but may, in its own strange way, have been one of the most important of the century. If it had been a little harder, or come a little sooner, Burns might have lost his title. Squires, who had already dodged Johnson once, would have been champion and unlikely to give him a chance in a hurry.

If it hadn't landed at all — and Australia could not crow about its man getting better and almost being the champion — McIntosh's plans of a big boxing tournament for the fleet might have gone awry. Furthermore, the new picture of black achievement, shoved in the face of the white world by Johnson, may never have been so dramatically painted.

———— 4 ————

IF JACK JOHNSON HAD TO write a ripping yarn of an autobiography riddled with tall tales to sell books — as if the bare truth of his extraordinary life was not epic drama in itself — Hugh D. McIntosh could well have written a plain-facts autobiography that would have painted its author as one of the fascinating adventurers of the time.

Few Australians before or since can claim to have risen so far from such humble beginnings. Even Jack London, who found his way to McIntosh's boxing stadium via the South Seas, must have realised that he was dealing with no mere entrepreneur.

As with anybody who makes pots of money through a combination of energy, cunning and bravado, McIntosh made enemies who branded him a grafter, opportunist, con man and political animal. But just as many admired him for his courage, generosity and buccaneering charisma.

Nellie Stewart, the most revered Australian actress of the era, was one such admirer.

Stewart came from a theatre family that traced back to Drury Lane and the Shakespearean productions of the 1750s. She started her stage career at the age of three in Melbourne's Haymarket Theatre and her whole family, led by her mother Theodisia, played the Australian vaudeville circuit. They were a huge success touring New Zealand, India, England and America with a comedy called *Rainbow Revels*.

In 1880 she met 26-year-old George Musgrave, who went on to become a great producer. They went to London where Musgrave staged a huge hit called *Belle of New York* and Stewart enjoyed her own success on Drury Lane. She would later become Australia's great opera star, and when her voice gave out she turned with equal aplomb to the stage.

Nobody could remember a woman who kept her looks so well (all thanks to a staple diet of prime steak juice seasoned with pepper and salt) and, as testament to this, stage-door johnnies were still courting her even in her late fifties. A horse named after her, Sweet Nell, won the Caulfield Cup, and for decades she was Australian society's darling.

But when World War I broke out Musgrave's finances took a dive. On his birthday in January 1916, Stewart found him dead on his garden chair.

The nation feared her devastation might be fatal. But it was the dynamic McIntosh (by now the owner of the Tivoli theatre chain) who came to her rescue with offers of work on some of his massive musical productions — Huge Deal was the kind of bloke who would bring in a camel from the Australian desert if one was needed on stage — and it was for that, as much as the historic Burns–Johnson fight, that Australia remembered him most fondly. The little hard man had a big soft spot inside him too.

McIntosh, Stewart explained in her autobiography, was a Highlander by heart, a man whose forebears 'rushed around the heather in kilts and occasionally descended on the towns to stick their claymores into fat superior persons'. There were some who suggested that McIntosh was the equal of Jack Johnson in his weakness for sticking his claymore into the artistes of the time, but sweet Nellie figured that it was usually Huge Deal who got shafted — he was mostly too easy a touch for his own good.

'I do know that Mr McIntosh himself is the most generous of men, and that he is at all times far more likely to suffer from brigandage than to resort to it,' she wrote.

She said that hospitality was almost a religion with McIntosh and he outsmarted the wowsers by turning the big fights into social events that Sydney could not resist. Never before had the society pages been atwitter about what hats a pug's wife was wearing, what car the basher and the little missus were motoring about in, or what theatrical production they had adorned with their presence.

Stewart had first met McIntosh in 1911 when he was staging a charity matinee at the Stadium.

'Hugh D. impressed me at once,' she gushed. 'A man of little less than medium height, broad in the shoulders, cheery in the eye, hiding under a rattling loquacity the fact that he is shy as a girl, a man all aglow with enthusiasm like a happy boy. One of the first things I discovered was that he had brains. In his discussions of people, and things, I don't think I ever heard him say anything really stupid. He had an almost eery [sic] knack of flashing his way to the core of a subject. His personality is almost startlingly vivid.'

Mind you, he was not exactly restrained in his opinions, and though a great raconteur, was perhaps was a little too fond of his adjectives for the tastes of the totally refined. Perchance he was overcompensating for his lack of a formal education, but his intuition for what would work in the theatre was superb.

Stewart recalled McIntosh as saying that he had developed a 'cordial dislike' of Jack Johnson. Burns may have figured that Johnson had a yellow streak, but Huge Deal reckoned the black American had a 'cheap streak running right through him'. However, that hardly gelled with Jack's reputation for spending up on a good time. He may have been demanding about getting his hands on the money, but he wasn't afraid to get rid of it once he got it. That, too, was the story of McIntosh's life and other reports spoke of a grudging respect between the two men, even if McIntosh had to pull a gun occasionally to enforce it.

Hugh Donald McIntosh was born in Sydney, in a tiny cottage on Macquarie Street, near Circular Quay, on 17 September 1886, on a night when a two-day gale was causing havoc. It was known as the 'Dandenong Gale' because it wrecked a ship called the *Dandenong* off Jervis Bay.

'I was born then for better or worse,' he once said. 'As far as I know there are only a few half-baked journalists who will heartily echo "worse".'

His invalid father, a policeman and former soldier who was badly injured while fighting in the Black Watch regiment during the Indian Mutiny, died when he was four. At the age of seven, he asked his mother if he could go to Adelaide with a man he knew, an itinerant jeweller. Having always encouraged her son to read about the lives of great men, she realised that he was itching to be on his way. She nodded her head distractedly and before she knew it, little Hughie was out the door and halfway across the continent.

All his life, McIntosh had the inclination to move from one job, scheme, or venture to another. In Adelaide he discovered there was not much of a living to be had as a jeweller's apprentice so he took off for Broken Hill to pick quartz out of ore in the silver mines. For a while he was making more in a week than most men supporting families, and he sent much of it back to his mother.

Then he took all kinds of jobs around the bush. At 12 he was working as a surgeon's assistant, holding instruments by the operating table. When he was 15 the doctor died so he moved to Melbourne and got a job in a dairy. He boasted that he became such a good milker that he entered contests and won championships.

But, for whatever reason, young Hughie had show business in his blood. At 16 he became a chorus boy in a production of *Sinbad the Sailor* at the Theatre Royal in Melbourne. It was an inauspicious start to a great career in showbiz — he played the hind legs of a mule.

'I had reached the inevitable stage of every ambitious youth who desires the limelight and desires it quickly,' he recalled. 'I wanted to become an actor. With me, to want anything was to go after it.'

But there wasn't enough money in it to keep him interested. He returned to Sydney and went into business. He bought a tray with a special strap on it, got six-dozen pies on credit from a Redfern factory, and started selling them at racetracks, beaches, prize fights, two-up schools, and brothels. As prize fights, cathouses, and two-up were illegal, and the coppers could descend at any time, the strap allowed him to take flight immediately and beat off any customers who figured they had wasted their money. He was learning to be tough as well as quick.

He started to expand his pie business, with other boys selling on commission, and before he was 21 had married the woman who would stick with him for the next 40 years, even if that unstoppable energy sometimes led him to stray.

He then went to work for a caterer who had a business in the Masonic Hall at North Sydney, and when the caterer died, took over the business. Most of his first year's profit disappeared when his wife had to have an appendix operation, which was very costly in those days. He kept at the catering until he had the biggest plant in Australia. But he was restless.

He was keen on cycling — a sport drawing huge crowds — and was made President of the NSW League of Wheelmen. He took a chance and offered a prize of a 'thousand sovereigns' for a one-mile 'world championship' at the Sydney Showgrounds. It enticed some of the world's best to come Down Under and race the nation's best.

It was said that in cycling the bull-necked McIntosh developed some of the management techniques which would later serve him well with Jack Johnson. A recalcitrant cyclist, for example, could expect a good clout with a spanner.

One of the most popular riders with Australian crowds was the black American Marshall 'Major' Taylor, who was described by McIntosh as 'the wonderful darkie who was almost as good a Baptist preacher as he was a cyclist'. Taylor had a bitter rival in fellow American ace Floyd McFarland, who tried to fix the Sydney Thousand. Taylor was riding off a handicap of 150 yards and McFarland organised a group of riders to clean up in a betting coup by running Taylor off the track. Everything went to plan: Taylor was ambushed and the 'pea' — the rider with the money on him — came home to win. But promoter McIntosh — setting a famous precedent — had appointed himself referee. He smelled a rat and disqualified the winner.

An enraged McFarland rushed at him, shouting, 'I'll kill you, you swindling bastard.' But the little bulldog wasn't backing down.

'Keep your fists to yourself, McFarland,' he snarled. 'You can't fight any better than you can ride.'

McIntosh made a lot of money out of cycling, but was tainted by the corruption in the sport. By 1908, the cycling boom was over and he had moved on to investing in holiday resorts, including one at Kosciusko in the Snowy Mountains where Tommy Burns would later train, hunt, fish and swim in the weeks leading up to his fight with Jack Johnson.

Bored and restless again, McIntosh began to think about the imminent arrival of Teddy Roosevelt's Great White Fleet, with its 12 000 sailors. While the rest of the country welcomed the fleet as both a strategic godsend, a great moment in history, and a chance for a grand patriotic celebration, Huge Deal saw a big quid in it.

First, he made a trip to New Zealand and cornered the market on bunting so that he would have a nice little earner from Kiwi flag-waving when the fleet arrived in Auckland en route to Sydney. Then he began to work on what (apart from grog, women and gambling) the jolly Jack Tars might conceivably spend up on while in port.

He hit on the idea of a big fight. Although Burns was actually Canadian, he was perceived as American. What red-blooded Yank wouldn't fork over a fistful of dollars to see the champ go up against another big-name American, or a local hero like Boshter Bill Squires?

McIntosh's initial idea was to rent the large Sydney Exhibition Building, but he found that there were too many city council palms to grease. There was, however, a large vacant block at Rushcutters Bay, near the tramline from the city, which had for many years been a Chinese market garden but was now owned by an ironmonger named Furness. Sensing a priceless opportunity, McIntosh got himself kitted out in a threadbare suit, battered hat, and shoes down to their uppers, and waltzed on down to meet Furness. The ironmonger listened to the bum's tale of wanting to rent the site to put on a little sideshow for the American sailors and agreed to a rent of £4 a week for two years, with an option at £8 a week for the next two years. The day after the lease was signed Furness knew he had been well and truly stiffed. McIntosh, in a snappy suit and puffing on a big cigar, turned up to oversee the arrival of truckloads of timber and galvanised iron, and an unroofed stadium began to grow like a giant mushroom. McIntosh was laying the foundations for history — even if Jack Johnson was furthest from his mind.

But McIntosh knew little about the intricacies of promoting boxing — the dealing and double-dealing that went with every major fight. And, as it turned out, his premise about the American sailors could not have been more wrong. However, he would make enough money out of Burns fighting Squires and Lang to grab Burns–Johnson from under the noses of the big players of world boxing. Burns was immediately condemned for rejecting the English offer, while the Americans were in shock because all the talk out of California and the Nevada goldfields had amounted to nothing.

So, in one those great ironies which shape history, the fight went to an Australian pie-salesman who was bankrolling the operation on a totally dodgy financial premise. For all his life until Boxing Day 1908, and for many grandiose years afterwards, McIntosh was a man who took the sort of chances that made luck.

5

THE CHAMPION OF THE WORLD arrived in Fremantle, Western Australia, by the steamer S.S. *Mongolia* in the first week of August, accompanied by Jewel in one of her 'Merry Widow' hats. Reporters gathered for the great moment were quick to remark what a dazzling couple they were, Jewel being most attractive and Tommy a 'keen, intellectual-looking individual'. As if to demonstrate that the town was no outpost of civilisation, unversed in the art of exploiting celebrity to make a quick profit, Burns was driven up to Perth in a four-in-hand, welcomed by the mayor, and hustled off to referee a couple of fights in a hall at the local Paddy's Market. For his trouble he was presented with a gold-mounted walking-stick.

Burns, knowing that he had a selling job on his hands — not everybody was convinced he hadn't carried Squires in Paris with the Sydney fight in mind — immediately began singing the praises of Boshter Bill to the press.

'Well, if you want to know all about Bill, you can set it down right here that he is one of the gamest men who ever stripped,' he said. 'I like Bill; he seems to me a determined, manly fellow.'

In their first fight, said Burns, Squires had rushed in so open that it all seemed too easy. Was it some type of trap? Clearly not. He simply settled the matter with a straight right.

'Oh, yes, he certainly fought,' said Burns. 'He launched some beauties, any of which would have made him champion of the world — if I'd been there when they landed.'

Burns said he believed Squires had been suffering from 'rheumatics' in that California fight, and was getting bad advice out of his corner about how easily his opponent could be taken. But in Paris it seemed that Squires had a better appreciation of the 'American' style. After that big punch in the fifth round, Burns admitted, he was happy to hear the gong.

(There was some truth to Burns' comments in that they echoed what he had earlier written in a book called *Scientific Boxing and Self-defence*. In the book, Burns spoke of the art of attacking while making the opponent feel that he is the aggressor.

'Glove fighting has passed out of its early stages of brute force and into the era of brain work and science,' he wrote. 'Brains are more important than fists today.'

He also claimed to have honed a new style of short, deadly punching — a far cry from the days of the old straightbacks — and told how he could thwart a man's attack with a paralysing tap on the shoulder.

Squires featured prominently in the book, but unfortunately in a chapter titled, 'How To Meet a Rusher'. In their first fight Squires had come out open like a bull at a gate, and Burns had been able to deck him with a short right. But he gave Squires credit for strength and gameness, even if it was a one-round affair, for Boshter Bill got up and landed one on Burns' mouth which had the Canadian reeling. He was forced to 'cuddle' the inexperienced Squires, and hold him and talk to him, until his head cleared and he could finish his challenger off. He didn't want to cop any more of Squires' big punch than he had to.)

Then came the question of why he wouldn't fight Johnson.

'If Johnson shows me as much money as I am making, then I am after him,' said Burns. 'Johnson is showing himself in music halls in London, styling himself unbeaten; but he was badly beaten by Marvin Hart, who has since been defeated by me. When Marvin Hart beat Johnson he tired himself nearly to death chasing around a 24-ft ring. I won't give him a chance to tire me that way for I'll fight in a 16-ft ring, when he will have to stand up. I will fight him just as sure as he is alive, but it will be on terms I have indicated.

'All niggers are alike to me, but I'll fight him even though he is a nigger.'

At this point, as if to put an end to something distasteful, the delicate Jewel appeared and commanded attention.

'I do hate him fighting,' she trilled. 'You don't know how it effects my nerves. I am ill for days after each fight, and I was in bed for three weeks after the Moir fight in London. He is always going to stop fighting, but he never does — just one more, he says, and so it goes on.'

Perhaps Tommy hadn't told her about that £400 bet, and how his greatest exertion and biggest worry in that encounter had been collecting his purse.

Squires had arrived a couple of days earlier in Western Australia on the S.S. *Aruba* and announced that he was 'just as good as ever'.

'I don't think that I am a world-beater,' he said, with typical candour. 'But I do think that with a little luck I can come to the top of the tree.'

In the Paris fight with Burns, he thought he had the world title in the fifth.

'I caught him a fair solid smack on the side of the head,' he said. 'Tommy almost went to sleep. His eyes dropped and fluttered, his arms fell down limply by his sides, and he shivered just as if he had ague. Just after I hit him the gong sounded. I was then ready to give him a touch which would have proved whether he or I had the most brittle of glass jaws. Had I smashed him in the same way in the middle of the round that would have been the end of Burns' trip to Australia.'

(It was in Burns' contract that he had to arrive in Australia unbeaten. If he had been beaten, and Squires had become world champion, the fight wouldn't have happened. Burns may have been greedy, but in this business he had a right to be.)

Squires said Burns was the fastest heavyweight who ever lived. He was no skite, just a shrewd Yankee out to make his fortune. And Johnson?

'I do say that fellow is a great, strong man with a touch like the delivery of a sledgehammer,' he said. 'American papers state that he has a yellow streak in him, but they don't know what they are talking about. He is very game and very honourable.'

On the question of Burns v. Johnson, Squires said it would be a great show. Burns wasn't frightened, and he had seen Johnson beat Fireman Jim Flynn like a real tradesman. In fact, in his considered opinion, Johnson was a 'white man', and certainly no big-head. But later he contradicted himself by telling another reporter that Burns would 'settle' Johnson because of his youth and his clean living.

'Burns could astonish the nigger,' he said.

In Sydney, McIntosh was moving quickly. He announced that the syndicate, now known as Scientific Boxing and Self-defence Limited (after Burns' book), had officially acquired the market-garden land at Rushcutters Bay. But it had not been without some powerful opposition within Parliament and among the wowsers.

'Friend Hughie's hands have been up all the time,' crooned The Amateur. 'He has shown remarkable readiness of resource and determination of character throughout.'

It was true that McIntosh, as they say in Australia, wasn't 'mucking about'. Overlooking the bay and right on the tramline, the open-air stadium was truly immense for its time. It was octagonally shaped and designed to hold 20 000 people with unbroken sightlines to the ring. Ticket prices would range from £1 to £5.

Meanwhile, Squires and Burns began making their way east. In Adelaide, Burns was entertained at the races and professed that he had been weakened a little by sunburn. In Melbourne, he hurried off the *Adelaide Express* and attended mass at St Patrick's Cathedral, unnoticed by the very class of people who were leading the fight against boxing. The next day he was at the Cathedral Hotel, at a reception hosted by John Wren. Johnson would have to wait, he told the audience. He would fight white boys first.

When Squires' train arrived at Sydney's Central Station, 4000 people were there to greet him. Squires had won only one fight in his 16 months away, yet the throng had gathered an hour before the posted arrival time and were still there when the train was running 70 minutes late. Huge Deal's right-hand man, Major George Wynne, pushed forward to shield Squires as he stepped onto the platform and had the buttons ripped off his coat in the push. Squires was then shepherded into a car by a scrum of McIntosh's men and police and taken to the Crystal Hotel where, among a privileged 300-strong audience, an assembly of windbags lay in wait.

Squires, a figure of slightly dented sporting royalty wearing a quiet country bloke's suit, low collar, and a brown American 'pee wee' hat on his balding pate, went to the window to acknowledge the motley crew in the street below. It had been the same at every railway station on the 800-km journey up from Melbourne.

McIntosh, third up on the lectern after a politician blowing his own bags and a military man warning of the coming Asian invasion, declared that Squires would almost certainly 'deliver the goods' and 'bring home the bacon'. (It was lamented among many guardians of the Queen's English that in speeches like this the 'Murkan' influence seemed to be increasingly prevalent.)

The well-nourished Major Wynne — known as 'the man who won the China war' — told how he had been forced to defend the fight to parliamentarians who worried that Rushcutters Bay, and the good name of the state, would be deluged in gore.

'Putting the boot in will not be allowed,' he said, earning a laugh.

With volleys coming from the churches and their newspapers, a running battle had ensued with the sporting sheets.

'Out handkerchiefs, brethren, and prepare to weep,' sneered *The Sportsman*, commenting on a letter in *The Watchman* which had invoked the tortured figure of poor Jewel — especially on fight nights.

'Look at that poor woman's face as she accompanies to the door the pride of her heart, he in whom centres all the happiness this world can give, save what true religion supplies,' *The Watchman*'s correspondent had sobbed. 'What artist can paint the anxious look on her face? Did God ever intend that man should enter on a line of life that would bring upon the face of any woman a look like that?'

Bloody oath He did, figured the all-male gathering at the Crystal, which preferred the following doggerel in *The Sportsman*, squarely aimed at the Temperance and Moral Committee of the Methodist Church, which had called for the fight to be banned:

So wowser man and wowser maid,
If down in prayer you must,
Pray that our William, sober, staid,
Lays Tommy in the dust.

Another of *The Sportsman*'s 'poets', Annie Howe, was moved to gush:

> *And these two men are, meeting face to face,*
> *A credit to the Anglo-Saxon race;*
> *Two men are they, beloved by British folk,*
> *Each with a heart as stout as English oak!*
> *Both have been manly in the battles fought,*
> *For nothing underhanded have they sought —*
> *Those are the warriors a world admires,*
> *Men of the kidney of a Burns and Squires!*

Larry Foley got up and said that the fighters of the day were pygmies compared to the world-conquering juggernauts he had trained so ably in the past. But Boshter was a rough diamond there for the polishing.

'You know, Blondin paralysed the world by walking on a six-inch rope,' said Foley. 'When Australians saw him perform they did the same thing on a clothesline.'

When it was all over, Squires headed off to a 2000-strong reception in Newcastle. He then went to Heddon-Greta to see his parents, and moved on to Toronto, near Newcastle, to set up camp.

--------------------- 6 ---------------------

THERE WAS AN EVEN BIGGER crowd, estimated at 7000 and including hundreds of women, to greet Burns' train from Melbourne a few days later. Tommy, with his bright steel-grey eyes, emerged from his carriage clad in a fawn Newmarket coat with a velvet collar, under which, some observed, bulged the shoulders of an ox. One reporter was so impressed that he figured the thumper could well be mistaken for one of those 'American beauty actors'. However, one self-appointed arbiter of style among the greasy sports hacks complained that the effect was undermined by a little, round, green plush hat that made Burns look like a bit of a dill. More coarse than Corsican.

Police had to force a way through the mob to get Burns to his reception at the Crystal Hotel. In the ensuing speeches, wowsers were heartily bashed, with McIntosh getting off a few stinkpots. Huge Deal himself was praised to the skies, and boxing was lauded as a manly art, with E.W. O'Sullivan, Member of the Legislative Assembly, going so far as to say it — along with other rugged sports — had made England the great nation that she was.

Colonel Ryrie MLA said that he wasn't hoping for a Burns win, but was sure that Tommy would acquit himself 'as a man', while Major Wynne let drop a rather interesting tidbit. There was, he said, sitting on McIntosh's desk at Sports and Amusements Ltd, a signed agreement — from the Australian end — for a match in Australia between Burns and Johnson, the coon heavyweight, providing certain conditions were met.

'It is well within probability,' he said. But it was a mere addendum to the day, and there was no mention as to where Tommy's mammoth purse might come from.

The ever-modest Squires, who had reportedly walked five kilometres to catch the Newcastle train down to welcome his opponent, promised Burns 'the best of treatment' on the 24th. Burns then dutifully rose, and in a quiet, earnest little speech, said he hoped the best man would win.

Then Bill Lang got up and said that he had changed his mind after all, and had accepted a fight with Burns in Melbourne after the Squires fight, and hoped he would emerge victorious.

Afterwards, Burns was ushered into a car to take him to a big stately home called The Gunyah in the posh harbourside suburb of Darling Point — and probably not a moment too soon, lest he choke on all the overblown rhetoric.

In Paris he had been welcomed into high society by Baron de Rothschild, and fêted at his palace as the *'champion du monde'*. Now he had gone from barons to bumpkins. Nonetheless, Jewel was provided with a spectacular backdrop. She had been given her own 'Reception by the Ladies of Sydney to Mrs Noah Brusso' at the Royal Hotel and by all reports had proven herself to be 'a splendid specimen of a Western girl'.

The Sydney fashion scene was in uproar with the advent of the *directoire* dress for spring. It was a variation on the French number of the early eighteenth century worn by the *'merveilleuses'* or 'female dandies'. Beneath them were to be worn a range of items including the sheath skirt, snake petticoat, and pantalettes. The bodice, however, was considered to be so 'insignificant' that it was feared that the charms of ladies would be falling out all over Sydney. Conservative fashion writers picked them up and failed to ascertain any foundations. It was almost as scandalous to the wowsers as the brutish violence at the stadium.

Imagine, then, the fine impression made by Jewel, who arrived attired in a very smart coat and skirt of shepherd's plaid, with black-braid trimming, sable muff, and large black hat. She was pale, dark-eyed, attractive, ethereal. She epitomised the wife of the stylish new brand of professional, world-travelled athlete.

Questioned by the good ladies about the violence, Jewel reiterated that she never went to the fights. But in reality, she said, there was little chance of Tommy being seriously injured in the ring. Boxing was not like football, in which he had once broken both of his arms.

'He is so scientific,' she smiled. 'He doesn't believe in the rough and tumble stuff.'

Meanwhile, The Amateur was lucky enough to get a scoop — an interview with Burns in his car. Perhaps not the most difficult of feats, considering that he was helping to manage the man, but not a moment to be wasted for his readers.

'No marks, no cauliflower ears?' he asked.

'Well, I've never bumped anything hard enough to cause more than a slight flesh wound,' Burns replied. He did have a little scar on the bridge of his nose, he said, turning to show his Napoleonic profile, but that had come from lacrosse. (He later told another reporter it had come from a dog bite suffered as a child.)

Burns told how he had once been taunted by a fighter named Ben O'Grady. O'Grady had taken four days to regain consciousness, but years later both men had shaken hands. Burns was just that sort of guy.

'In boxing the good sportsman who loses should never bear a grudge against the winner,' said Burns. 'Because, well, the next thing to winning is losing, isn't it?'

Did the world need any more convincing that this man was the noblest and the greatest of them all? To drive the point home, The Amateur managed to dig up a comment from a Catholic priest in London, where Burns had put on an exhibition for the Young Mens' Catholic Association.

'Self-discipline is the secret of this champion's work. It is not mere brute force that's the game to play,' said Father Bernard Vaughan, the punching priest.

If that wasn't enough, The Amateur also dredged up a comment about Johnson from New York fight expert Bob Edgrens: 'I am unable to call to mind any feat of Johnson's that would entitle him to a fight with anyone. Ever since he started as a fighter Johnson has shown nothing to indicate that he can fight a good heavyweight. Marvin Hart whipped him in 20 rounds. He fought Mexican Pete Everett, little George Gardiner, and a score of other third-raters without scoring a knockout. When Johnson is stung in a fight he immediately becomes the cleverest human turtle in the ring. He pulls his head in and takes precious good care of his handsome features.

'Johnson looks like all kinds of a champion. But in reality he is only a shell. He has the looks and the skill, but he hasn't the heart.'

Burns' financial adviser, W.C.J. Kelly, later got in his own little dig: 'Jack Johnson has a yellow streak as wide as a mountain.' He then repeated Burns' allegation, never quite believed in London, that the Canadian had put in his $10000 for a fight and Johnson had chickened out.

Tickets to the Burns–Squires fight began to sell quickly despite complaints about the cost, while movie rights were snapped up for £1000. Huge Deal's position was starting to look better all the time, even if the final cost of the stadium had been £15000.

McIntosh, for all his humble background, was proving to be quite an impresario. A big marquee was set up for Burns' training and ladies were invited to sip Jewel's tea and admire the physique of the champion, resplendent in emerald-green tights and a Stars and Stripes sash, as he punched a ball adorned with the flags of England, Ireland, and America: nations whose champions had all bowed to his prowess.

In an open challenge to the clergy, McIntosh issued a public invitation to anybody engaged in 'sky-pilotage' to drop by and gain a finer appreciation of the sophistication of the fight game. Curious, 30 Catholic priests turned up one day and mingled with the ladies.

Never had Australia been so starstruck over a basher and his bride. Forty-eight ladies soon applied for tickets for the fight but, this not being Paris, McIntosh regretfully declined to issue them, saying, 'When the battle grows hot and the claret begins to spurt, we don't want any hysterics or such rumpus.'

In training, Burns was showing the locals a few new angles. He went for 16-km walks around the harbourside hills in the mornings, punched the bag with one-lb dumbbells in his hands — building strength rather than speed — and did a lot of stomach work and shadow-boxing.

The sparring, with Irish middleweight champion Pat O'Keefe, was always full-on. One writer described Burns dancing round the ring like a 'snake-haunted drunk who had swallowed a spring mattress'.

The day before the fight Burns, wearing a cloth cap and chewing gum, appeared at the Stadium to referee a fight between heavyweights Peter Felix and Sid Russell. When the diminutive Burns went over to shake hands with the 206-cm Felix, the crowd broke into laughter at the disparity in size. Could this man really hold off the new, improved Boshter Bill?

Those watching Squires figured the Australian faster and stronger, for he had adopted a lot of American technique — certainly enough to turn the tables this time. Australia prayed that the punch which had deserted him after leaving home had finally returned.

7

'AS A FRIENDLY HAND ACROSS the Pacific comes to Australia the Great White Fleet,' wrote the respected monthly, *The Lone Hand*. 'In flashing white it comes, as it were a symbol of a racial ideal to be upheld, and yet of a pacific purpose. And we Australasians can find no words great enough to express the thought of our welcome.'

The Persians under Darius, the Tartar hordes, the Huns, the Saracens — history had been blighted by the westward pushes of Asian barbarians against the fortresses of the White Race, it argued. Now it was the turn of the dominant Whites to push east and absorb. But the fiendish Asiatics had put on the Whites' armour and were not only demanding to shape their own destinies but were looking greedily to the south.

'It is without a doubt a challenge to the long-accepted hegemony of the White Race ... if there is one clear principle amidst the welter of wrongs and reprisals and deceits called "international politics", it is that the supremacy of the white man must be maintained. "My country, right or wrong", may be questioned as a maxim of conduct, but most will confirm without a moment's doubt, "The White Race Right or Wrong".'

And so, *The Lone Hand* railed, Asia had never produced a stable democratic power devoted to human liberty. Whatever the merits of the other races — even the lotus-eating Kanaka — it was the white man's burden to elevate the species to a higher state of being. Another brandy, Carstairs, the natives are restless.

Nobody wanted war, of course. But the fleet was a welcome policeman, one which had recently whipped the Spaniards and taken the Philippines to its bosom.

Japan, too greedy for the state of her economy, was not to be trusted, even if Britain was her ally. And there was concern over the weakness of the Chinese in the matter of the seizure of the Japanese steamer *Tatsu Maru* which had been running guns into Macao to prop up Chinese bandits and revolutionaries. Japan had got into a snit, demanding full compensation, and China's Manchu rulers had cravenly backed down. This brought Canton close to rebellion, and there had been a boycott of Japanese goods in the southern province. The whole Pacific was jittery about the effects of 'jujitsu diplomacy'.

Japan was seen as an tyrannical oligarchy that overspent on its military machine. Its people were deplorably ignorant and had no real power in the Diet. The press was censored. In no way could it be described as a constitutional nation.

'The danger of Japan is that, still being so Asiatic, uncontrolled by public opinion, holding fundamentally different views from ours about human rights and progress, it possesses an Army and Navy, efficient, fanatical, directed by an ambitious, aggressive, and reckless oligarchy which at any moment can be turned loose as a destroyer in the Pacific,' argued Louis Esson in a major series of articles on the Asiatic menace written to coincide with the arrival of the fleet.

Why, Esson asked, when the Japanese people were earning only an average of a shilling a week, and taxed to the bone to pay war debts, did Japan need a two-million man army, even greater than the one which had defeated Russia, and a navy three times the size, if not to make a land-grab on foreign shores? If not to create her own empire? If not to append others the way she had barbarously appended Korea? If not to spread her cancer into China?

'It is a game of international poker,' he wrote. 'Japan is taking desperate chances, staking her national existence on a mad gamble. She holds a poor hand, but is risking a big bluff. When the cards are thrown down nations may look to their shooters.'

And who knew what might happen when the great 'Dragon' of China fully woke from her torpor? There were signs of a new national patriotism, and a more Western approach to the economy and the military, despite the decay of the Manchu dynasty. The shackles of an ancient society were being shaken off. China was no longer a large melon there for the slicing by foreign powers, the so-called 'Outer Barbarians'.

'The future of China is the core of the Asiatic problem. Everything depends on China, but what China will ultimately do no prophet is able to foretell,' wrote Esson. 'Asia is threatened with many warclouds, and when they burst the long-sleeping Dragon may startle the sceptic world by blowing from his mouth and nostrils smoke and brimstone.'

It was no wonder then that the Americans were treated as conquering heroes. There were predictable whinges that the Jackies would nick off with all the women and that the local 'dagos' would jack up the price of oysters, but poet Roderic Quinn best summed up the overwhelming sense of relief when he wrote, with straight face and sturdy pen:

America, proud, puissant
Mighty by sea and land,
We of the World's White Outpost

Welcome you heart and hand.
We are linked though the seas divide us,
We are wedded each to each
By the pure high thought of Milton
By Shakespeare's golden speech.
'Ere ever the starry banner
Was flung to the wind unfurled
We were one in high achievement
And one against the world.

We might have been a nation of bad poets but we were people with good hearts. When the battleships finally arrived in Sydney on 20 August, four days before the Burns–Squires fight, an estimated 40 000 people milled at the Heads with every imaginable conveyance jamming the road to Watsons Bay. The roads were lined with ice-cream carts advertising 'Uncle Sam hokey-pokey'. Cars and buses which could make no headway on the roads crashed through the scrub. Tommy and Jewel, keen to be among the first to greet them, were out on a steamer at 6 am.

The next day, at the official reception hosted by Governor of NSW Sir Harry Rawson and Governor-General of Australia Lord Northcote, Admiral Sperry was overwhelmed by the locals' affection, believing the 'immense mass of humanity had been drawn there by some deeper feeling than curiosity', namely 'the bond of feeling and sympathy between the English-speaking people'.

Then, on fight day, a crowd estimated by *The Sydney Morning Herald* at 250 000, almost half of Sydney's population, poured into Centennial Park to watch a parade of the fleet's sailors and marines. Marching with them were 10 000 Australian troops.

It was the biggest crowd ever gathered in Australia, and a shining testament to the importance of American might in the Pacific to Australia's national security. It was also the first time that Australian and American fighting men would stand side by side.

The great irony in all of this was that Admiral Sperry and his battleships had muscled into the Pacific to ease the 'white man's burden', but the result for America would be a giant black headache in the form of Jack Johnson. The Great White Fleet would unwittingly precipitate the era of the Great White Hope.

8

AFTER THE HUGE TURNOUT FOR the march in Centennial Park, the biggest sporting event for the American sailors was not Burns–Squires at the Stadium for the world heavyweight championship, but a baseball game at nearby Rushcutters Bay Oval between the fleet and a combined NSW–Victoria team, won by the visitors.

The sailors didn't take to the fight. In fact, only two turned up — drunk — and both men were itching to take on anyone who wanted a fight. The reason for the no-show? Word had spread around the dockside bars that the fight was a stinker, a set-up for the Canadian. The visitors were convinced that their money would be better spent on beer and the most hospitable local ladies.

McIntosh had taken a huge gamble on the patronage of the Jack Tars only to find that he didn't need them after all. There was enough interest among the locals in Australia's first heavyweight title fight, and sure enough, a great crowd gathered for the fistic summit of 'American' and Australian boxing.

The Stadium was filled with more than 15 000 spectators, while some 25 000 lingered outside the gates for a sniff of the action. Some daredevils had even scaled telegraph poles, standing out like sentinels against the bright-blue sky.

Squires entered the ring to a tremendous ovation, culminating in 'Three Cheers for Our Bill!'. He was wearing blue tights with a red, white and blue sash and looked gaunt at 80 kg. Burns came in wearing trousers, a sweater, and a motoring cap, and looked pale to some and a ghastly yellow to others. Whatever the hue, he certainly appeared to be suffering from a cold which had hit him a few days earlier while refereeing the Felix stoush.

He weighed half a kilogram lighter than Squires and when stripped revealed maroon trunks with a Stars and Stripes sash and fingerless leather gloves — instead of the usual bandages — to protect his hands. McIntosh, ever aware of Jewel's frailties, sat with a telephone to call her at the end of each round.

The two men shook hands warmly and tossed for corners. Burns won and chose the corner with his back to the sun: Squires would have to begin each round staring straight into it.

Reports of the fight varied wildly. A reporter from one of the dailies counted Squires landing ten thunderous rights in the first round, but the old hands from the sports sheets didn't bother to record any of them. What did become clear was that Burns, after testing Squires' punch and confirming that it still wasn't the famous one Australia had known to drop one opponent after another, allowed Boshter to carry the fight around the 24-ft ring until he tired.

Squires piled up the points — landing consistently (according to the local argot) on the bingie, boko, napper, tater trap, pantry, optic, and listener — but Burns remained unperturbed. There were roars for the local man as he landed a left hook to end the first round in front. And it was Squires again who drew first blood with a right to Burns' nose in the second. But, for all Squires' efforts, Burns was using his footwork well in the open and placing his punches well in the clinches.

By the third round, referee L.H. Nathan's shirt was splattered with blood from Burns' nose.

'Suddenly Bill electrified the crowd by scoring with the left and right hook square on the champion's mouth,' wrote *The Sportsman*. 'But Tommy, taking the gruel like a duck takes to water, smashed a heavy right in return to the ribs. Burns was spitting the ruby fluid at the bell.'

Burns drew Squires' blood from the chin in the fourth. He was smiling at some of Squires' efforts, but not, it was noted, in a 'flash' manner. Even so, the smile was temporarily removed by a bash on the mouth at the end of the round.

In the fifth a couple of good lefts started a dark swelling under Tommy's left eye, and in the sixth the crowd was in a fever as Boshter Bill rained in punches from all directions, though the local hero was beginning to grow anxious at their apparent lack of effect. In the seventh however, he landed a series of uppercuts and the crowd began screaming as Burns hung on for a full six seconds. Those screams became a chant in the eighth — 'Go Boshter Bill!' — as Squires kept up his battery of stingless punches, but by the ninth it was clear that Burns' short body shots were beginning to take their toll on the Australian.

In the 10th round, Burns was beginning to treat Squires' punches with contempt and the end was in sight. Burns dropped his hands and took three taps to the head. When Squires tried his own body attack Burns calmly went to the head. Then he went back to the body and Squires looked near collapse at the gong. But Squires raised a few notches in the 11th. As the round began Burns' sash fell to the floor and had to be adjusted. The two men then shook hands and proceeded to blaze away at each other, but in the frenzy neither man heard the gong.

There was a lot of clinching in the 12th as Burns again let Squires play out his hand. Burns reportedly sat down 'strong and cool'. But in the 13th the end came suddenly and emphatically. They swapped punches and Squires reeled away with blood spurting from his mouth. He came in again with his guard down and tried to clinch but Burns stepped back and crashed home a short right to the chin.

Boshter went down and sat on the canvas for an eight-count, which included some rest time. He got up and lashed his last punch, a right, at Tommy's eye, but another right put him down on one knee. He was up at eight for the dispatch, but Burns hit him with another piledriving right and he went down face first.

As the referee counted him out, the towel was coming in and the policeman in charge was yelling, 'No more of it!'. Boshter Bill's third tilt at the world heavyweight title was over.

A bloody exhibition was certainly not welcomed by the wowsers of Sydney society, but *The Sydney Morning Herald* did not hold back in lionising Burns. Its writer might not have known how to count punches but he knew how to shower accolades.

'The difference between the two men is that Squires is a pugilist — a pugilist who has developed his powers to a high degree,' he wrote. 'Burns is a scientist who has applied his brain to solving the problem of the knock-out. That he did not become an eminent bacteriologist or chemist is merely the accident of circumstances ... added to his scientific precision is a capacity for taking punishment which is almost superhuman. It may be possible to hurt Burns with a battle-axe, but most of those who witnessed his performance of yesterday would be inclined to doubt it.'

This must have bemused Burns. The only scientific thing known about him outside the ring was that he and Jewel had once tried egg farming with incubators, but Tommy had quit when he found that it was costing him £1 per egg.

Tommy was now most definitely Australia's Boy, even if there were mutterings among some of the old ringsiders that Squires had been carrying cream puffs in his hands, not battleaxes, and that Burns had probably held him up as long as he did to make sure of a good movie — who would have paid to see the film of a first-round knockout?

Burns had performed like the finest matador in the open and in-close, had made his short punches tell. The world now knew what he meant when he said that he fancied his chances of pounding Johnson's 'pantry' in a smaller ring, but there were to be no 'yellow streak' gibes against Burns for adopting similar tactics to those often used by Johnson: fighting within himself, and not taking risks until his man was worn down.

As soon as the fight was over Burns had the telephone handed up to him.

'Hello Jewel, is that you. It's Tommy, it's alright.'

Then, before the decision was announced, Squires fronted up to his victorious opponent.

'By Jove, Tommy, you gave me a very heavy punch in the throat in the third round,' he said.

'Sorry for that, but a man had to do something to stop you, you know.'

Burns would later complain about coming into it with a cold (which had made him slow and tired) and a sore right arm from sparring. But he had a lot of praise for Squires.

'You can take it from me Bill is one of the gamest and strongest fighters I have ever met,' he said. 'He is certainly no "false alarm" as the American press called him, and he could beat most of the heavyweights in the world.'

Meanwhile, the indomitable Squires declared that it was far from over for him. 'I had a bit of bad luck,' he said. 'If I had my old punch back I would make him sit up. What I want is two or three more fights, and then if I don't win my name's not Bill Squires.'

It was a bit like a tenor declaring that if he hadn't lost his voice he could still sing Pagliacci.

Bill Lang said he was confident he could beat Burns the following week, while Burns said he would be ready for Johnson after Lang, if McIntosh so wished. It looked like McIntosh would need a killing on the Burns–Lang fight in Melbourne for that sort of arithmetic to add up.

Nevertheless, with huge ticket sales, the stadium had begun to pay for itself. The film rights for the fight were sold for £1000, with Burns receiving £2000 and Squires £400.

9

Ladies it is to you I dedicate this description;
nor let it seem out of character for the fair to
notice the exploits of the brave. Courage
and modesty are the old English virtues,
and may they never look cold and askance
on one another! Think, ye fairest of the fair,
loveliest of the lovely kind, ye practisers of
soft enchantment, how many more ye kill
with poisoned baits than ever fell in the ring,
and listen with subdued air and without
shuddering to a tale tragic only in appearance,
and sacred to the Fancy.

– William Hazlitt

HOVERING IN THE GENERAL ORBIT of the Napoleonic one seemed to have dizzied The Amateur, and it was with these words from the nineteenth-century English essayist, concerning a legendary bareknuckle rumble between Bill Neat and 'The Gasman' Tom Hickman, at Newbury, England, in 1821, that he introduced his interminably waffling coverage of the Burns–Lang fight held in Melbourne just ten days after Burns–Squires.

With typical gusto, McIntosh's builders had whipped up another octagonal stadium on City Road in just 12 days. Tommy and Jewel were billeted to a St Kilda hotel and ladies were again invited to training. The purse was £1000 to Burns, with a generous £600 to Lang.

The fleet was in Melbourne but once more McIntosh didn't really need the visiting Yanks to make up the numbers. The Jackies seemed more interested in a series of three ice hockey matches between their best and a Victorian team, and a baseball match against the Melbourne Cricket Club. Three of the sailors, who weren't handling the local grog too well, went looking for a place to kip in the railyards. One was run over by a train and killed after falling asleep on the tracks at Flinders Street station. Another died after falling under a train he was trying to jump. Another fell out of a train and fractured his skull.

Meanwhile, Burns' handlers knew the champ was in the best possible spirits — he had been singing his favourite song 'Wait 'Til the Sun Shines Nellie' on the train down, and after all the ringing prose about how much punishment he had soaked up against Squires, he was fresh and unmarked for Lang, who had won 11 straight fights since losing to Jack Johnson.

On fight day, there were about 10 000 in the crowd but many of the most expensive seats were unfilled. Before the main event, a 'quiet-looking josser' with a little brown hat and a cigar entered the ring to challenge the winner. Who else but Boshter Bill! He was now starting to look like one of those American carnival game gophers: you keep banging them on the head with a mallet but they keep popping up out of their holes again. Even so, he got a big cheer.

Lang entered the ring wearing no sash, just trunks. Burns, wary of the cold, entered wearing a fawn overcoat (with a 'howling swell's' long-tailed box coat underneath) over his regular boxing gear. But he had forgotten the elastic bandage for the arm he had jarred before the Squires fight. The highly strung Lang had to wait 10 minutes while someone raced back to Burns' hotel to fetch it. As the preliminary had already taken the main fight well past its advertised time, it looked for all the world like Tommy was indulging in a little gamesmanship. When the bandage finally did arrive Lang objected to it, but referee Nathan snapped, 'He doesn't punch with his forearm, and if he does I'll know how to deal with him!'

There was to be no handshake either, puzzling some who had been reading about the spotless character of the little champ.

It was not a great fight but it would be remembered for one sensation. Burns had stalked Lang like easy prey, and punished his body in-close in the first round, drawing catcalls from some of the fans who didn't understand American-style infighting. But excitement was high and hundreds whirled their hats with approval at the gong.

Burns came out over-confident in the second and threw a loose right. Lang reacted swiftly, hitting him square on the chin with a big left hook, and the world champion dropped and rolled onto his back. It was his first knockdown as champion. The crowd was in such an uproar that Burns couldn't hear referee Nathan's count.

But this time Burns was genuinely demonstrating his durability. He watched Nathan's hand signalling the seconds, got to one knee after two and was up at eight. He then sprang at Lang and they swapped punches. However Burns, feeling that Lang was still too dangerous, backed away. Lang hit him with an uppercut in a clinch and Burns threw a couple of illegal punches while holding, which earned him a warning. The champ had survived the round, and was even smiling as Lang received a mighty ovation.

When the bell rang, Burns bore in and roughed up his man, opening a cut on Lang's left eyebrow. A short, brutal uppercut snapped Lang's head back and those who knew Burns' pedigree figured the fight would not last much longer. To many, Lang was proving himself to be no 'squib' — although some would later accuse him of losing his nerve after Burns got up from his whistling left hook in the second round.

In the fourth, as they parted from a scrimmage, Burns threw a big looping right that hit Lang on the back of the head and dropped him for a nine-count. Lang survived the round, with his corner yelling, 'Get away, keep away, run away!' In the next round however, an uppercut put him down for eight seconds. Then the same punch dropped him for another eight. After Lang got up Burns tried to end it with a huge right swing, missed, and went sprawling on the floor himself. With one desperate surge left in him, Lang went for Burns as he tried to get up, but a left-right combination put him down again and he was saved by the gong with the count at eight.

The sixth round was clearly going to be the last. Lang was totally spent and Burns poked his chin out and grinned, for which he could well have been branded 'white flash'. He pretended to be hurt and the crowd called out: 'He's done — finish him Bill!' But Burns got tired of toying with him, and moved in to drop Lang cold with a flurry of punches. The count had barely started when the towel came in from Lang's corner.

This was the signal for the crowd from the outer section to rush the ring, smashing chairs and tearing out the ringposts in their path as the police struggled in vain to hold them back: a far cry from the gentle exodus of the crowd in Sydney. Burns, taking the initiative, calmed them with a little speech: 'Gentlemen, I've travelled the world, and must say you're the finest sports I have ever met.'

———————— 1 0 ————————

AFTER THE FIGHT, BURNS DECLARED that he needed some rest and took off to one of McIntosh's resorts at Kosciusko.

It was then that *The Lone Hand*, taking time off from its probing analysis of the 'yellow peril', decided to weigh in with some serious coverage of the world heavyweight champion, and so dispatched a writer called 'Byrock' and the great Australian artist/illustrator Norman Lindsay to the Snowy Mountains.

On their arrival, Burns greeted his guests from an armchair in front of a roaring log fire. Byrock reported his face pale and his eyes small — not grey, but an impassive blue. His thighs were heavy, but it was his shoulders which were truly startling.

'They give to their owner, as he lolls back with his feet crossed before him (a favourite attitude), the appearance of a mighty wedge of flesh — a human triangle.'

In the tale of the tape Burns may have seemed long in the reach at 188 cm, but so much of that was shoulder, not arm. With a torso like that, observed this clinical writer, he would have been 193 cm, and not 170 cm, on the scale of the old Greek sculptors. All of his movements were as slow and ponderous as an old, tired man, yet he was as scrubbed clean as a child.

'I never in my life saw a human being of his age — white, brown, or black — who was capable of sitting quite still for so long a time,' Byrock noted.

Yet when he rose to demonstrate a boxing move he was electrified. Every muscle was controlled and hair-triggered. This was plainly the fastest heavyweight the world had known. He was also obviously intelligent — his business acumen was now the stuff of legend.

Byrock quoted George Bernard Shaw: 'The intelligent prizefighter is not a knight-errant; he is a disillusioned businessman, trying to make money at a certain weight and at certain risks, not of bodily injury (for a bruise is soon cured) but of pecuniary loss.'

Tommy nodded at that one.

'A man is only a champion once in his life, and not for long at that,' he replied.

Byrock concluded that any talk of Burns being afraid of Johnson was claptrap. He had probably never been physically afraid of anything in his life. Making Johnson wait was purely good business.

'And so, like any other reasonable citizen, he endured the gibes of critics with cheerful fortitude, and his banking account has been his solace,' he wrote.

Lord Lonsdale and his chums at the National Sporting Club in London may have sneered at Burns' fiscal management, but Tommy was fighting Johnson on his own terms and, win or lose, he would walk away — set up for life — at just 26. He was in perfect health and he never drank, smoked, or swore. He was, the writer concluded, 'the adult human animal in its most regenerate and highly bred form'.

He breakfasted on prunes, boiled eggs, toast and jam. Then, after a digestive rest, he would play handball, or ride, or shoot, or walk the mountains with a heavy stick. Then he would run as much as 10 km home. At lunch, he would feast on chops or steak, vegetables, and stewed fruit. By mid-afternoon he would do his boxing exercises with the same attention to detail that a watchmaker might give to a fine piece. It was not dissimilar, mused the writer, to the sort of regimen common to an English gentleman wishing to stay in good fettle for partridge-shooting or steeplechasing.

'What an exquisite fighting engine the Burns body is,' swooned Byrock. 'It is a block of speed and power. The massive legs support the stomach, chest and neck of a Hercules. Above them is the ideal pugilists's head — one of the champion's main assets.'

It was explained that Burns appeared to have a skull of iron, and appeared to take enormous punishment on it without flinching. How ironic, for it was the fashion to disparage blacks for having concrete heads, just as it is with Mexican fighters today. You didn't hit niggers on the head, you would hurt your hands; you attacked the body the way Burns planned to deal with Johnson.

'The brow is not only strongly boned, but is thickly padded with flesh, and the cheekbones are also of tremendous strength,' Byrock rabbited on. 'There is no fullness about his eyes. They lie back and are protected by heavy ramparts of flesh and bone. The nose is small and strong. The skull resembles a cannon-ball and is about as hard. The hand that comes into contact with any of these iron surfaces stands in danger of being maimed or crippled outright.'

This adamantine pate was supported by a neck like a tree trunk. When he came in with head down he was like a battering ram. And once in there he defended his chin, kidneys, and stomach with great skill. Everything about him was Napoleonic.

'For my part,' summed up *The Lone Hand*'s man, 'I find it impossible to believe that any human being in this particular year of grace is capable of outpointing or knocking out — unless by the sheerest of accidents — the extremely effective punching machine which is Tommy Burns.'

His vote was for the small white man against the big black coon, who would be depicted in Norman Lindsay's fight poster as a massive bear towering over Burns.

— 11 —

AFTER BURNS–LANG THERE SEEMED to be little new information on Jack Johnson, but negotiations were underway and Burns certainly wasn't going to hang about for nothing. It was common knowledge that John Wren and bookmaker Sol Green were trying to raise the £6000 that Burns was demanding, plus something for the black man.

Burns decided to set the world straight about the 'big smoke'.

'I particularly want to meet Johnson and get out of the boxing game forever,' he said. 'I want to meet Johnson; firstly, to make it plain that I draw no colour line, nor bar any man in the world; secondly, to establish my own opinion that I am Johnson's superior; and thirdly, to quit the game as champion of the world. If Johnson refuses to meet me, then I will retire for good and all, for the match with him is the only one I desire.'

There was Tommy again, making out that Johnson — who had been tracking him around the world like a bad-tempered bloodhound — was doing all the dodging.

'There could be no better time and place than Melbourne at Cup week,' he said.

Indeed a date close to the nation's biggest horserace would have filled any stadium a promoter could throw together. Burns said McIntosh had cabled another offer to Johnson and was anxious to see if the lippy American could 'nerve himself up' to accept it.

Even before any announcement, the demonisation of Johnson was well underway. On his previous visit he had mostly been treated kindly and regarded as a sportsman who, like Peter Jackson, had been dealt harshly by the colour line. Now he was being disparaged as a coon, big smoke, big buck nigger, and dinge with a yellow streak who had never done anything worthwhile in boxing — even if most of the boxing world regarded him as the only serious opponent left for Burns.

McIntosh opined: 'I like Burns' fighting, and think the best he can do has not been forced from him here, but what we have seen has been good enough for anything pretty well. The contest will surely prove a treat to watch, and in the end Burns will have a big coloured man's scalp dangling from his belt, but only after a desperate struggle.'

Harry Clayton, one of Burns' seconds, said he had seen Johnson fight Sailor Burke the year before and that Burns would bring him down heavily. The black would be knocked off his pedestal where he had been placed by well-meaning but misguided people. Johnson was only kidding, he said. Wild horses couldn't drag him into the ring with Burns.

Clayton said that in England Johnson had been served up a real lemon in Ben Taylor for an eight-round KO. The win was credited more to Taylor's exhaustion than to the punching of Johnson. If Johnson didn't hit harder against Burns it was 'guineas to gooseberries' that a couple of good ones from Burns would put him away.

Even Jim Jeffries said that it would only take a couple of body punches to eliminate the 'Senegambian'.

Bill Lang said he was a comparative mug when he met the big blackfellow, but had lasted nine rounds after a lot of money had been bet that he would be knocked out in four.

John Wren confirmed Johnson had been told by his backers to finish Lang quickly after the fourth. Even then there was no clear knockout as the towel came in.

'There we have something to go by,' said Wren. 'Burns did in six rounds what Johnson couldn't do in nine rounds, with the task very much more difficult when Burns tackled it, because of Lang's improved form and great weight.'

There was even gossip published in one sheet that the 'cullud pusson' Johnson had become infatuated with a frisky French lady in Paris and was sidestepping Burns because he was more interested in chasing dubious white women than genuine white fighters. Maybe that was why he hadn't replied to McIntosh's offers.

One paper said that Johnson had been talking about an offer to finish Burns inside 20 rounds. That was what his own countrymen would call 'guff', a feeble attempt to talk big. There were no conditions about stopping anybody inside 20 rounds, and Johnson would be the last fighter to talk about knockouts as he had no punch — unless, of course, it was a ploy to alienate McIntosh and wriggle out of the fight.

In response to all the criticism and slander, Johnson put his case forcefully in an article written for the British press.

'At last I am convinced that Burns, although he styles himself the champion boxer of the world, is, nevertheless, uncommonly anxious to avoid meeting me at any price — and that is to say except at such an utterly absurd price that no-one will be likely to put up a purse of the amount Burns says he requires,' he wrote.

'True, Tommy says that a purse of £7000 has been offered for a match to take place between us in Nevada, but it seems to me that it takes two to bring off a sporting contest between boxers, and up to date only one acknowledges to have received any intimation of this huge prize packet — and that is not your humble servant.'

As for the 'yellow streak' insult, which had long been attributed to Burns, Johnson said every sporting man in England knew that he had been chasing the champion around the world to get a match with him. Everywhere he had turned up, Burns and the white contenders had just managed to depart.

'After that there was a lot of talk in Australia about Squires, who was the champion of that big island, and who threatened to come right over to America to meet James Jeffries, who was then champion [Johnson had his dates mixed up again] but who, by the way, refused to defend his title against me, giving as an excuse the fact that I was colored.

'Now I don't want to make "pertinent" remarks [Johnson must have meant "impertinent" because he was now to the heart of the matter] but in athletics or any form of sport it seems to me that this colour line is way out of sight the poorest excuse any athlete can possibly bring up in order to slide out of meeting an opponent.

'Still, as Squires at the time was saying that he wanted to get on a match, I just got aboard a boat and "trekked" out to Australia to try and catch the Kangaroo heavyweight before he left his home,' Johnson wrote. 'But, like the "villain in the play" I was "foiled again", for no sooner had I landed in Australia than Squires sailed away to America. So there was I, having gone half round the world, just dead keen for a fight, while the white fellows were beating it faster than ever to keep out of my way.'

Even in England, where all athletes got a fair go, good purses were raised but Burns had taken the easy fights and dodged him again. It was enough to drive an ordinary man crazy. But, being no ordinary man, Johnson would continue the 'Burns hunt'.

'However, I do not for a moment wish to under-rate the man I am so anxious to meet, and right here I say that I consider

Burns is a great boxer, for he is both clever and game, while he does not do any "featherbedding" work when he starts hitting.

'I would point out, too, that in these days boxing is no longer a brutal sport. It is a contest of brains and skill, and I would wager the "maximum" on the chance of a clever man who fights with strategy against an opponent who relies on mere brute force and sledge-hammer hitting.'

Johnson said that there would be no groaning, or false excuses, if he lost to Burns. A bad workman should not blame his tools. Let the best man win.

'But say,' he concluded, 'it's downright weary work chasing a man around the world. It makes one real tired, it does indeed.'

In Australia Burns was the noblest of them all, even if he had dodged Johnson and now wanted an exorbitant sum to meet him. In London the black man undoubtedly felt that he had taken the higher moral ground. But who wanted to listen to a flash black about morality? If Johnson really wanted a fight why wasn't he here? Why hadn't he signed? It was less than two months to Melbourne Cup Day.

—————————— 1 2 ——————————

B Y LATE SEPTEMBER A CABLE did arrive. Johnson had signed with McIntosh.

'De big coon am a-comin',' proclaimed a sports sheet.

The press reported that the purse would be £7000, of which Burns would receive 60 per cent and Johnson the remainder. The fight would be after 30 November — forget the Melbourne Cup — most probably in Sydney on the morning of Boxing Day, and before the Randwick races. The fight might have had the ring of destiny about it, but McIntosh would not risk going up against the ponies.

The Amateur, ever concerned with the McIntosh reputation, wrote: 'Australia has succeeded where England and America failed.

Hitherto America had a monopoly on such things, and it will prove a staggerer indeed for the people of that country to hear that this little continent has outbidden and out-generalled them in the matter. Purses varying in value from £4000 to £7000 have been offered by different promoters and syndicates in the States — the two biggest (£6000 and £7000) coming from Californian speculators.'

(The most lavish of these speculators, Jim Coffroth, was reported to be in trouble with the law. It was said that in an argument during the counting of the gate takings after a Joe Gans–Battling Nelson lightweight fight, he had attacked Nelson's manager with a carving knife.)

The Johnson cable said that it would be a fight 'to the finish', which was nonsense. It would be the now-standard 20 rounds. It also didn't explain how Burns would get his £6000 demand — 60 per cent of £7000 being a mere £4200. If all his talk about retiring — having beaten all the champions on their own continents — was to be taken seriously, he did not seem like the type to give up £1800. Especially if those other offers had been genuine.

There was a provision in the agreement that both men would have to agree on a referee, something that would come back to haunt McIntosh. It was also alleged that during the negotiations Johnson, anxious to seal the deal, had offered to pay Burns £1000 if he managed to last 20 rounds.

Burns commented: 'Never mind about that. Johnson is too generous. I'll put up £2000; £1000 that he can't beat me in 20 rounds, and another £1000 that I beat him. If Johnson has not got the money himself, some of his admirers may find it for him.'

It was said that critics around the world were polarised, some feeling that Australia had not seen the best of either man. Johnson had beaten a raw Lang and a hopeless Felix, while Burns had undertaken a fight with Squires only ten days after getting off the boat; strangely, there was no mention that Squires had fought under the same conditions.

Burns had also contracted that terrible cold before the Squires fight. That was largely the reason why the fight went on so long: Burns could not force the pace. In fact, the fight almost had to be postponed, so ill was Burns.

But not all sportswriters were as eager to rationalise Burns' knockdown by the ordinary Lang. The Amateur was ready to declare that Johnson didn't need a medical condition as an excuse for his mundane habit of keeping a fight going until his man was wobbling.

Johnson, he said, was not even in the same class as Peter Jackson as an infighter, and certainly not in Burns' class. Burns had the brains. Burns had the art. Wait until Johnson had to face that deadly switch to southpaw.

The champ wasn't quite as agile on a horse, however. Down at Kosciusko he had fallen off one while fox-hunting, landed on a rock, and suffered a gravel rash upon his Napoleonic visage.

Perhaps that — or a session in the artesian bore baths at Moree for his 'rheumatics' — inspired Boshter Bill to publicly declare that he was prepared to deal with Johnson after Burns was through with him.

Johnson meanwhile, was boarding the *Ortona* in Naples with his wife and his Australian manager Sam Fitzpatrick, a former trainer of Peter Jackson and ex-pug who had been around the American fight game for 20 years. To make the trip, Johnson had cancelled a fight with the black middleweight Sam Langford.

And so the country waited. A big dark shadow loomed over its love affair with Tommy. The coon was set to arrive around 31 October.

After leaving Kosciusko, Burns made a quick trip to Tasmania, and indulged in an entertainment at the Albert Hall in Launceston. It consisted of a commentary on the film of his defeat of Gunner Moir, followed by a change into tights for a training routine and spar.

A week later at a boozy lunch at Sydney's Café Français, dutifully attended by the alleged teetotaller champion, bank cheques for the stake for the fight (said now to be £7500, less £400 sent over for Johnson's expenses) were handed by McIntosh to The Amateur. McIntosh said there had been a lot of blab about bigger purses in America, but this was truly the tops. He still did not explain how Burns was to get his £6000.

There were the usual speeches. The interminable self-serving jabber of E.W. O'Sullivan was interrupted by a drunk smashing crockery with a beer bottle. Another speaker, Alderman English, roasted a deputation of 'womenly men and unmanly women' of the church who had unsuccessfully appealed to Premier Wade to have all boxing banned in New South Wales. There was also a big raspberry for a meeting of anti-boxing 'Christian women' in Melbourne which had turned into such a ruckus that the rozzers had been called in to shut them up.

'Could anything as disgraceful happen at a boxing match?' English asked the assembled imbibers.

The Amateur ran his educated eye over Burns and pronounced him only a few grams over fighting weight after his month in the mountains. *The Sportsman*, which had developed a more jaundiced view of Burns, cackled that he looked 'as fat as mud'. But *The Referee*'s man was unperturbed, declaring it would be a devilishly close contest. (Burns must have wondered how his superior art had now suddenly been somewhat devalued.)

Bored witless, Tommy rose and made a short speech about what a nation of great sports Australia was. Then to make good his published boast he handed over two cheques for £1000 each. There was, however, now only one to be bet with Johnson. The other £1000 was a guarantee to McIntosh that he would turn up.

He also announced, yet again, that it would be his last fight. This was greeted with derision among the press. The thought of Tommy and Jewel going off to raise chickens when there were even fatter promoters to be plucked just didn't ring true.

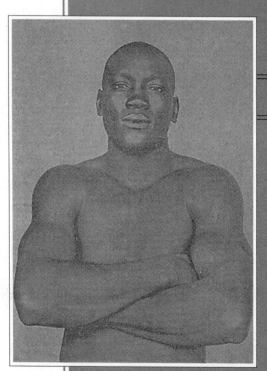

PART THREE

JACK

1

WHEN JOHNSON DID ARRIVE — 'The Coon Arrives' was one headline — he quickly realised that this visit wouldn't be anything like the last.

One cartoonist portrayed him — over a caption of '"Modest" Mistah Jack Johnson' — as balloon-headed, thick-lipped, garishly dressed, sporting a huge diamond stickpin, smoking a cigar, and donning a pork-pie hat, and telling a reporter: 'I hab chased Burns all over de world – yah sir! I am a larger fellow and cleverer than Tahmy, and know more about de game – by gar! Goodness I do hope nothing will happen to little Tahmy. I do want him so bad, sure! Guess Burns will quit de game when I've finished with him — he's nothing but a bluffer!'

From the time he arrived in Perth, the press had refused to quote him in regular English. Burns had a 'Murkan' accent but was quoted like a nobleman. Johnson had a Texan accent and was quoted like some kind of comical yokel ('I jes have the greatest regard for Tahmy's health, and if anything happened I'd take it bad', they had him saying).

'Bah,' interrupted the gruff Fitzpatrick. 'Burns is a bluffer, and I don't know whether we've got him yet.'

Johnson had the Canadian well and truly in his sights: 'He is the man who is going to play for my body all the time, and win out. I am going to keep my hands up above my head ... I have been fighting 16 years now and I reckon I know more about the game than any man.

'I am a larger man than he, and am cleverer. Does Burns want it fast and willing? I'm his man in that case. Does he want it flat-footed? Goodness, if he does I'm his Moses again. Anything to suit. But fast or slow, I'm going to win.'

Later in boxing history it would be said of Muhammad Ali that it ain't bragging if you can do it. However, coming from Jack Johnson it was considered bullshit of the worst water. This darkie, this coon, this big buck nigger, this labourer from a race which was no match for the wit and the grit of the white man, was running off at the mouth.

Johnson said he figured Burns had not beaten anybody that tough. Philadelphia Jack O'Brien, for example, had been only half-trained. Right now, he said, the black American Sam McVea, all the rage in Paris, was probably a better fighter than Burns.

'I think Burns is a good little fellow with brains,' he said.

When asked about his loss to Hart, Johnson finally set the record straight — as it had long been recognised in America.

'I beat Marvin Hart easier than any man I ever downed, and yet the decision was given against me.'

Reporters then dropped a bombshell. They informed Johnson that McIntosh had been negotiating to get Jim Jeffries to referee the fight. Nothing could have been a greater insult to the man. Jeffries had refused to fight him, and had consistently derided him in the world press. He had every right to suspect that the fix was in.

'I would never agree to allow that man to referee over me,' he complained. 'He has always been very bitter against me, and would not fight me after I beat his brother. Guess Jim was sore over that, and has never forgiven me. I calculate Mr Nathan [the referee in Burns' two Australian fights] might suit me.'

And what about that diamond and ruby scarf pin he was wearing?

'That's something I got from Lady Dudley for being the best-dressed gentleman at a ball given on board coming over. I got myself out for the occasion,' he grinned.

And the great Bill Squires challenge?

'I don't mind another fight,' he said, 'though your Bill treated me badly by refusing to fight me when I was in Australia. I offered to pay all expenses incurred by Bill ... I think Bill would have fought me but Reynolds, his manager, wanted to see a bit of the world, and put his foot down on it.'

The Amateur was singularly unimpressed. He attacked as a 'heap of bile' a London newspaper's opinion that Burns had fought as many 'stiffs' as Johnson and that he had no better a record than the black man.

Burns, meanwhile, had totally swallowed the hook and had given Johnson the psychological advantage that he needed. In Fremantle, Johnson had called him a 'bluffer'. Then when he got to Adelaide, according to some newspaper reports, he denied the 'bluffer' jibe. But when the Johnsons got to Melbourne and found that the champ was not around, Mrs Johnson got into the act by declaring that Burns was once again demonstrating his uncanny ability to disappear from any place where her husband had just arrived.

Burns was not copping any of this sweet. Heading to Sydney ahead of Johnson, he was interviewed on the train. He said that by backing away from the Fremantle statements Johnson was already 'squibbing'.

'And he'll squib it in the ring,' he said.

Burns said that there was only a three-minute gap between the time that Johnson's train had arrived in Melbourne and his had left for Sydney. He was certainly not hiding, but being three minutes together in the same place had clearly rattled Johnson.

'When he was told I was getting away he thought he had succeeded in chasing me out of Australia,' Burns said. 'One of the station porters told me this ... but Johnson has never chased me out of a country yet, and he never will … we are down to bedrock now, and you just say for me that what has been said of the "yellow streak" in Johnson is all right. By denying what he said about me he is showing it, and my honest opinion is that he will show it in the ring on Boxing Day.'

So there it was, finally made plain to Australia. Until that time the yellow streak had been only newspaper talk, and foreign newspaper talk at that. In Australia, Burns had built up a following that almost amounted to worship. Everywhere he went there was talk of the rectitude of the man, and his majestic image had thwarted those who sought to ban boxing as a subhuman spectacle. But now he was openly calling a man a coward — a man who had chased him demanding a fight.

In Australia, there was still enough of the 'fair play' ethos for many to gag on one athlete calling another a dog. Even today, with boxing at one of its lowest ebbs — disorganised, corrupt, greedy, riddled with drugs — there is no honour in one man calling another yellow. But Burns' following had been too well-established for the nation to see it Johnson's way.

Hugh D. McIntosh had never promoted a boxing match until Burns met Squires and now he had grabbed the one fight that the world wanted to see and it was coming to the boil with a rush. He had two choices: he could play up the racial hatred for all it was worth to sell tickets, or he could try to hose it down. To his credit — before the Great White Hope phenomenon, and long before the Joe Louis–Max Schmeling bouts were fought purely along racial lines for profit and propaganda — he chose the latter.

Maybe he didn't need race to sell the fight, but he also knew that he needed a 'sporting' contest to appease the Australian sense of fair play. There was a lot of self-serving bluster about this 'fair go', and even though it often made his countrymen seem naive in the eyes of a more sophisticated, cynical world, McIntosh did not doubt that it was truly out there. The hysterical debate prompted by the fight would prove him right.

Even the racy Sydney daily *The Australian Star*, known to all as 'The Twinkler', was moved to editorialise.

'Nowadays a boxing match is not a matter of a few brisk rounds with a sharp and decisive finale,' it wrote. 'It is rather a glorified exhibition of 'chin music' extending over months, and in the course of which the principals bathe constantly in the limelight of frequent publicity, slangwhanging each other freely in the newspapers, and annihilate each other with pen stabs until their quarrel is so far submerged in a sea of ink that the public are liable to get the impression that the actual encounter is only a detail in the carnival of wind and bluster.'

This, however, didn't stop The Twinkler from following every move of the combatants as breathlessly as any other publication. And McIntosh and his people were among the few who knew just how little bluster, and how much genuine hatred, there was between Burns and Johnson. What was not reported was how close the men would come to blows in his office on several occasions when important matters — especially the issue of the referee — had to be thrashed out in person.

———— 2 ————

JACK JOHNSON HAD A LITTLE chin music of his own with reporters on the train up to Sydney from Melbourne. McIntosh must have flinched when he heard the big man open up to debunk Burns and his 'yellow streak' talk — there had even been a report that Huge Deal had pulled a gun on Johnson during the journey to try, albeit unsuccessfully, to get him to keep his big black trap shut about yellow streaks and purses.

'I have got him now,' Johnson told the press. 'We'll see where the yellow streak is on December 26. He has been talking about having the fight in a 16-ft or 10-ft ring. Well, he can have an 8-ft ring if he likes — that is if he does not 'squib' out of it ... tell him that I've got a yellow streak, but that I'm looking for someone to bring it out ... to tell you the truth I do not think Burns is a game fellow.'

Johnson told how he had tried to talk to Burns at the National Sporting Club in London but Burns had deliberately cut him, claiming to have more important business. Now he was giving Burns the 'best of everything' just to get the fight.

However, the stories of Burns and Johnson getting a 60:40 split were nonsense. Tommy was getting no more or less than he had been demanding all along: more than any fighter in the past. He was getting his £6000 and Johnson was getting only £1000 plus a £100 share of film rights, though this wouldn't stop the black man from pestering McIntosh for more. For reasons of their own — maybe to avoid the public perception of both greed and unfairness — all parties were keeping the financial arrangements close to their chests.

The Bulletin, an unashamedly bigoted 'white Australia' magazine, commented on Johnson's apparent personality change from his earlier visit. In 1907, he had been a humble, jovial stousher, but now he was coming across as a blowhard and a boaster, and was being held up to 'scorn, hatred, ridicule, and contempt'. It was hard to believe these reports of 'mouth butchery' about him.

But on the train Johnson had lowered his guard. Not only had his disdain for Burns spilled out (the money issue was eating at him), but as the big picture of the fight began to unfold, with the anticipated crowd and huge takings, he grew more agitated, angry and resentful.

There were no big receptions along the way for Johnson and his plain white 'wife' — who was colourfully described as being 'addicted to jewellery' — and there was to be no soiree held in her honour by the 'ladies of Sydney'.

The ladyfolk of Sydney may well have done their homework for she was not Mrs Johnson at all. She was an ex-prostitute, a New York Irishwoman named Hattie McLay, whose father, according to Johnson, had helped to finance his trip to Europe on the Burns trail.

Johnson claimed in his autobiography that she was the first of his white women. Those who had read the Lola Toy case, however, would have doubted that Jack had held himself back for so long. It is more than likely that Johnson, as his fame grew from around 1906 onwards, had a string of white girlfriends, mostly prostitutes, before he met Hattie.

Hattie, he found, was a 'splendid pal' with a 'sporting' bent. He always called her 'Mac'. Unfortunately, she had one habit which displeased Johnson: she was an alcoholic; a beer-guzzler who regularly embarrassed him in public. When he finally put a beer ban on their house she simply smuggled the suds in.

'I frequently found her much the worse for her indulgence and was mystified concerning the manner in which she obtained it,' he wrote in his autobiography. 'The secret was solved to some extent when one day I found numerous empty bottles hidden under her mattress which attracted my attention because of the bulging appearance of the bed.'

Those bottles under the mattress were the last straw for the new world champion. In 1911 Hattie was kicked out and he paid her $500 for letters and telegrams she had written.

In Sydney the Johnson mob were booked into the Sir Joseph Banks Hotel, scene of Johnson's imbroglio with Miss Toy. Mrs Johnson would handle the cooking and Jack would run around the hotel pavilion's indoor 140-yard track.

On his arrival in Sydney, an enthusiastic crowd of several thousand gathered at Sydney's Central Station — with cries of 'Good boy, Johnson!' and 'Good luck, Jack!' — and like Burns, Johnson needed a police escort to get him to safety.

A reception was arranged at the Café Français and big Jack ('de boss slogger of de Colored Races') arrived in a gorgeous new car. He was to find that most of McIntosh's invitations to those who had gathered at the feet of Burns had been more or less ignored.

McIntosh lamely tried to lay the blame on the Post Office. He said he had posted 250 invitations with penny stamps but the Post Office had refused to carry them at that rate.

The 'dusky Cyclops', it was noted by the press, had packed on a fair amount of beef since his last visit, and was at least four and a half kilograms overweight. He must have had his nose well into the feedbag in London and Paris, but Johnson maintained that he needed only a few weeks to get into fighting shape.

'He was encased in a check suit of faultless cut, and his white silken tie was ornamented by a solitaire, which flashed like a heliograph, and the amount of gold in his ivories that gleamed as he smiled a smile was a prize calculated to arouse a base thought in the mind of a bodysnatcher had one happened to be present,' guffawed *The Sportsman*.

First up on his feet, of course, was E.W. O'Sullivan, who was quick to reassure Johnson that Australians were really not such bad chaps. No colour line here: this was the home of the great Peter Jackson and, of course, that great patriot Bill Squires.

McIntosh rose and vented his rage at Sydney's 'penny dreadfuls' who had accused Johnson of slagging Burns for having a yellow streak of his own. The hosing down of the racial embers had well and truly begun. He said it was a pure fabrication that Johnson had called Burns a 'bluffer'. But they were hollow words, as Burns and Johnson had since been at each other's throats in print.

'Let us see the fight and the public can then say which, if either, of the pair possesses a yellow streak,' said McIntosh.

But, said McIntosh, all credit was due to Tommy Burns for giving this man his chance, the only champion in modern times to do so. Now, in the interests of fairness, the fighters would have to agree on a referee.

(Jim Jeffries, it was revealed by W.W. Naughton, had been miffed that McIntosh's cabled offer had not been 'return paid'. Who was this clod from the Antipodes? Big 'Jeff' had been vocal in support of Burns against Johnson but also critical of Burns' hunger for a dollar. He claimed he had never been so plain greedy himself. Having said that he cabled McIntosh a demand for $5000 and 'transportation' to do the refereeing job, but not even McIntosh was biting at that price.)

McIntosh went on to assure Johnson that he had not been playing favourites with Burns by travelling with him around the country. That was just business; if Johnson had been here first he would have done the same.

Johnson then got up to say his piece. He was smiling broadly but wasn't going to dodge the issue of the yellow streak, no matter what McIntosh had just said. He wanted it made clear that he was not the one who had started this thing.

'The words I am about to speak to you, gentlemen, I speak from my heart,' he began, drawing a hush. 'Each and every one in this room who has read the sporting papers knows that I have travelled the world over trying to get Mr Burns. I don't believe in making a lot of noise because I believe in the old saying that a barking dog won't bite.

'I, myself, have picked up several papers with interviews from Mr Burns saying that I have a yellow streak. I have travelled all over the world and nobody has yet found that yellow streak. I am a man and I say it is a thing that any man would take offence at — any man in the world would ... we will see who has the yellow streak. All I ask for — I don't want any favour — is a fair field. I will do my best to win and I won't try to mislead the public through the papers.'

Missing from the reception table, however, was his much-celebrated opponent, along with The Amateur. It was written that

Burns was miffed at the way Johnson had 'let himself loose'. He also felt that there was a distinct lack of style in the black man's entourage. There would certainly be no fashionable guest list down at Botany.

Tommy and Jewel had in fact been motoring about Sydney in their new 15–20 hp Fiat — Tommy's Christmas present to his beloved — looking at prime real estate. They had also driven up to the Blue Mountains and enjoyed a roadside picnic of billy tea and broiled chops.

'It was glorious,' said Jewel of the swagman's beverage. 'And I never before thought chops were so nice.'

The loving couple settled on Sheilah, a cottage with a big garden, at Medlow Bath, in the grounds of the Hydro Majestic Hotel resort. That would be the last seen of them before Boxing Day. Johnson, meanwhile, was seen whizzing all over town in a big hire car looking up friends from his previous visit.

While all this was going on, The Amateur, who had been steering well clear of the big black man, sought out his 'old friend' Sam Fitzpatrick. Showing 'a great wealth of tweed about the waist', Fitzpatrick sucked on a cigar and told The Amateur of Johnson's exploits since his last visit.

Despite having no apparent knockout punch, Johnson had felled Bob Fitzsimmons in two rounds in Philadelphia in July 1907. There was a big crowd, said Fitzpatrick, and Fitzsimmons, even at 45, was given a chance.

'Bob let a few weighty punches go and had any of them landed Jack would have been hurt, I tell you, but he was too clever,' said Fitzpatrick. 'Fitz tried the same shift with Johnson that brought Jim Corbett down, but it didn't work.'

In September, at Bridgeport, Johnson had had a points-win over Sailor Burke in a six-rounder. Burke, said Fitzpatrick, had shown a great fondness for the deck, hitting it any time Johnson hit him — maybe 24 times — to see out the distance. In November,

Johnson had stopped Fireman Jim Flynn in 11 rounds in San Francisco. The following month Flynn knocked out Squires in six.

'They boomed Flynn as a sure trip up for Johnson's reputation,' said Fitzpatrick. 'He was going to do everything to Johnson and sports piled coin on the white man very freely. The same old yellow streak was talked. You don't want me to tell you what a punching bag Jack made of Flynn that night; he never put a glove on Johnson.'

That was a form line which didn't seem to get a lot of play in Australia. Johnson had beaten Flynn, and Flynn had beaten Squires much faster than Burns. Ah, but our Bill had the 'rheumatics' in America, and he was only learning the American way. All in all, he was a much truer test for Tommy. Better to go back to Hart beating Johnson and Burns beating Hart.

Fitzpatrick said that Johnson was a ring tactician much in the mould of Peter Jackson — but was he really as good? Fitzpatrick was perhaps more qualified than anyone to answer that question.

'It is very hard indeed to judge between the man of today and the man of years ago,' he said. 'But I feel sure there isn't much difference one way or the other.'

Jackson stood up straight, the old way, to get full advantage of his height. Johnson had a bit of a stoop, but that was the new way of making it harder to land. Jackson was strictly a straight-puncher, while Johnson had all kinds of hooks and uppercuts. Both men were safe fighters who didn't like to take risks. Today, most fight critics studying pictures of Jackson — who was slimmer and much-less developed in the shoulders than Johnson at his peak — would doubt Jackson's ability to stand up to the power of Johnson, who was the prototype modern heavyweight.

The English certainly had a high opinion of Johnson, claimed Fitzpatrick. If the Burns fight was on over there at least £50000 would be bet on Johnson — there was perhaps no limit to what 'sports' in England would be prepared to risk. In fact, the

National Sporting Club was running a lottery on how many rounds it would take Jack to finish Tommy. Johnson had predicted it would be done within 12 rounds.

Australia, however, remained unconvinced. It had seen what Burns could do, while Fitzpatrick's opinion just sounded like a lot of hot air — especially as Johnson was nowhere near fighting shape.

But with Burns up in the Blue Mountains, the public were privileged to watch Johnson get into peak condition. Advertisements appeared for his daily routine at the Sir Joseph Banks, which had been renamed the Olympic Recreation Grounds for the occasion.

Bright, breezy, boxing bouts were promised: scientific exhibitions of skipping, ball-punching and shadow-sparring. Trams were running daily from the city. Admission was 1s. Ladies would be admitted, too. At the time there weren't many opportunities to see a big hunk of a black man stripped to the waist, with muscles flexing and an engaging bulge in his tights.

Women turned up in huge numbers.

Even with the 'wife' around, Johnson was not averse to advertising his manhood (although he was wrapping it in gauze bandages to exaggerate its size). And when photographers were present, he certainly didn't seem to shirk from side-on poses.

However, many women might have been more impressed by the power in Johnson's arms and shoulders. He was light in the legs but up top he would have compared well with 1990s heavyweights like Mike Tyson and Evander Holyfield — he astonished some of the fight types by picking up local heavyweight Mike Williams and walking him around the ring like a child.

But equally, the local women might well have been charmed by his roguish smile and prowess on the bull fiddle. Some were even flashing the hosiery beneath their side-split *directoire* dresses in a scandalous fashion. When one lady tripped over a chair and exposed her abundant charms, Sam Fitzpatrick screamed, 'For the love of heaven somebody lend the lady a barrel!' and sent the crowd into an uproar. He then tacked up a sign: DIRECTOIRE GOWNS AND OTHER ROUGH STUFF BARRED.

3

FOR A DEEP AND MEANINGFUL appraisal of Johnson, *The Lone Hand* commissioned a writer named 'Leonce' and the result — as one would expect from the sister paper of *The Bulletin* — was not quite as hagiographic as it had been with Burns.

'Six feet and a quarter of an inch of copper-colored brawn and muscle, a small closely-shaven head, suggestive of the knobby handle of some monstrous blackthorn walking stick, a pair of gleaming dark eyes, and a wide mouthful of golden teeth — that is Jack Johnson,' Leonce wrote.

'He is just a big, and for the most part good-natured black-fellow, with a U.S. State school education, a somewhat quaint wit, an unabashed liking for the limelight, and a regard for his chosen calling that amounts to worship,' he continued. 'He means to stick to it until he drops.'

Indeed, Johnson refused — correctly — to take seriously Burns' talk of giving up the fight game for a life of poultry management. To him, that was plain chicken-witted. However, the big black did not score well on the humility index. Leonce wrote that Johnson adored himself, regarding his fighting ability with 'wondering veneration'.

Which hand did he prefer?

'Wal, thar,' Johnson was quoted, ever the yokel. 'They're both so good, it's impossible to rightly say.'

Johnson was clearly enjoying himself, with Leonce taking careful notes of his line of bull. He spoke of examinations by eminent European physiologists who were astounded by his wondrous heart, which, within four or five minutes of a brutal 20-round battle would beat at its normal, languid rate. He had never suffered indigestion, even if he did suck champagne through a straw and scoffed all kinds of puddings, cream, jam, and ices, and smoked cigars even when in full-training.

Leonce wrote that Johnson had become known throughout America as 'The Iceberg' for his cool style. Furthermore, he had once been a flat-race jockey, not just a stablehand. He had also excelled in athletics as a sprinter, but would leave the long-distance stuff to 'Tahmy'.

Johnson was prominent in the ward politics of Texas, too, even though he was never around much these days. And not only that, he was also a leading member of the Methodist Church back in Galveston. (One can imagine the scenes of hilarity in the Johnson camp as all this solemn nonsense was gobbled up by *The Lone Hand*'s man.)

Leonce was not that impressed with Johnson's work on the bag: it was neat but lacked the devil of Burns' routine. He would be the first to admit however, as the English writers had rightly observed, that Johnson was superb in his sparring because of his science and variety of punches, although he did not share Johnson's view of the Hart fight.

'If Johnson is as good as he thinks he is, Burns will crawl out of the Stadium on the 26th of this month an anguished, reputationless wreck,' he wrote. The fight, Leonce argued, would probably be decided on gameness and the only certainty was that a 'level and willing' fight would occur.

Leonce perceived that Johnson's willingness to fight, indeed his unmitigated hatred of Burns, was most intense. This detail had been washed over by The Amateur and others interested in promoting a 'clean' contest in the wake of wowser objections to a primeval spectacle.

'Johnson does not like Burns,' he wrote. 'Far from it. It is his normal habit to direct upon the whole world a beaming auriferous smile of friendliness. The beam fades swiftly away, however, when the name of the little Canadian is mentioned.'

'Johnson thirsts to humiliate his detractor. He hurls no charge of streak-ownership at Burns, but he does say that Burns is a grossly over-estimated battler ... Johnson condemns Burns for his niggardliness. He considers it beneath the white man's dignity to have but one attendant to perform the multitude of duties that are required by a world's champion ... Burns is his conception of a thoroughly rude and offensive person ... the struggle with Burns will be the first, he claims, in which he will enter the ring with a feeling against his adversary.'

Here should have been the true warning to those doggedly making Burns the favourite in this fight. Johnson was much bigger and stronger, highly skilled, and intensely motivated. Australia had seen Tommy Burns knocked down by Bill Lang, the footballer who had been treated as a joke by Johnson, but still it couldn't swallow hard enough to concede the black man the advantage. Nowhere was this logic more tortured than in *The Bulletin*.

Despite all the rumours about Johnson's bad habits, Johnson had worked tremendously hard, reported *The Bulletin*'s column, 'Sporting Notions'. His arms, legs, and shoulders were as hard as vulcanite. He was so strong that big men would clasp their hands around his neck and he would swing them around like little children. In sparring, Lang was a baby in his hands who could be laid out at any time. In clinches he would lock those logs of arms around his sparring partners and render them powerless. He had shown, in these spars, an extraordinary ability to protect his unmarked head and face. Nobody had come close to landing a punch on the noggin of this 'big, brawny, good-natured, over-grown boy'.

So how on earth was Tommy Burns going to beat him? Sporting Notions had some ideas about that. For a start, Burns' shoulders were 'Atlantean'. His arms and biceps were as big as legs. They tapered down to little fists, but that just made them 'wedges' of bone and muscle. There was no hint that he had indulged in any 'Babylonian orgies' — even if some American writers claimed that, on the quiet, and far away from the adoring gaze of The Amateur (among others), Tommy was addicted to cigars and strong drink. And while Johnson hit with his arms, Burns had body behind his blows.

That wasn't all. Johnson had a weak 'bingie', or stomach. For weeks, Sporting Notions alleged, his trainer had been trying to dry it out and toughen it but had been thwarted by Johnson's need for liquid refreshment. It would be there that the giant blows of Burns would land on Boxing Day. Burns would be fighting out of his crouch, giving Johnson little to hit and opening up Jack's breadbasket.

The writer said he had examined the Johnson equator and found it to be 'a fair round belly with fat capon lined' — a reference to Johnson's allegedly enormous appetite for chickens. It was soft-looking and resembled a little heap of sheeny brown satin. It had dimples in it and a 'rude touch' might destroy its symmetry, so Johnson was not allowing a glove near it in sparring. It certainly didn't compare with the washboard that Burns was sporting.

'In plain English, Burns has trained himself to a point at which all his vitals are protected with a thick coating of muscle and hardened tissue, and Johnson has not,' it surmised.

Burns, it was concluded, knew the weak spot and should win somewhere between the ninth and 13th rounds.

4

JOHNSON MAY HAVE TRAINED HARD but he figured he really only needed three weeks to prepare for the fight, even if it was the biggest of his life. And although he paced himself, he didn't exactly spare himself a good time.

Between morning and afternoon training sessions he was regularly spotted motoring rapidly about town and pulling into bars and cafés. Enquiries at the kitchen at the Sir Joseph Banks — about the only place anybody seemed to see Mrs Johnson during the day, although she accompanied him on piano in their nightly after-dinner music sessions — revealed that he was getting through three chickens a day.

Meanwhile, Tommy and Jewel were driving down from the mountains to put on charity workouts at the Stadium which drew up to 5000 people — 1500 of them women. To add a touch of style, McIntosh had a string band playing while Tommy went through his ball-punching routine.

Once more the ladies were all agog at the boyishness of Burns, one remarking that he looked very much like the new young curate at her church. Others complained that it seemed awfully cruel that he was being made to fight the enormous black. Jewel had volunteered to serve tea to the ladies, but was overwhelmed by the numbers. When she failed to turn up again it was reported that she had had an attack of the vapours and that doctors were being relayed in and out of the Burns' cottage at the Hydro Majestic.

McIntosh, however, was aglow. On the first day of ticket sales, five weeks before the fight, he sold £1074 worth. The question of Johnson's purse was still muddy, but that day's sales just about made sure that it would be covered.

If there didn't seem to be much joy at Sheilah, with Jewel laid up, there was plenty going on at the Johnson camp. Bill Lang turned up one day to spar and soon had one eye opened up. But he wasn't to be outdone by Johnson in the new recreation of wallaby-chasing.

A hapless wallaby had been brought to the camp in a crate and released on the grounds to be chased and tackled by Jack and the lads. There were men diving in all directions at the poor beast, with Johnson loudly proclaiming himself the champion wallaby-chaser of the world. The locals, however, reckoned Lang, with his superior Aussie Rules footwork, had finally secured a victory over the American.

With the wallaby no match for the two fighters, a greased razorback pig was brought to the camp for more sport.

'He was a long, tall and lanky member of his species, built like a racehorse,' Johnson recalled. 'Furthermore, he was undomesticated and valued his liberty exceedingly high. He had no wish to be coddled and manifested a rather vicious nature.'

Johnson claimed he ran it down. Then came a further test: a 'jack rabbit' — a common hare to the locals — which was considered 'the last word in animal speed' in Australia. They let one loose and Johnson ran it to death.

Well, almost. Sam Fitzpatrick had wagered that if the hare was released on the nearby cricket oval Johnson and his sparring partners, Lang and Bob Bryant, would not be able to run it down within 20 minutes. A large number of punters gathered to make bets and the hare put up a good show until Johnson grabbed it with three minutes to spare. It was still kicking when he carried it triumphantly back to the pavilion.

Johnson claimed he had never been in better shape. With a month to go he was — courtesy of 32 km a day of running and walking — only two kilograms over his fighting weight.

Pressure? There just didn't seem to be much in the public face of the American. He had even convinced some earnest sections of the press that his artistic talents extended well beyond whacking a bull fiddle to a higher appreciation of Shakespeare, especially *Othello*.

What a picture: the former Galveston streetfighter up at night with his hooker de facto reading him the great play, the couple making plans to bring their own production of the tragedy of the Moor and his white wife Desdemona to the stage. Hattie was now being described as a 'very striking white woman of the Venetian type' by The Twinkler.

James Brennan put on a charity night at his Amphitheatre and Johnson, in a tuxedo, played his bull fiddle in a quartet. Later, he treated a bevy of showgirls ('artistes') to a champagne supper at the Paris House club.

Burns, however, was not to be overshadowed. It was revealed by The Twinkler that Prince Pu Lun, the heir apparent to the throne of China, was a great fan. Burns was flashing an autographed photograph of the prince to reporters.

One strange aspect of the lionisation of Burns by the Australian press was that, like Johnson, he liked a good time with the lads — at least when Jewel wasn't around — and had quite a reputation as a practical joker. His sparring partners were always wary of copping some itchy powder in their shorts — he even tried it on the ladies at dances — and he owned a novelty book with the racy title, *A Night in Paris*. Open it and it would explode in your face like a trick cigar ... or a Jack Johnson punch.

5

AT CLOSE QUARTERS IN McINTOSH'S office neither Burns nor Johnson was in the mood for joking. McIntosh had been compelled to call them together several times to sort out the matter of the referee, and Johnson, bristling at the disparity in the purses, was constantly at McIntosh for a bigger cut.

Norman Lindsay walked into Huge Deal's office one day close to the fight and found an iron bar on his desk wrapped in sheet music.

'What the devil is this for Hughie?' asked Lindsay.

'It's for that black bastard, if he tries any funny business,' growled McIntosh.

Lindsay wasn't surprised, as he too had heard the story about McIntosh pulling a gun on Johnson in the train up from

Melbourne. However, he noted with some amusement the song McIntosh had chosen to wrap around the bar: 'Sing Me to Sleep, Mother'.

But Burns was also a handful. He wouldn't accept Nathan as referee and bickered about other choices, in turn riling Johnson who feared another sidestep. McIntosh was forced to step between the fighters to keep the peace. It was just like his old cycling days.

Johnson later recalled attending one of the meetings with seven-year-old Phyllis Bain, daughter of James Bain, manager of the National Amphitheatre. The little girl followed him around like a puppy. One day, he said, Burns got angry at a meeting and told him: 'You used to be a good fighter but you are all shot now. You might as well take your medicine.'

Johnson then claimed that Burns began to swear at him in front of the little girl.

'Burns,' he retorted, 'the newspapers are describing you as a gentleman, so be careful what you say. If you swear any more before this child I shall give you a lacing right here.'

Burns, he said, made a movement like he might draw a gun. McIntosh, who had more of a reputation for pulling an equaliser, stepped between them. Burns reached for a chair to smash Johnson, but McIntosh ripped it away from him. Not to be outdone, Burns then grabbed an inkwell from McIntosh's desk and made to throw it.

'Let him loose, he's tame and harmless,' said Johnson — or so he claimed.

There was no agreement on the referee that day. For one thing Johnson, who didn't trust any referee that McIntosh wanted to appoint, demanded two judges for the fight, as well as a referee, claiming that this was the standard in America under Queensberry rules.

Burns disagreed: 'I feel quite satisfied to leave the decision to the referee and the public of Australia. I don't want any new-fangled notions at the eleventh hour, and am satisfied to be

guided by the universal custom, recognised the world over ...
I will not be a party to make demands which I consider an insult
to the sporting public of Australia, and a reflection upon the
honesty of the men who have the contest in charge.'

Johnson appealed to fair-minded sportsmen to back him.
The Bulletin reckoned that if pieces of Tommy were going to be
strewn around the ring as Johnson was boasting, there would be
no need for judges. But local fighter Snowy Baker, returning from
London with a silver medal from the Olympics, where he was
beaten by Englishman J.A.T. Douglas, and preparing to spar with
Burns, backed Johnson, saying that two judges was now the rule
in England. All the same, Burns was to get his way. The Amateur
drew up a 'revised' set of Queensberry rules for the fight with a
referee only, and no judges. This only served to convince Johnson
that he could expect no favours and would have to scrap for any
conceivable advantage.

Burns' problems with Nathan as referee had stemmed from a
fight between his sparring partner Pat O'Keefe, the Irish
middleweight champion, and Australian welterweight Jack
Blackmore, who had been on a winning streak and had even
stopped a heavyweight.

It was one of the worst fights seen in Sydney for years — it
even looked like Blackmore was laying down — and Nathan
called it a draw at the end of 20 excruciating rounds of scrambling
and holding. Most critics declared that it should have been
declared 'no fight'. It was pure 'cocktailship'.

A livid Burns, who had been in the limp O'Keefe's corner,
bombarding him with instructions to go for the kill, told Nathan
that it was a 'rotten decision'. Nathan, who had already refereed
Burns' two fights in Australia, wasn't copping that, not even from
the world heavyweight champion. He fronted Burns and told him
that he was 'no gentleman' and should know how to conduct
himself better. That effectively ended his chance of refereeing the

great fight, but not before he and The Amateur had slugged it out in print.

The Amateur had written that he had long held the impression that Nathan's point-scoring was peculiar, and didn't allow for the sort of evasive skills that at least one fighter might display on Boxing Day. Nathan, in a letter to *The Referee*, wondered how long The Amateur had really been thinking this way — there had been no complaints when Burns beat Squires and Lang. And he vehemently denied an allegation that he had threatened a dozen times to disqualify Blackmore — without doing anything about Blackmore's tactics — against O'Keefe.

The Amateur, having the last word on the matter, replied that since 1893 he had been concerned about Nathan's ability to give a decision when there was no knockout. So he had recommended to McIntosh that Nathan not be used in the big fight.

But this was a slap in the face for Boshter Bill, who had been so cynically built up for his third fight with Burns. It was obviously in the interests of Burns to have a referee in that fight who would make a decision. There had been no objection from The Amateur at the time about Nathan, probably because there had been no real chance of Boshter going the distance.

Meanwhile, Johnson had shifted camp to a cottage by Manly Beach and was bodysurfing with the locals every day. *The Sportsman* ran a big-lipped cartoon of him in a bathing suit, with children admiring his suntan ('My word he's sunburnt'). The caption was pure doggerel:

Hi! here he goes, de fighting coon, he's getting right in trim,
For Tahmmy and he will meet soon — see Yack goes for his swim.
The Manly folks they fairly gasp each bloke and pretty peach.
When they see him, dis 'ansome coon, come striding
down de beach.

And it had more to describe the resplendent Johnson on one of his walks downtown:

W'en de colo's man come a walkin' down the street
You kin heah de ladies all aroun' repeat;
'Ain't he handsome? Ain't he gran'?
Ain't he splendid? Goodness, lan'?
W'y he's pu'fect from his fo'head to his feet.'
An' sich steppin' to de music down de line,
Tain't de music by itself dat makes it fine;
It's his walkin' step by step,
And de keepin' time wid 'Hep'
Dat makes dis colo'd gen'lman look divine.

Ten thousand people turned up at the Stadium on a Monday night to welcome back Snowy Baker and to watch him spar with Tommy Burns. Once more McIntosh had catered to the ladies and there were hundreds of them in the crowd. Sir Francis Suttor, president of the Legislative Council, led Baker into the ring.

It was to be a lively four-round spar, although Baker flagged towards the end. The crowd gave both men a standing ovation and Burns' popularity was now at its peak. Afterwards he certainly said all the right things: he had boxed the Englishman who beat Baker for the gold medal and said there was nothing to choose between them. Snowy was one of the best amateurs he had seen.

McIntosh announced that he had already sold 50 per cent more reserved seats for Burns–Johnson than at the same stage before Burns–Squires. He also had to issue a warning about scalpers who were buying up big lots.

Crowds packed Castlereagh Street when Burns turned up to perform his stage routine for an annual charity show to raise money for Christmas dinners for the poor. The audience was almost in tears when he made a short speech about how he too had known great poverty in childhood.

Meanwhile, the Burns' had shifted camp and were back at Darling Point. Jewel had been out buying new outfits — despite her reported illnesses, she had put on 12 kg since arriving in the country — and would serve tea as her husband got in an hour or two of handball. The Amateur wondered why Australia had not adopted such a fine game. If it was good for Tommy, why not the nation?

Johnson was now sparring at the Stadium too, and it was reported that one big punter was ready to unload on him — but only at inflated odds. However, Australian bookies were aware that their American brothers had Johnson as favourite — they would not take the risk. The Amateur pooh-poohed this. The 'Murkan' people, he said, were lousy gamblers. The Yanks had made John L. Sullivan favourite against Gentleman Jim Corbett. (The Amateur had snaffled £25 from a visiting American comedian on that fight.) Burns had also been the 5/1 underdog against Marvin Hart, and Boshter Bill had been favoured to beat him over there. So much for them! In this country Burns would justifiably start favourite.

To illustrate the grip that the fight had on the public, 12 000 people turned up at the Stadium on a Wednesday night to see Burns' sparring partner Les O'Donnell go against Johnson's sparring partner Bob Bryant. The main attraction was that Burns and Johnson would be in the corners.

It was reported that the two men, somewhat embarrassed, met in a corridor outside the dressing-rooms.

'Hello Burns,' said Johnson.

'Hello Johnson,' said Burns.

'Don't be sarcastic.'

'I'm not sarcastic. I'm always a good fellow.'

The tension from the meetings with McIntosh was simmering, but nonetheless the two men shook hands and went to their charges. When the fighters were in the ring, however, there was aggravation. Johnson — with his trousers tucked up to show a pair of rainbow-coloured socks — marched over to discuss tossing for corners. Burns faced him and reportedly called him a 'son of a gun', or worse.

Things got heated and the crowd began to rumble. Could it all explode right then and there? McIntosh, with what The Amateur described as his famous 'fierce and menacing expression', jumped straight between them and gave them both a gobful — a slice of 'piquant tongue pie' — to stop his massive investment, with its unprecedented profits, being blown away in an eruption of egos. Johnson walked away in disgust.

Then, to the dismay of The Amateur (who had been watching O'Donnell spar Burns, and had declared Les the bright new hope of Australian boxing), Bryant, who weighed over six kilograms lighter, proceeded to give O'Donnell a hiding. Yet referee Snowy Baker, to the chagrin of the crowd, called it a draw. So much for the nous of the Australian punters: they had made O'Donnell the heavy favourite. But was it an omen?

—————— 6 ——————

THE MATTER OF A REFEREE was still boiling, and Johnson's mood was not helped by an announcement from McIntosh that it was now estimated that he would make £40 000 from the film rights and would be off to Europe and America with the footage a week after the fight.

Johnson's mood was further darkened a week before the fight when he put on a show for an orphanage at his sparring venue, the Manly Skating Rink. He had promised to spar with Larry Foley and Bill Lang, but turned up in full evening dress with his bull fiddle and a band and played some tunes. His regular sparring partners put on exhibitions but there was no Foley and no Lang. Johnson made an announcement that their boat was late.

'Tommy will not be late, though,' yelled a spectator.

The mob demanded that Johnson spar but he refused — Sam Fitzpatrick wasn't risking anything unarranged so close to the 'great bashing match'. The crowd began to hoot Johnson — looking at the suit they figured that he had never intended to spar. It was starting to get ugly, so Jack signalled the band. It broke into a chorus of 'Auld Lang Syne' and he bolted for the exit.

Four names had been put up for referee, including Colonel Ryrie and Snowy Baker. However, Ryrie was ill and McIntosh could not get the fighters to agree on any one of the other candidates. Not only that, but he was having to deal with scaremongering that the Stadium would not hold the weight of the crowd and might collapse, like matchwood, killing thousands.

'Nonsense,' he announced. 'It could carry a regiment of elephants and you wouldn't even hear a plank creak.'

The issue was finally settled two days before the fight when McIntosh, who had never refereed a fight before — but had tried his hand as an amateur boxer — appointed himself. Baker was the last name on the table but Johnson, after that stinker of a decision in the Bryant–O'Donnell fight, would have no bar of it.

But eventually, after much consideration, Johnson counted on McIntosh not daring to give a blatantly biased decision. It was a risk — there was little that Huge Deal might not dare. But to Johnson it looked like McIntosh was in boxing for the long term; he would not risk making a fool of himself in front of the world.

So he turned to Burns, who was sitting across the table, and said, 'Before going any further with this match, I want to know if you and McIntosh are good friends.'

'We are friends, the best of friends,' Burns replied. Johnson asked the same of McIntosh and got the same answer. He and Burns were friends. He and Tommy had confidence in each other.

Fitzpatrick began to wonder what the hell Jack was up to.

'If you and Burns are such good friends, then you must referee the fight,' Johnson said to McIntosh. Fitzpatrick almost fainted.

'I am fighting this fight and am going to have some part in naming the referee,' Johnson said. For once McIntosh was taken aback — he began to mutter doubts. But when Burns agreed he realised that he really had no alternative.

There was grumbling in the press and around the pubs about the decision. But it was barely heard beneath the din of excitement which had gripped the city and the nation. The time for talk was over. The final advertisements appeared in the papers: 'Burns v. Johnson. For the Championship of the World. On Saturday Next, Boxing Day'.

7

MᶜINTOSH PRODUCED A SPLENDID PROGRAM befitting the occasion. Prominent was a magnificent photographic portrait of himself: dark, handsome, strong, an early Errol Flynn. He was proclaimed as 'a Justice of the Peace and prominent in many big Australasian ventures', including government tourist houses, and a developer of 'clean straight sport and tests of athletic skill', especially boxing, of which he was himself an exponent.

Above all, of course, he was now 'the greatest handler of boxing contests the world has known'. He had beaten the American and English 'speculators' to this fight, with its £7500 purse (Johnson's £400 expenses and £100 for the film had been included to inflate his share to £1500).

It would be the richest gate in history but Johnson's light cut — £1000 to Burns' £6000 — would make it only the third biggest purse. In the Jeffries–Corbett match of 1903 the fighters had shared $43 638 (£8727).

Huge Deal, however, was outdoing his international rivals in the looking-after-the-promoter department. The Burns–Squires match had hauled in £13 400, with only £3000 going to the pugs.

In the program, a history of the sport in Australia came with a timely political punch. The 'noble art' had flourished on the Ballarat and Bendigo goldfields, wrote McIntosh, producing a long list of 'splendid specimens of grit and endurance' which had ended with Larry Foley, the last of the bareknuckle champions.

But the age of science had reached Australia 20 years ago with laws compelling the use of gloves, so that the chance of injury was no greater than that of other sports.

The 'offence' of bareknuckle fighting had disappeared the world over. In a sophisticated nation like Australia men with differences chose to settle them in the ring under recognised rules — except, of course, for public-house brawls. The bareknuckle fights around the harbour, or at the back of Randwick Racecourse, which the police had been powerless to stop, were almost a thing of the past.

Whether this healthy situation was allowed to continue, McIntosh railed, depended on how the limelighting wowsers of the community — who were intent on having boxing banned — were met by the 'virile' in the community.

'The annals of the old country, from the invasion of the Romans downward, sufficiently demonstrate that the native Briton trusted more to the strength of his arm, the muscular vigour of his frame, and the fearless attributes of his mind in the hour of danger, than to any artificial expedients, and that, whether in attack or defence, the combination of those qualities rendered him at all times formidable in the eyes of his assailants, however skilled in the science or practice of warfare,' thundered McIntosh, pre-empting some of the red-hot debate which the fight would generate.

McIntosh even got literary, producing a passage from Sir Arthur Conan Doyle's story, *Rodney Stone*: 'It is a less evil that two men should, of their own free will, fight until they can fight no more, than that the standard of hardihood and endurance should run the slightest risk of being lowered in a nation which depends so largely upon the individual qualities of her citizens for her defence. Do away with war, if the cursed thing can by any wit of man be avoided, but until you see your way to that, have a care in meddling with those primitive qualities to which at any moment you may have to appeal for your own protection.'

That, said Huge Deal, was what the great writer had to say in support of bareknuckle fighting. Imagine, then, how glowing he might have been about fighting with the 'thickly upholstered fist'.

Perhaps McIntosh, in seeking literary support for his enterprise, had conveniently ignored the opinion of an even greater writer, George Bernard Shaw, a one-time contender for the English amateur middleweight title.

In 1882 Shaw had written a novel called *Cashel Byron's Profession*, the romantic tale of a handsome son of an actress who ran away to Australia and returned to England as its greatest fighter. When the book — which Shaw regretted writing — was republished in 1901, he added a 'note on modern prizefighting' which argued that the Queensberry rules had at first turned off the fans because it seemed to have made the sport as harmless as 'a fencing match with buttoned foils'. But the reality of the bareknuckle days was that more rounds ended with a trip, or a fall, than a genuine knockdown blow. Most of the time it was the pretended knockdown which earned the fighter a half-minute's rest.

But, said Shaw, time had proved that gloves, and a minute's rest between rounds, and the 10-second knockdown rule, were much more dangerous than anybody thought when Queensberry devised his rules, and most people figured that boxing had now become 'a spar for points before three gentlemanly members of the Stock Exchange ... awarding marks only for skill and elegance'.

Men now had to stagger to their feet inside ten seconds, many to be battered into insensibility.

'And the shortest way to the heart of a big audience is to stick to your man; stop his blows bravely with your nose and return them with interest; cover yourself and him with your own gore; and outlast him in a hearty punching match,' he wrote, in words that even today echo the sorry story of the preliminary fighter who builds a reputation for guts rather than ability: the fighter who is too brave for his own health.

The old fights, said Shaw, mostly ended in exhaustion. Now they ended in savagery. The crowd was no longer interested in skill: it bayed for blood.

The final step along this wretched path had been taken by the Americans, with their huge audiences, and cinematographs rolling to transport the scene to London and elsewhere.

Shaw mused about the spectacle of a match between 'the Church and the Ring' drawing a colossal crowd. He was not to know that McIntosh's fight was about to instigate such a ruckus in Australia, and around the world.

He also regretted that the trend in American fighting seemed to be a victory for brawn. Brain, he wrote, often appeared to end in a state of concussion; a loser after performing miracles of science.

Whether or not McIntosh, or the Australian public knew it, Jack Johnson represented not only the brawn but the brains in this affair. Both fighters were asked to contribute pearls of wisdom to the program to educate the Australian sporting public on their methods.

Burns, in 'How I Prepare for Battle', spoke of the dangers of becoming musclebound. He was no weightlifter, he said, and tried to keep himself supple and quick. Then there was his love of a good walk, a 'jaunt' of 10–12 km.

'Yes,' he revealed, no doubt to nods of agreement, 'I am a believer in trudging through hilly country, despite the moss-grown notion that an athlete's pace is injuriously affected by that class of exercise … after one has been going a couple of weeks one may walk to the summit of the steepest at a fairly brisk gait and run here and there as I do.'

So the physical side wasn't exactly *Rocky*. And Burns was also into good, plain food — excepting bread and potatoes.

'I run to fat too easily,' he wrote.

Maybe it was because he couldn't walk it off after dinner.

He was also a devotee of shadow-boxing and liked to spar for 20 minutes a day, his partners being replaced as they tired. He liked ball-punching for 'cultivating dash' and was using a stuffed kapok item, supplied by The Amateur, which had been used 17 years earlier by lightweight champion George Dawson before he pounded 'Dummy' Mace. But Burns didn't believe in trick work — he was no showman.

'Fight the ball, or bag, as if you had an antagonist to deal with, moving around and about and driving your blows well home,' he wrote.

Burns was typical of a breed of small, sharp fighters — not much more than what we would today call built-up middleweights — who had been able to dominate bigger men in the heavyweight division before the emergence of Jeffries.

'A nice quiet stroll between dinner and bedtime assists sleep materially; and slackening up to a fair thing, two or three days before the contest, will cause the storing of a goodly stock of vim and desire for fight,' he concluded.

Jack Johnson was not noted for the purity of his nocturnal habits, but he had not neglected study of his art. Anybody who held the popular racist opinion that the black man was incapable of sophisticated thought was in for a rude shock, for Johnson was the true analyst of the pair — even if Burns had written a 'scientific' book — as he showed in his discourse on 'Timing and Feinting'.

'A few hints on boxing for the Souvenir? Why certainly. S'pose you don't want a big bookful?' Johnson was quoted, his contribution being presented as an interview. But he wouldn't talk about punches; he was smart enough to know that hitting without being hit was the secret to the fight game.

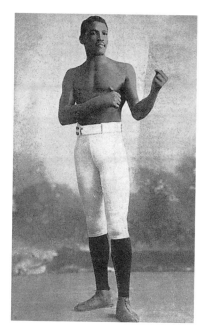

LEFT: Australian folk hero and adopted black West Indian Peter Jackson was said to be the greatest heavyweight of his time, but the so-called 'colour line' denied him the world title.
Image Library, State Library of NSW

RIGHT: Australian 'Boshter' Bill Squires was a sinewy basher from the bush who lost his punch when he hit the big time. Without him, the Boxing Day fight would never have happened.
Image Library, State Library of NSW

ABOVE: Johnson's 1907 Sydney camp. *Back row, from L to R:* F. Dorrington, Steve Hyland (Johnson's trainer, who testified at the Lola Toy trial), A.A. Maclean (Johnson's then-manager who had his nose literally put out of joint by Johnson in an argument over money), George Rignold, George Darrell, and Fred Parkes. *Front row, from L to R:* James Brennan (promoter), J.J., Larry Foley (former Australian champion), and W.F. Corbett (boxing writer 'The Amateur'). *Image Library, State Library of NSW*

ABOVE: Jack Johnson was in the best shape of his life for the Boxing Day fight.
Image Library, State Library of NSW

THE LATEST MANLY SURF-BATHER.

ABOVE: Johnson was constantly lampooned in racist cartoons before the fight. This one, from *The Sportsman*, shows him bodysurfing with the locals at Manly Beach.
Image Library, State Library of NSW

ABOVE: Johnson and his 'wife' Hattie McLay, pictured at the Sir Joseph Banks Hotel with a small and unknown admirer. Johnson frequently played his famous bull fiddle (accompanied by McLay on the piano) in musical evenings at the hotel in the weeks leading up to Boxing Day. *Australian Consolidated Press*

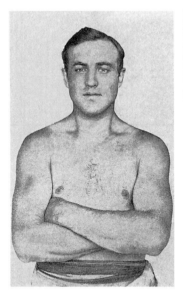

ABOVE: As the smallest world heavyweight champion in history, Tommy Burns couldn't compete with Johnson in the muscle department. He was built like a fire hydrant.
Image Library, State Library of NSW

ABOVE: The impossibly stylish Jewel Burns, or 'Mrs Noah Brusso', was fêted by the ladies of Sydney society.
Image Library, State Library of NSW

LEFT: Great Australian artist Norman Lindsay drew several portraits of Burns and Johnson, including the fight poster. Here are some of Lindsay's portraits of a brooding, 'Napoleonic' Burns at his Snowy Mountains retreat.
Jane Glad

LEFT: Hugh D. 'Huge Deal' McIntosh (pictured in the program) was a fearless risk-taker who made a fortune by selling the film of the Boxing Day fight. *Image Library, State Library of NSW*

RIGHT: Jack London looked the quintessential bohemian socialist in this photograph. However, the world's then-most famous writer started the racist 'Great White Hope' campaign against Johnson. *Mirror Australian Telegraph Publications*

A Prophecy. "The Lone Hand"
Dec. 1st 1908

ABOVE: This stylised Lindsay sketch of the two fighters accompanied a prediction in *The Lone Hand* that Burns would win the fight. *Jane Glad*

OPPOSITE PAGE, TOP: The 20 000-strong crowd is stunned as Burns gets the count in the first five seconds of the fight. The single movie camera is under a canopy to the right of the ring. Referee McIntosh is in the white outfit and motoring cap.
Image Library, State Library of NSW

OPPOSITE PAGE, BOTTOM: Burns could never get close enough to hurt the towering Johnson. As the fight progressed, his battered face began to look more and more desperate.
Image Library, State Library of NSW

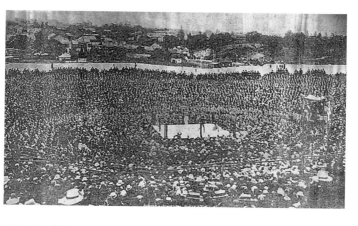

LEFT: Johnson wasn't just a great fighter and a great talker, he was also a 'sport': a snappy dresser who changed his suit three times a day. Here he is pictured in one of his favourite Australian ensembles.
Australian Consolidated Press

RIGHT: Johnson, like Burns, became a fire-and-brimstone preacher after finding God in prison.
Australian Consolidated Press

'Good countering depends on good timing,' he said. 'Every move possible should be studied to save all the time you can, thus increasing speed and force, and conserving strength.'

People had branded Johnson a lazy fighter — an inconsistent performer who didn't always take the chances offered, and who didn't cater to the crowd. Now, whether they knew it or not, he was revealing a long-view motive for his actions. In his autobiography he told how, by the end of 1906, with 56 registered fights, he figured he was ready for the championship. Every move in every fight after that was calculated to preserve his body and his skills. Getting hit back just wasn't part of the plan.

'Don't telegraph punches by moving your shoulder back. Only bring your arm back for the left rip. Make up your mind about a counter when his punch is on the way.

'Your eye sees the blow start, your brain telegraphs the desired move to the muscles, and they obey the command of the brain, all in a flash. If you hit with accuracy and force, your feet must be on the floor, or the left foot raised before the blow is delivered,' he said.

'But don't lift the left foot when countering, it wastes time — enough time for the opponent to land a punch. The counterpunch is launched by a straightening of the right leg. And no matter where the body has to be moved to avoid a punch you must never lose balance.

'A feint is a move of the head, hands, or feet, and sometimes of all together, to deceive an opponent as to the real purpose. I have seen many amateur boxers and some professionals make feints, not knowing themselves why they did so. A feint should never be made without some good reason.'

A good feint, said Johnson, would deceive the best fighter, make him bring his hands up or down, or throw the wrong punch, or back-pedal. If the other man feints too much throw your lead at him and he will stop.

'Never move the feet when feinting; if you step forward with the left foot and your opponent jumps away your feet will be too close together for you to hit well,' he wrote. 'If your opponent lifts the left foot when he feints at you, let him think he is deceiving you, so that he may do it again. When he does, jump back a few inches, not far enough to get out of reach, but just enough for his blow to fall short, and when he places his right foot on the floor he will be off his balance for an instant. Before he can recover himself step in and hit him.'

Johnson was a bigger man than Burns. If he could apply all of the science rolling off his tongue he might make some kind of opponent. In fact three pages of Johnson on the art of feinting — always from the punching position, sometimes feinting to beat a feint, tiring the man who brings his guard up and down — was enough to make a seasoned pug dizzy.

Then there was Johnson's set of rules which Boshter Bill should perhaps have committed to memory:

* *Keep a good position at all times.*
* *If the opponent swings at your head, guard.*
* *If he hits straight at your head, duck.*
* *If your opponent ducks when you hit straight, swing at him.*
* *If he guards when you swing go to the body.*
* *After you hit, get away, back to your position.*
* *Work to the left if he favours his left, and use your right.*
  Work to the right if he hits straight and favours his right.
  If he uses all kinds of blows work to the right and away from
  him, if on the defensive, and forward and to the right if on
  the aggressive.
                                          Yours Truly. Jack Johnson.

Was this big black man all mouth and no action? Tommy Burns, and his starstruck Australian fans, were about to find out in a hurry.

THE FIGHT WHICH WAS TO bring together not only the champions of the black and white races, but also, for the first time in many a year, the men recognised as the two best heavyweights, was due to start at 11 am in a 24-ft ring.

Thousands camped outside the stadium and the queue at the 10s windows began filling at 2.30 am, knowing that business would begin at 4 am. At 6.15 am a shuttle service of 12 trams began rolling in from the city. A dozen more would be brought into action later. People were hanging off them like monkeys, as cabs and buses also disgorged their loads.

At 6.30 am Superintendent Mitchell arrived with 250 police, followed by Superintendent Edwards with a force of traffic cops, and things were running smoothly. When the first gates were thrown open at 7 am about 5000 people swarmed into the 10s seats, which were filled by 9 am. Half an hour later the £1 and £2 seats were gone. By 10 am, when all the reserved seats had been taken, with the crowd inside the 360-ft circle of the stadium swelling to 20 000, it was estimated that 30 000 men and boys were milling outside or perched in trees, on roofs, or up telegraph poles, just to get a sniff of the action. Five thousand complained that they had bought seats but couldn't get in.

The unprecedented numbers brought in an enormous gate of £26 000 for McIntosh and it was reported that as the crowd grew and grew Johnson became more and more agitated about his pitiful cut. He was broke and living on credit and figured he could squeeze another £500 out of Huge Deal. He sent a message to McIntosh that he would not fight unless the ante was upped. Furthermore, he wanted the money in his hands before he would lace on a glove.

McIntosh stormed into Johnson's dressing-room and looked Jack square in the eye.

'So you want your money first do you cobber?' he said. 'Where's my chequebook.' McIntosh reached into his coat, but instead of pulling out a cheque he produced a huge pistol. 'If you're not in that ring right on time I'll skin you alive,' he glared. Johnson looked at the pistol, and then looked at the cold fury in the little man's eyes. He would, he muttered, be in the ring on time.

The sky was overcast that morning, and ominous for those who feared for Burns. Johnson was first into the ring, wearing a robe, and was greeted with a mixture of polite applause and hoots. The hoots were put down to his pre-fight bragging that he would be off to the races in the afternoon and Tommy would be in bed recovering. Certainly, he was sporting a big grin and looked totally relaxed as he went to the eastern corner.

Burns entered to a tumultuous reception. Men stood and howled 'Good boy, Tommy!' and waved rattles. But he looked anything but a champion. He was wearing an old suit and a battered green felt hat and one of his seconds trailed him with a cheap suitcase. Some critics pronounced him perfectly fit but to those who knew him better he seemed sallow and drawn, as if hungover. There were stories circulating that the whole Burns camp had celebrated well into the night, bellowing choruses of 'Where the Shannon River Flows' in anticipation of victory.

If Burns was being arrogant about his chances, he wasn't letting on. The fears of his backers were confirmed when the weights were announced — Burns was 76 kg, three kilograms less than had been expected. If he looked pale he also looked tiny — the world heavyweight champion was going in a fraction under today's light-heavyweight limit. For what it was worth, The Amateur would claim that a cold had peeled weight off him. He also claimed that Johnson was even heavier than the official figures.

Johnson was announced at 87 kg and it was solid muscle. He was, to the horror of many onlookers, looking much like the overpowering monster that Norman Lindsay had drawn. Yet such was the infatuation with Burns that he was still the 7/4 favourite in ringside betting. In some places small punters could get 3s/1 if, for whatever twisted reason, they fancied the darkie.

Johnson walked across the ring to shake hands with Burns but Burns looked at his hand like it was a stale fish and touched it diffidently. He insisted on feeling Johnson's fist as if the bandages were concealing a horseshoe. First insult to Burns.

There was trouble immediately. After the gloves had been weighed and Burns had peeled off his suit and stuffed it into the suitcase, Johnson saw that he was wearing the same sort of elastic elbow bandages that he had worn against Squires and Lang.

'No, no!' yelled Johnson. 'He must take them off.' He then sat in his corner as stone-faced as a huge black Buddha and refused to fight. The officials went into a huddle and the crowd wondered what was afoot. It was the perfect moment for Boshter Bill Squires. He jumped in and challenged everybody — the winner of Burns-Johnson *and* Bill Lang. He got his usual reception but then an announcement was made that Johnson would not fight until Burns removed the bandages. The crowd went ballistic, jeering the black man, and roared for 'Tommy Boy!'. Referee McIntosh, done up in a white outfit with cap, seemed at a loss and huddled with officials.

'The referee says the bands on Tommy Burns' elbows are fair,' the announcer blared into his megaphone. The crowd was delirious but Johnson was totally unmoved.

'Don't care,' he said. 'I'll sit here for an hour if necessary.'

It was the biggest moment of the black man's life. He had chased so long and hard. Why would he risk everything over such an innocuous matter? Surely he didn't believe that the bandages would give Burns any physical advantage? But Johnson had reached the point in his life where he was doing things his way, no matter what the consequences. He felt humiliated by the purse and was making no more concessions. And annoying Burns would not hurt his cause.

Johnson was well within his rights to protest, even if the bandages were flimsy items. No fighter is supposed to wear any added protection. If they were sparing Burns any pain they had to go.

McIntosh tried to convince Johnson that the bandages were within the rules, but Johnson knew that the rules were no more than what The Amateur had drawn up to deny him the judges he had originally requested.

Burns, meanwhile, wasn't budging — it was a standoff. Then McIntosh called Larry Foley to ringside. Foley took one look at the bandages and declared that they were illegal. Burns stood up and petulantly called for a second to strip them off. First psychological jab to Johnson. To the crowd Burns was being the sportsman, making a sacrifice just to get the matter under way. The mob was now almost totally on his side, and already beginning to feel that the coon wanted to play this one unfair. But Johnson was, as they say today, in 'the zone'. No crowd had ever upset him enough to make him fight badly and this one would be treated the same. The two men were brought together to pose for photographers, with McIntosh pressing their hands together for the symbolic shake.

McIntosh lectured them on the rules and comically gave his impersonation of what constituted a clinch. What follows is a 'compilation' of the way — apart from the loudest voice of all, Jack London (he comes later) — that various Australian and American newspapers (*The London Times* disdainfully ignored it) covered the fight:

ROUND ONE

It was 11.07 pm when the gong sounded and the two men bore in. 'All right Tahmy here I am,' grinned the big black man, showing his teeth: gold-filled tombstones.

Johnson swung at Burns but the Canadian evaded. 'Good boy Tommy!' screamed the crowd, according to The Amateur.

But in five seconds, Burns would be sprawled on the canvas, half-sitting, with a look of incredulity spread across his 'Corsican' countenance. The cranial fortress had been breached; those bridge pylons of neck muscles had been of no use — his bowling ball of a head had been attacked from beneath! Johnson had hit Burns with a right uppercut and he had toppled like a tenpin. After all that talk, speculation, rhetoric, and Social Darwinian nonsense, 'de big coon' had dumped Napoleon with his first serious punch.

According to the Sydney *Sportsman* (which later ran headlines like 'The Coon Outclasses Tommy and Makes Him Look a Mug' and 'The Flash Coon Holds a Carnival of Comicalities at Tommy's Expense'), 'a roar like a discharge of artillery went up from the crowd'.

Burns stayed down for eight seconds, and nodded to his corner that he was OK, just a little stunned and very surprised. He got up and launched himself at Johnson. He was, if anything, game. But Johnson drove two lefts to the body then hit him with another right to the head that sent him staggering back across the ring and down again.

He was up immediately — like Antaeus bouncing off Mother Earth, said The Amateur, getting into the Greek classics (perhaps forgetting that Antaeus copped a smacking from Hercules and was crushed to death).

After only 20 seconds there was no doubt in Johnson's mind, and probably Burns' too, that the fight was already over as a contest. Johnson had tasted Burns' weakness, and Burns had been shocked by Johnson's true power. The rapidly diminishing Canadian sought refuge in the clinches, which McIntosh had trouble breaking, but looked dwarfed and helpless. Johnson, for his part, remained sublimely cool.

'Oosh, oosh,' was the way The Amateur heard the body punches of Burns thudding into the great mass of Johnson, the 'son of Ham', but he must have had a keener ear than any other writer at ringside.

'They scuffled, and they embraced, and they broke, and Burns pummelled the body with a will until those brawny black arms gripped both the little fellow's weapons and held them as if in a vice,' he wrote.

It remained for Johnson to paint the picture the way he wished. The fight was now a canvas for the artist in Johnson, and he was never one to deny his public a tutorial in technique. Burns would now have to endure humiliation from the man he had called yellow, but endure it in a way that would bring him credit. To illustrate that this was going to cost him dearly, Johnson hit Burns with a stinging left and a right square before the gong. As it sounded the dreaded 'mouth-fighting' had begun. They were muttering at each other. Burns went back to his corner with his elbows grazed (maybe he had been prescient about those bandages), his ribs reddened and his hopes forlorn.

His cornermen began rubbing him with champagne, which was supposed to have some restorative effect. Then they began to talk about a set of pre-arranged gridiron-style verbal signals to get him into his fight plan and provide a tactical advantage.

According to a typically enraged *Bulletin*, Johnson sat back on his stool and roared for water. He took a mighty gargle and then sprayed the pressmen in the seats below.

ROUND TWO

Johnson yelled across the ring: 'Come right on!'. Immediately his best punch, the uppercut, was working. There had been so much written about how hard it was to punch down on a crouching Burns, but Johnson was well-versed in the skill of punching up. Then Johnson swung a right to the chin and the champion went down for the third time, his ankle twisting and giving way under him. He was up instantly to clinch, but got tattooed, and his left eye had started to swell. Johnson dug a big left into his 'bingey'. Burns was doing little and now he was bleeding from the mouth and already seemed to be tiring.

According to The Amateur, Johnson's sneering and taunting already had the crowd enraged. But he saw a couple of lefts to the head by the champion, which gave them cause for optimism. He didn't see a punch put Burns down to one knee with a twisted ankle, but only a 'rush' by Johnson. And he was awarding Burns points for defence! — for not getting hit with everything that Johnson threw.

'If Burns didn't have a little the better of this round,' wrote The Amateur, 'he certainly had none the worst of it.'

ROUND THREE

Most of this stanza was spent wrestling and Burns, getting a breather, landed some shots to the ribs and head in the clinches. In the same holds Johnson pounded Burns' kidneys. The Australian press, awed by these exchanges, was still making the mistake of thinking that punches in clinches — supposedly Burns' best weapon against Squires — could stop a man.

The Amateur, however, wished to point out that it was pure spite by Johnson to aim a sinister punch at Tommy on the break.

'Carm 'ahn,' sneered the 'ink-pelted pusson' in The Amateur's report. Had there been the same dialogue when Johnson was thrashed by Marvin Hart? Burns came on and had his ribs rattled, which caused Johnson to grin like a chimpanzee.

Wrote The Amateur: 'Johnson grinned that grin which was so much and so objectionably in evidence that one sighed for a Peter Jackson so that it might be wiped out forever.'

The Amateur had to admit, however, that the 'brave white-skinned fighter' had not had the better of this round. Burns was leaning on his back toe and lunging foward but Johnson's chin was always just too far away. According to *The Sportsman*, this caused Johnson to jeer: 'Great blows them!' and he retaliated with blows to the 'napper' and 'dinner box' of Burns. *The Sportsman* had developed a dislike for Burns, but was not about to give the 'coon' any accolades either.

The Bulletin accused Johnson of dropping his hands and mocking Burns. But it had to admit that when it came to generalship in the ring, he appeared to have read all of Burns' book on the subject.

ROUND FOUR

According to *The New York Times*, this was when the wild talk began, each man trying to goad the other. But after Johnson landed a heavy right to the ribs early on, there were more insults being landed than blows. Burns landed a right to the head but Johnson answered it with a one-two. *The Town and Country Journal* wrote that Johnson was now breathing heavily from the exertion of mastering Burns. But he was also looking calm, and Burns was looking rather anxious.

The Amateur heard Johnson jibing, 'Good boy, Tahmy. Carm ahn Tahmy!' and the crowd hooting, 'Why don't you go on yourself?' Burns rewarded them with the grittiest exhibition ever seen in an Australian ring. But all Johnson had to do now was wait for Burns to figure some kind of move, with his corner yelling numbers like quarterbacks, and thump him as he came in. *The Sportsman* feared Burns was copping a terrible pasting. *The Bulletin*, putting the best possible spin on things, figured it had espied a heavy punch by Burns to Johnson's black heart during the course of the round.

ROUND FIVE

Appearing refreshed, Burns opened briskly with a right to Johnson's head and both hands to the body. Johnson slipped over a few rights to the head. The Melbourne *Herald* saw Burns go down from a heavy body blow. Other witnesses missed it. One reporter heard Burns' corner calling, 'Don't let him kill you Tommy, that's a sickly smile!' But Burns was being punished too heavily to believe it.

The Amateur heard Burns wearily complain with an air of disgust: 'Why, you won't fight at all.' As if three knockdowns didn't count. But he was still giving Burns points for avoiding punches. He also had Johnson getting desperate, and more willing than Burns to clinch.

The Sportsman, sitting in the same press seats, had it a 'fearfully one-sided contest'. It also had Burns yelling, 'You yellow cur!' This was far more scandalous than any of Johnson's standard American fight palaver. In recognition of this Johnson smashed a left into Tommy's middle and retorted, 'Can you fight at all?' From that point, anytime the fighters halted in a clinch, Johnson began a running dialogue over the ropes with the crowd, which was not short of an opinion about his manners.

The Bulletin railed that Johnson considered the crowd 'white trash' and had commenced a most beastly exhibition of 'rubbing it in'. Looking down at a photographer he said, 'Did you get that? Anyhow I'll give you a good picture.'

ROUND SIX

Johnson rushed and Burns clinched, only to have Johnson nail his ribs a dozen times. Burns got in a few short jolts — punches which had disintegrated other men — into Johnson's body. But Johnson just laughed and joked with the crowd as he pushed Burns around the ring, sometimes almost throwing him to the ground. That old Social Darwinian maxim about the black man's lack of stomach for a stoush was unravelling before disbelieving eyes.

The Sydney Morning Herald was astonished that Johnson could be almost, but not quite, as clever as the white man in the ring. Johnson was holding Burns' right arm, the way Burns had disabled other men, but the scribes had to swallow it as it was allowable under Queensberry rules. Burns' body was now covered in welts.

The Amateur heard Johnson joke to the crowd: 'Look, he's gaht me now,' while he hammered rights to the kidneys 'for all the world as a butcher would handle a chopper'. And once more he exhibited his 'mouth jewellery'. But, hello, a body shot from

Burns made that big-lipped orifice snap shut, much to the mirth of the crowd.

For a moment, at least in The Amateur's eyes, Johnson appeared to have lost his balance and was in danger of going over. Burns was looking good. Johnson did send him sagging against the bottom rope but the crowd cheered again when Tommy avoided a 'desperate' Johnson charge late in the round.

The Sportsman, however, had the 'vengeful demon' toying with Burns and couldn't abide Burns' later comments that Johnson didn't hit hard. Those big black arms pressed Burns down, and Johnson leaned down on him, making him almost helpless. The coon landed a brace of right jabs square in Burns' comely countenance, followed by a left into the pantry. It was ludicrous, pathetic. Tommy's left optic was beginning to swell and look purple.

ROUND SEVEN

The tempo was now increasing. Johnson rushed Burns across the ring, landing a barrage of rights. Burns got a left up under Johnson's chin, but still he had no power, and his right eye was now bloodied, making it a target. Johnson chatted with the crowd and then landed a hard left to the body and a right to the side of the head which sank Burns for a second. When they were close again Johnson, much to the disgust of The Amateur, appealed to McIntosh to stop the holding.

The crowd yelled, 'Get away Tommy!' and Johnson yelled back, 'I thought Tommy was an infighter!' Burns seemed bamboozled by Johnson's body defence and was reduced to forlorn longshots at that distant head.

ROUND EIGHT

'The coon came cake-walking vaingloriously over to the battered Thomas,' complained *The Sportsman*.

Burns was bleeding from the mouth when he left his corner, and Johnson simply resumed his domination. Burns could land but the blows appeared to have absolutely no effect. Johnson was cackling at Burns' corner as they sang out their gridiron signals, none of which had the least effect, and had the superior strength to push Burns away with a glove in his face and follow up with a straight left. But there was also a little blood on Johnson's teeth — it could be seen because he was still grinning.

The Amateur heard a voice in the crowd call: 'Stick to him Tom. That yellow streak's there, you'll find it!' to which Johnson answered back: 'You won't find it.' The Amateur accused him of being so flash that his molars were now on display.

With his superior eyesight, The Amateur observed Burns shake up Johnson with a couple of body punches and a rap in the mouth which 'added ruby to the yellow, white, and pink of Johnson's facial jewel-case'. Burns ducked a punch and the crowd, wrote the esteemed scribe, rose en masse. Johnson waved 'ta ta' to Tommy at the end of the round, causing outraged spectators to rise and howl 'The Cur! The Brute!' and some unprintable things as well.

ROUND NINE

'Come on Tommy, swing your right!' goaded Johnson at the gong. 'Yellow dog!' Burns yelled back, according to *The New York Times*. The Amateur missed the 'yellow' part. Both men took a breather in this round, swapping more verbal raps than rips.

The Amateur did, however, hear Burns complain about the clinching: 'You're holding again you cur. You're always holding.' Spurned on by those remarks Johnson swung and missed and looked down at the little fellow 'as a gorilla might upon something just captured'. Johnson, in The Amateur's view, was starting to get out of breath. Maybe, just maybe, mused our man, it was possible that the thought was passing through the weaker mind of the coloured chap that Burns just might wear him down. No-one else shared his optimism.

'Thirteen now!' screamed Burns' corner, relaying some new stratagem.

'Here's fourteen!' said Johnson, thumping Burns again.

From *The Bulletin*'s press seat the dialogue was a little different.

'Come on leedle Tahmmy, come right here where I want you ... no good, Tahmmy, I'll teach you,' said Johnson.

'Let go — break Tommy!' screamed McIntosh.

'He can't hurt, he can't hurt,' sniggered Johnson.

Just before the gong, wrote *The Sportsman*, Burns speculated a knockout punch at the coon's jaw, but missed by a foot. Johnson laughed derisively.

ROUND TEN

Both men seemed to be tiring, said *The New York Times*. Burns still lacked steam, and the crowd was yelling for him. Johnson smiled. It seemed that any time Johnson chose to exert himself Burns was at his mercy. He finished the round with a flurry of punches.

However, according to The Amateur, Burns did manage to sting Johnson in this round. He opened up with his tongue: 'Say, you can't fight a lick.' Johnson looked quite hurt, and he rushed in only to sprawl all over Burns like an old woman.

Sadly, by the end of the round Tommy was again a 'comparatively easy mark' — which was a polite way of saying punching bag. His jaw was swollen and droopy and he was a chopping block when edged into a corner. His body shots were like the flapping of mosquito wings against an elephant's head.

ROUND ELEVEN

Perspiration was now pouring off Johnson, making him look like a highly polished walnut. All that meant, however, was that he was properly warmed up and enjoying himself. Johnson was invulnerable. It was *his* show all the way. Not one theory about the superiority of Burns or the white race had been proved, except, of course, white courage epitomised in the smaller man. Now, however, 'nobility' was debatable. For Tommy's 'yellow' slur on Johnson was a lesion on his own character.

Burns' ribs were now red-raw from the tom-tom of Jack's right hand in the clinches. It seemed like he was trying to muster a final desperate effort, but once more he was forced back on to the ropes and hammered. 'Now, come on Tommy,' Johnson said.

The Amateur was moved to comment: 'Johnson's failure in an attempt to uppercut the right was bad indeed for a champion and might have brought trouble to him had Burns been a bigger fellow.'

One moment The Amateur had Johnson holding on for dear life and the next pounding at Burns' ribs like a butcher at a carcass. But, still, after all the one-way traffic Burns was described as being 'as strong as ever' at the gong. In most eyes, however, he had never been strong at all.

Even *The Bulletin* had Burns in a 'horrible plight' by this stage. His jaw hung like it was broken, his mouth oozed blood.

'Outgeneralled, over-reached, overmatched in strength, insulted and treated like a helpless mouse by a great black cat, he came up heroically to take his punishment ... it was magnificent but it wasn't pugilism, and all against the tactics laid down in his book,' it lamented.

It observed that every time Burns went to his corner he had his hair combed and parted — ever aware of the cinema camera grinding away on its platform.

ROUND TWELVE

Johnson now seemed intent on finishing the fight and poor Burns was strafed. All Burns could do was hang on and suffer while Johnson bullied him and landed that merciless uppercut. Burns was bruised and scraped all over — pulped. Johnson, on the other hand, was pristine.

The Amateur, however, still credited Burns with the 'vim of a tiger', and discoursed on the lack of true accuracy in Johnson's jab. In his eyes, Burns managed to bounce to his corner after landing some fine punches.

ROUND THIRTEEN

Burns' seconds pushed him out into the killing ground with the cry: 'This is your lucky round, Tommy!' (One of the yarns that Burns had been feeding the press was that 13 was his lucky number.) Either way, Johnson continued to mash Burns' Napoleonic dial. Then he rattled his ribs with three straight punches. When Burns staggered to his corner, after a vicious right uppercut, it looked as if the gong had saved him.

But the Amateur still had Burns going for Johnson like a bull-terrier. His opinion at the end of the round: 'Nobody could say, and feel confident in the tip, that Burns might not do something yet.' How might The Amateur have covered the sinking of the *Titanic* had he had a financial interest in its success? Would he have still been pencilling notes on its invincibility as the freezing water closed over his hand?

Some in the crowd were convinced that Burns' jaw was broken, and that Johnson was a swine for taking aim at it. Between rounds the police, with their power to stop the fight, moved in to confer with McIntosh. The end was nigh.

ROUND FOURTEEN

Johnson was now hitting Burns at will. He jabbed with the left and swung the right into Burns' bloated face time after time. They clinched, Johnson pushed him away, and drove home a smashing right to the jaw. Burns finally fell, a limp mass on the floor.

He listened to the count and was rising again at eight as a policeman began shouting 'Enough!' and attempted to climb through the ropes. Johnson didn't hear and moved in to finally finish Burns off, to stretch him out in the way he had always imagined. But his corner was yelling over the pandemonium of the crowd for him to stop and he backed away as Superintendent Mitchell stepped in to demand an end to the slaughter.

'Stop Johnson!' bellowed McIntosh, in a voice fit to raise the dead.

The Amateur alone insisted that Burns was not really through, as he wobbled back to his corner while McIntosh prepared to make his famous announcement to a silenced and stupefied crowd: 'I declare Johnson winner on points.'

'Burns was not done. He could certainly have gone on: how long one can hardly guess,' The Amateur wrote. 'But there was no help for it and Mr McIntosh had to, in accordance with an understanding arrived at beforehand, declare the winner on what had taken place up to the moment of interference. He therefore awarded the palm, and the Championship, to Johnson and we now have a black champion of the world. Who will dethrone him?'

9

HOW COULD AUSTRALIA HAVE GOT it so wrong? How could Burns have been beaten so easily — some observers declaring that he hadn't even landed a blow?

In London, the boxing writers had mixed views. 'Cestus' of *The Sportsman*, a man with no love for Burns, declared that Burns had never had the class of past champions. In this fight he had plainly lost his head and his generalship. *The Sporting Life* said Johnson was too big and clever and could have won much earlier on in the piece. *The Daily Mail* said that the fight was not 'heroic' and that Burns had obtained the title in a period of 'decadence'. *The Referee* said that the odds favouring Burns were the result of either racial prejudice against Johnson or a belief that something was wrong with him. *The Observer* merely dismissed it as a 'degrading spectacle'. There had even been one report in England that Burns had died from his injuries.

In San Francisco, Johnson had been the 10/9 favourite but W.W. Naughton revealed that there was a rush of money for Burns because it was believed the fight was a fix — how could it not be some kind of stunt if Johnson was getting so little of the purse? Even weeks after the fight there were still stories doing the rounds that Johnson had agreed to fall, and had doublecrossed Burns.

At the same time Jeffries recanted his earlier opinion that Burns would win. With the benefit of hindsight he now believed Burns had never stood a chance against the big coon.

'In my opinion Johnson is the greatest fighter in the game today,' Jeffries said.

Naughton said that before the fight John L. Sullivan had declared it a fake. Now he was saying, 'I never could see how a good little man had a show with a good big man.' But Sullivan, who was given to talking twaddle, had also said that Burns was never the champion — Johnson, therefore, could not assume the title.

Larry Foley was scathing about the contest, calling it the worst championship fight he had ever seen.

He said of Burns: 'He beat Squires and Lang and Roche and Moir and the others but if you could do 100 yards in 12 seconds, and all the other men you had to race could only do it in 14 seconds, you'd look like a champion sprinter, you see; but what would you look like when a man who could do it evens — in 10 seconds — came along?

'Well he would make you look slow wouldn't he? Burns met his 10-second man today, and we found that Tommy was only a 12-seconder. That's it, all right. He is a good middleweight. He's a good plucky, natural fighter, with a hard hit, and some good footwork; but he is not in the same class as Johnson, who has length, weight, reach, strength, cleverness, and brains. You don't want much more, you see.'

He said that even if the fight was a 'barren spot' in boxing history, Johnson was now a worthy champion and his reign would be a long one. Foley wasn't ready to endorse a comeback by Jeffries.

Over at *The Referee*, The Amateur was examining the good big-man-versus-good-little-man theory. One prominent bookmaker was likening the fight to 'a bantam against a game rooster'.

It was a fair-enough theory, The Amateur mused, but there had been many notable exceptions. Smaller men could beat bigger men. Burns had beaten Hart who had beaten Johnson, he said, still ignoring the fact that the decision for Hart over Johnson was a rort.

Burns had given the bigger Gunner Moir 'the father of a hiding'. Lightweight Young Griffo had held his own with strong middleweight Dan Creedon — the man who taught Johnson — and Creedon later became the English heavyweight champion. And maybe — if you believed one story doing the rounds — big Jack had not entirely escaped punishment by little Tommy. How about two broken ribs?

Johnson had been seen entering Manly Hospital, The Amateur revealed. The rumour had it that X-rays had picked up busted ribs. Johnson denied it, of course, saying that it had been nothing more than the routine check he undertook after every battle. But The Amateur wasn't satisfied. Why not just call a doctor to his hotel room?

The Amateur also supported the 'broken jaw' theory. He said that it was a common tactic for a corner to try to inveigle the police into the ring to stop a fight with claims that the opponent was badly hurt. And, predictably, he was not about to back Foley's opinion, or any belief of the 'many-headed' mug public, that Johnson was the true champion.

A 'great fighter' maybe, he said, but not in the same class as Peter Jackson or Young Griffo.

'Johnson's left is by no means the fine weapon it should be, and usually is, in the equipment of a first-class boxer,' he wrote. 'Especially it is not up to requirements at long range.'

Nevertheless, he conceded that Johnson's infighting had been a revelation to Australia and, for the moment the only fighter given a chance to beat him was Al Kaufmann, who was around Johnson's size and had recently knocked out recognised fighters in Mike Schreck and Dave Barry.

Trust *The Bulletin*, however, to demean the debate.

'Serious consideration of the fight leads to one of two conclusions. Either Burns is an abnormally tough man or Johnson's blows are not nearly so heavy and forceful as they seem,' it wrote.

'Had they been what they seemed Burns' jaw must have assuredly been broken. He received 17 right smashes on exactly the same spot in the first three rounds — and was not knocked out. Talk about the man with the iron jaw! Had those blows been anywhere near what they looked like, iron itself should have been bent if not broken by so much accumulated shock.

'He received 19 right-hand smashes over the left kidney, and was not bent, let alone broken in two. After the fight the place showed practically no sign of injury. Therefore either Burns is gifted with tissue like no other man on earth, or Johnson's tremendous-looking smashes are more showy than effective,' it waffled.

The giant black might look good winning, it argued, but look at his head from the back, and consider what sort of scrap he would put up when things started to go against him. As a head it was more like a gooseberry on the top of his neck. A man with that 'top-piece' was incapable of Burns' brand of courage. If Johnson ever got tired in a fight, and started losing, his moral fibre would crumple.

The Bulletin chose to go with Burns' own line that he was waiting for Johnson to tire — no doubt falling down occasionally to hamper his progress. Burns should have waited for Johnson's 'undersized shins' to weaken, and after soaking up his punches, administered the coup de grâce.

Unfortunately, it had to admit, Burns didn't have the speed, and he certainly didn't have the strength. Nevertheless, it dismissed the opinions of London and Foley about his true ability and still could not find 'any particular reason' why Burns should not have beaten the 'dark gentleman'.

'To begin with, Burns was not as he ought to have been,' it wrote.

This was a theme in the reportage, and there may have been something to it. But history doesn't look at boxing that way. It looks at results. Any fighter can find an excuse, and preparation is as important as performance on the day. If Burns had overtrained it may well have been because a fear of Johnson had already taken over his mind. Mike Tyson certainly won many fights on fear, until he took Buster Douglas lightly and paid the price.

'His nerves had given way; he was over-trained, and had gone stale,' *The Bulletin* droned. 'To beat Johnson, or even hold his own, it was necessary that he should have superior speed, should keep off, and should lead the inky antagonist around the ring for a dozen rounds or so till those spindle-shanks of the top heavy blackfellow began to tire.'

And Burns should have forgotten any idea of hurting Johnson's head. It was too hard and too far away. To reach it, Burns had to come within the bear-like grip of a man who was strong enough to hold him and twist him into any position. *The Bulletin*'s plan for Burns seemed, in retrospect, exactly what Burns had done all along: play the punching bag and wait for Johnson to faint.

But the early knockdown could also be blamed (as if Johnson had no part in it) on Burns forgetting his own fight plan, throwing away all of his 'beautiful maxims'. This had allowed Johnson to play Burns' game. He got Burns mad and made him do all the work.

Summing it up, Johnson got lucky early, and there wasn't much hope in Jeffries, who had ballooned up to 127 kg and was rolling in money. The best chance for the white race seemed to rest with McIntosh promoting a rematch, for big money, in London or Paris.

Meanwhile, the conspiracy theories — the fight-fix yarns — were so outlandish that not even *The Bulletin* was prepared to endorse them. The biggest furphy that had circulated the Sydney bars was that a rich syndicate had contrived to pay Johnson an extra £2500 to take a fall. Then Burns would swallow dive against Squires. Then Squires would turn turtle against Johnson. If there was such a plot it seems Johnson had chosen to cut out the middlemen.

Also, it was lamented, there appeared to be no currency in the rumour that Squires and Johnson had 'bumped' in a bar and that Squires had knocked Johnson through a glass door.

'So it looks as though the destruction of Johnson will be left to some of his own countrymen,' *The Bulletin* concluded. They were prophetic words, but it would not be a fair or manly destruction in the ring that would bring down Jack Johnson — it would be an ugly political ambush.

The Sydney Morning Herald concluded that Burns' signal system had failed him. Bill Squires said, to the surprise of nobody, that a good big man should beat a good little man. Still, he was ready to beat Johnson. Tommy's trainer simply said that Johnson had to be a great fighter to beat Burns.

Well-known referee Harry Beckett said, 'When I saw Johnson beat Felix I marked him a great fighter. He is the best the world has seen — another Peter Jackson.'

Soon, however, *The Sportsman* could take no more. It had been proved conclusively that Burns had no hope of beating the coon, it said. Johnson walloped him fair and square. Nobody would want to pay to see a rematch.

'With Johnson's coon-like tactics in the ring and Burns' excuses since the fray, the bubble has entirely burst,' it editorialised.

'We were glad to see them come; we were glad to see the fight, but that is the end. They have occupied the stage, they have had the limelight, they have reaped the boodle, and the time for the fall of the curtain on the whole affair is now right here.'

---------- 1 0 ----------

THE CROWD DEPARTED IN ALMOST eerie silence, not knowing what to make of the spectacle — their thoughts would come spilling out in the newspapers later. The combatants, however, were already talking.

'Burns can't fight,' were Johnson's first words after he had reluctantly let reporters into his dressing-room.

'No,' interrupted a member of his entourage. 'He doesn't mean that.'

Sure enough, as he was rolled on to a table — totally unmarked — to be rubbed from head to toe with eucalyptus oil, Johnson changed his mind.

'I don't want to say that,' he said. 'He's a game, straight fighter. But I will say this: some of them have been talking about me being yellow, having a yellow streak, and all that sort of thing.

'Well he looked as yellow as I did, I reckon, when I got him in the ring. I made up my mind I'd not only win, but I'd give him a beating he'd remember into the bargain. I beat him proper and I did it on purpose. I wanted to beat him down bit by bit, and show him and the public how much yellow there was in me,' he said, and let out a big laugh.

'He did not give me as much trouble as Bill Lang gives me in the training ring at home.

'I just laid myself out to beat him all the way and not too quickly. He fought much gamer than I expected, but never seriously troubled me at any time.'

Burns, of course, saw things a little differently.

'That blow in the first round settled my chances. I would have given Johnson a great shaking but for his lucky punch. A round or two later my ankle went badly, and endeavouring to hide the fact handicapped me a lot because of the pain,' he said.

'No, I never really felt myself. I was lighter than I have been for a long time. He can't hit worth a cent. He had me dazed all the time, and got his favourite blows home often. But I was there till the police interfered, and would have been there through the other six rounds, and might have won, because the big nigger was tiring fast.'

On the face of it, Burns was proving himself a sore loser, a man of much less nobility than he had been acclaimed. And Johnson, while cocky, was within his rights to complain about having been branded a coward, and was well justified in having responded to the man who was doing the branding.

While Burns had given him little credit, Johnson had publicly acknowledged Burns' gameness. In fact, all his life Johnson maintained his admiration for Burns' bravery in that fight, and so should have been lauded rather than vilified. But it was his failure to hide his delight that the world found so unforgivable.

Later, Burns was prepared to admit that Johnson was 'too big and strong for me', and said that he would stick to his promise to retire, having made between £50 000 and £60 000 from the fight game. However, it was revealed that he had also sent off a cable to *The Sporting Life* in England claiming that Johnson's seconds had influenced the police in stopping the fight while he still had a chance. The rival *Sportsman* described the cable as 'childish, mean, contemptible, and quite unfounded'.

When Burns was called to account in McIntosh's office he refused to back down, although he said that the English *Sportsman* had been running a vendetta against him since he had beaten Gunner Moir. He repeated the allegation that Johnson's corner had been shouting 'His jaw is broken!' before police had stopped the fight. If they had not, he said, he could have waited until Johnson tired.

None of the detailed accounts of the fight bothered to report Burns' claim, though *The Sydney Morning Herald* agreed it was true, but maintained that the shouts could not have been heard by the police above the din of the crowd. It was plainly obvious that Burns, far from quitting the game, was now pushing for a rematch, but not in Australia, where there were too many eyewitnesses to the extent of his humiliation.

Burns also spoke darkly of unspeakable references Johnson had made to Jewel during the fight. There were some reports — not noted by the ringside reporters — that Johnson had goaded Burns with the words: 'Jewel won't recognise you.'

'Johnson said things to me that it would not do to print,' said Burns. 'He said something about my wife in the ring and if the public had heard him they would have lynched him. I tell you that if he had made the same remarks about my wife in America, or about any white woman, that he did to me, he would have been lynched very quickly.'

Then there was the weight fantasy indulged by Jewel's brother Larry Keating, in which he claimed Johnson's weight advantage had blown out to a colossal — and impossible — 19 kg. Johnson dismissed the theory as 'bunkum'.

If Burns wanted a rematch, Johnson was now dictating terms. He put a minimum £6000 on his own services and said he might accept a challenge from Burns if the Canadian would settle for a £2000 purse. When Burns heard this he went to McIntosh's office to lodge £2000 as a guarantee. But Sam Fitzpatrick had killed off the idea, reckoning that after such a one-sided affair a second fight would not draw a crowd. Besides, there were arrangements for Johnson to fight Sam Langford in London on Derby Day (something Johnson never quite got around to during his reign).

It was also feared that the police would prevent another fight, and there were moves in the New South Wales Parliament to ban boxing altogether. Then it was reported that McIntosh, at Jewel's insistence, had procured a 10-year agreement to promote Burns and would not allow him to fight again.

McIntosh said that there was no doubt that Burns was stale and overtrained. And, he said, Jewel was ill again and her devoted husband was very worried about her. Above all, said Huge Deal, Burns had not stuck to a plan — he should have made Johnson lead. However, Burns had told him that he had received much worse punishment in other fights. Poor Jack, still no garlands.

McIntosh was questioned about the rumour sweeping Sydney that both men had kept the fight going to make a better picture. He said the picture rights were his sole property — the fighters had no interest — and it did seem one of the sillier pieces of scuttlebutt given that five-second knockdown. He also confirmed the world-record £26 200 gate, doubling the previous figure set for the Joe Gans-Battling Nelson fight in 1906.

McIntosh stated that he had cabled Jim Jeffries with a £10 000 offer to fight Johnson (in Melbourne, John Wren was doing exactly the same thing) and would soon be on his way to America to meet him. He recalled that Jeffries had promised to come out of retirement if the title was won by a coloured man.

'He is morally obliged to come back,' McIntosh said.

It was intriguing how Huge Deal figured he could pay Jeffries that amount knowing that Johnson would want more. He had just staged a £7000 fight — and would be looking to jump to more than £20 000 — but McIntosh had long ago given up thinking small. However, few commentators gave him much chance of snaring Jeffries in the immediate future. Philadelphia Jack O'Brien and Twin Jack Sullivan were immediate propects though, having already cabled challenges from America.

Still in Australia, Burns and Johnson went on lucrative music hall tours for showman Harry Rickards — who was willing to pay Burns £225 a week but Johnson only £200 — while McIntosh had started showing the film of the fight at two venues.

Burns was not as close to death as some had made out. Most fighters healed quickly and he was no exception. The day after the fight he and Jewel, suddenly better again, had attended church and then went motoring through the Royal National Park.

Jewel was to leave the following day. A few days later a big dinner was thrown in his honour and he was fêted as a better man than the winner. At another dinner Jack London said that if Johnson had been subjected to half the punishment Burns had suffered he would have been counted out.

Johnson was obviously getting fed up with this line of patter. Where was the glory in winning? So, when collared by a *Sydney Morning Herald* reporter at a garage where he was checking the latest fast cars, he proceeded to give the most astonishing interview in the history of Australian sport — one which had the sports sheets ululating that he was responsible for the biggest leg-pull imaginable.

It started out with a question about Burns' ability — something Johnson regarded with contempt. Burns, he said, was considered a mere 'bluffer' in England and America.

'Why the man was a mere child in my hands on Boxing Day,' he said. 'I could have beaten him in two rounds but I was in a merry mood that day.'

In fact, he said, laying back in the seat of his latest auto, he could beat Burns at any sport.

'We hear daily bulletins about Tommy in his motor car, how he drove from Medlow or went to the National Park and other places in so many minutes,' he said. 'Bah! I met Burns the other day on the road to Tom Ugly's [an inlet south of Sydney]. I was in an old rattletrap of a car hired for the day. None other was available so I had to take it.

'Who should come up behind us but Mr Tommy on his auto. Didn't I laugh. "Shake her up," I said to my chauffeur. But Tommy went fast and hung on inside a mile. Then I took the wheel, and if our old buzz-cart didn't hum I'm not champion of the world. In less than five minutes I was alongside,' he grinned.

'The struggle was short. I simply left Tommy as if he'd been walking, and I did so by skilful and superior handling of the motor as the old crock I was on was decidedly slower than his.'

Was this not the first coming of Ali? For Johnson was now on a roll, the earnest pencil on the notepad flying to keep up.

He could beat Burns at any sport Tommy liked to choose. He would put down £20 to say that he could wallop Burns at cycling, running, swimming, tennis, baseball or golf. He was so good at bowls he would like a match with a local champion. Burns would not even know what bowls were.

And sculling was getting popular. He could soon be out there against Dick Arnst — the world champion who, some claimed, could turn his hand to boxing and beat Johnson because of the quality of his whiteness. He was just sick and tired of hearing about Burns' merits. He could beat Burns at billiards and give him a 30-yard start in the 100-yard dash. But by no means was he confining himself to sport.

'Find out if he will tackle me on the piano, the guitar, the fiddle, or the banjo, or even the concertina,' he said.

And, after fending off a question about chasing chickens and rabbits, he turned to his superiority in culture.

'I spend most of my spare time in the art galleries and the museum,' he said. 'My principal hobby is archaeology. When I visit your museum and see the numerous specimens of prehistoric man's art, your boomerangs of many varieties, your stone axes from various states and the many examples of Paleolithic and Neolithic man's skill — I simply envy you,' he said.

America had its rude implements but they did not show anything like the same forethought, he said. The Australian natives must have been geniuses to invent such weapons. Moving right along, he turned to modern science.

'You won't believe it, I know,' he said, 'but I'm real interested in aeronautics. I have an idea of a new kind of flying machine which will turn out, I think, a fine success. It has got the usual motor engine and planes and a propeller, and all that, but in addition possesses some innovations of my own invention that should make it fly better than some of the machines now on the market.'

Johnson certainly had his rap going. It was mostly a load of bull but it was a fine riposte, a firm finger in the face of those who were writing that he should be back in Africa up a tree. But it was just a little too much for *The Lone Hand*, which crafted an editorial in response to his outburst. A new humorist had been unearthed in the flamboyant negro, it sneered.

'These utterances of a great muscularist are worthy to rank for naive fun with the best of contemporary humour,' wrote the editor, at his 'uneasy chair'.

So Johnson had views on art, aeroplanes, and archaeology, with a special interest in Neolithic man?

'This allusion to the stage of *genus homo* most nearly approaching his own, was made delicately — not pressed home ... taking the risk of it being unappreciated.'

Johnson had also been quoted as saying that as the 'champion of the world Christian church' his fellow Methodists had not rallied to his cause for the fight. *The Lone Hand* could not equate this religious bearing with his wilful destruction of Burns into a state of helplessness on Boxing Day, a day of peace and goodwill.

'He had battered his brother-man well and truly, but no triumphal tea-meeting or service of praise was the recompense,' sniffed the editor. 'Nary a "Te Deum" did he get and he felt aggrieved.'

Johnson — who must have been having a whale of a time — had also brought up the subject of literature. He said he had engrossed himself in the study of the Bible, Shakespeare's *Titus Andronicus*, and Bunyan's *The Pilgrim's Progress*. (They were all good books taught in Sunday School back in Galveston.)

The Lone Hand could see nothing funny in this at all. In fact, it hissed, *Titus Andronicus* was 'a revolting tragedy, a bombastic and gruesome record of unmentionable crimes.'

So much for the negro gentleman's attempts at humour.

PART FOUR

AFTERMATH

1

H AVING JACK LONDON AT RINGSIDE was a happy accident for Hugh D. McIntosh but a savage twist of fate for Jack Johnson.

McIntosh was an unknown quantity in world boxing; to overseas authorities he was just a garrulous colonial with only a couple of sucker fights for Burns under his belt. He had stolen the great fight from the English and the Americans and they had no interest in publicly regarding it with anything but suspicion.

A world-title fight staged in Australia might have been painted as little more than a stunt had there not been witnesses of impeccable reputation. And for that task, McIntosh could not have hand-picked anybody more impressive than London, quintessential man of action and peerless wordsmith.

In fact, McIntosh was so smitten with the Londons that he allowed Mrs London to be seated at ringside as the only 'official' female spectator; Jewel, of course, was not in attendance and it was suspected that the only other woman was in the 10s seats disguised in dark men's clothing. Years later, while reminiscing about the fight, McIntosh said, 'Funny thing, while I was in the ring all I thought of between rounds was good old Jack London and his wife.'

When the world read London's account of the fight, there could be no doubting Johnson's superiority, yet his words echoed around the world as a battlecry for the white race. This is the enduring tragedy of Burns–Johnson: that the convergence of four phenomenal soldiers of fortune in Burns, Johnson, McIntosh and London produced little more than a grubby racist campaign, the search for the 'Great White Hope'.

It was hard to tell who had the bragging rights among this unlikely quartet for the toughest start in life. Each had been hardened early, and had roamed and lived on their wits and courage. London, for his part, was the illegitimate son of an itinerant Irish fortune-teller and a 'loose' woman named Flora Wellman. It was reported that Wellman had pulled a gun and had defiantly put it to her head when her lover ordered her to abort the child. Jack, born in Oakland, California, on 14 January 1876, got his name from a widower she married eight months after his birth.

By the age of 11, London was supporting his family with all kinds of oddjobs. He fought other boys for paper-rounds and mingled with seamen, eventually becoming an oyster pirate pillaging private beds in the Oakland Estuary. At 15 he was chesting the bar and going whisky for whisky with gnarled sea dogs, and later became a sealer in the waters off Korea, Japan and Siberia.

It was when he was working in a jute mill, during the financial slump of 1893, that London entered a newspaper story contest with a $25 prize. His yarn about a typhoon off Japan won. It gave him a start as a writer, but not before he had taken off across America as a hobo, dodging railyard bulls and sheriffs — although he had one 30-day spell in jail as a vagrant — and learning to spin yarns around campfires. Not yet 19, it was an experience that sowed the seeds of socialism in his soul. He went home to get a high school education but was lured to Alaska by the goldrush of 1896. He went broke, but money had begun to trickle in from the magazine stories he was writing about his experiences.

He paid off the family debts and married a schoolteacher named Bessie Maddern. Then followed a spate of best-selling sociological and adventure novels like *The Call of the Wild* and *The Sea-Wolf* — 50 books in 16 years — which would make him world-famous. But in 1903, to the astonishment of his friends, he dumped Bessie and their two young daughters for an older, unattractive woman named Charmian Kittredge. This was the Mrs Jack London who sat ringside at Rushcutters Bay.

In 1904, London showed remarkable courage and endurance by sailing a junk across the Yellow Sea and crossing the icy Korean Peninsula to get to the front of the Russo-Japanese War. It earned him a spell in a Japanese jail, but also a great world scoop. He then got the idea of sailing around the world with Charmian in a 50-foot ketch, which he designed himself, and spent $30 000 on the finest materials and latest comforts for what he thought would be an epic seven-year voyage. He christened it the *Snark* (after a mythical creature in a Lewis Carroll fable), hoisted an old football sweater as a flag, and set sail for Hawaii with hopes high for hair-raising adventures and penworthy Odyssean tales.

In Hawaii, London wrote stories which later had him branded as more of a race supremacist than a socialist. But in the early part of the *Snark* voyage he also punched out, at his usual rate of 1000 words a day, scrawled by hand and typed up by Charmian, the 145 000-word novel *Martin Eden*, which he described as 'an attack upon the bourgeoisie and all that the bourgeoisie stands for'.

The Londons did have the adventures which Jack craved when they sailed deeper into Polynesia, but they were encounters in which he failed to appreciate the humanity of the islanders. To his eye, the natives were little more than savages, cannibals, and headhunters who would fit conveniently into scenarios of white derring-do for his book- and magazine-readers back home.

By the time they reached the New Hebrides (Vanuatu), London was suffering from deep sores around his ankles from scratching mosquito bites, which he treated with mercury from his meagre medicine chest. Charmian, too, had an ulcer which refused to heal, and the entire crew began to suffer the crushing headaches which are among the first symptoms of malaria.

But they plugged on to the Solomon Islands, hoping to find a doctor. The *Snark* was now infested with copra beetles and huge centipedes. When they hit the Solomons their fears about hostile natives were soon realised. At Port Mary, on Santa Ana, the *Snark* was surrounded by canoes full of the wildest men London had seen in his life, armed with spears and bows, and screaming their heads off.

Young crewman Martin Johnson — who was later to become one of the most celebrated photographers of African wildlife — wrote in his diary on 28 June 1908: 'They had big heads of bushy hair. Half of them wore nose rings of tortoise shell and wild boar tusks ... their cheeks were tattooed in monstrous designs ... their teeth were filed to points and were dead black; their lips, large and negroid, were ruby red.'

All wore earrings. One was made from the handle of an old teacup, another from a sardine-can opener. One man had the shell of an alarm clock hanging from his nose.

A native who spoke pidgin English was allowed on board and claimed he was a Christian. Peace was established and next day the locals paddled out to the *Snark* to trade. London happily dudded them, getting a big stash of jewellery and weapons for what was described as 'vile trade tobacco'. Then the *Snark* was nosed towards the island of Malaita, which was said to be the home of the world's most primitive headhunters. Their biggest prize? The mummified head of a white man, in which was captured his magical powers. The Londons managed to impress the locals by dynamiting fish off the reef, did some more trading, and then headed for Guadalcanal and the biggest plantation in the Solomons, Pendruffyn.

There they joined a ketch called the *Minota*, under a Captain Jensen, on a 'blackbirding' cruise. Blackbirding was the great white atrocity of the South Seas. Young men were grabbed off islands — some kidnapped, some sold — and pressed into labour under brutal conditions on plantations as far away as Australia.

Martin Johnson refused to go along as he could see that blackbirding was no different to American slavery. He wrote later: 'When I think of this practice I do not really wonder that the natives are so savage against the whites.'

All the same, those great 'humanitarians' Jack and Charmian happily went along for the ride, sniffing another ripping yarn in the offing. Jensen had warned them to bring their guns, so the Londons went on board toting rifles for any native-potting.

After staying with a missionary at Malu, the *Minota* put out but a wind change blew her back onto the reef and her stern got stuck. The 'recruits' on board panicked and soon, once more, the Londons — having a great run of luck — were surrounded by canoes full of hostile barbarians. A boat from the mission came out and Charmian, with a suitcase full of manuscripts, was taken ashore. London stayed on board as the *Minota* was battered. Eventually they were rescued by a whale boat with an armed crew.

The *Snark*, after being careened, roamed for two more months before returning to Pendruffyn. But by this time London's health problems were too serious for him to continue. Beside the sores on his legs his hands had swelled, and the skin kept peeling off them, making sailing work agonising. London began to fear that he had leprosy and in November boarded the steamer *Makambo*, for Australia, with Charmian, Martin Johnson, and their Japanese 'houseboy' Nakata.

London would later write that in Sydney he had two fistula removed from his legs, but a strange skin condition which caused his toenails to become infected and grow at an alarming rate baffled Australian doctors. It was later diagnosed as pellagra, which is caused by a niacin (Vitamin B) deficiency. It would mean the end of the voyage of the *Snark*, and London's return to California, but not before he had accepted a £275 commission from *The New York Herald*, and other newspapers including *The Melbourne Argus* and *The Australian Star*, to cover the Burns–Johnson fight.

Sydney now had another dazzling couple to match Tommy and Jewel. But for all of Jack London's noble works, it seemed he wasn't entirely fond of the noble savage. After Boxing Day, he certainly didn't find anything noble in Jack Johnson.

'But one thing remains,' he would write, in one of the immortal sentences about boxing. 'Jeffries must emerge from his alfalfa farm and remove that smile from Johnson's face. Jeff, it's up to you. And M'Intosh, it's up to you to get the fight for Australia. Both you and Australia certainly deserve it.'

Before the fight, London realised that some of the wiseheads in the American press already knew that the title was for Johnson's taking, and that American bookmakers were nowhere near as generous with their odds about the challenger. And though he was aghast to have Johnson as champion and generally scathing about the merit of the fight as a contest, he would leave no doubt about the completeness of the victory — he didn't give a single round to Burns, despite some of the local critics having the Canadian even after six rounds.

For a great writer, London wrote lousy leads as a journalist with a deadline. He began: 'Full credit for the big fight must be given to Mr H. D. M'Intosh, who has done the unprecedented, and had the nerve to carry it through. But equal credit must be given to Australia: for without her splendid sport-loving men not a hundred M'Intoshes could have pulled off the great contest of Saturday.'

Even The Amateur looked good up against this stuff. London had witnessed a bitter, bloody, cathartic race struggle and that was the best he could manage for a fee of a quarter of

Johnson's purse! He continued by declaring the Stadium and the crowd magnificent. The event was square and fair-minded — a lot fairer than he would be when he got warmed up.

It was hard to imagine, he wrote, that the 50 000 to 60 000 men inside and outside were descended from the same rabble which had watched bareknuckle fights in England, 'slugging each other, smashing the top-hats of gentlemen promoters and backers, and swatting away with clubs at the heads of the poor devils of fighters whenever they came near the ropes.'

London made the old 'fancy' sound as nasty as those brutes up in the Solomons.

Rushcutters Bay, he said, had seen a remarkable display of inhibition from a crowd which had rallied behind the man copping the beating. But, he said, there was no point in minimising Johnson's performance in order to spare the feelings of Burns. It was part of the game to take punishment in the ring and to accept unbiased criticism from the press afterwards. Having thus established some credibility for the press, he then stated that he was, however, biased himself.

'Personally, I was with Burns all the way,' wrote London. 'He is a white man and so am I. Naturally I wanted to see the white man win. Put the case to Johnson. Ask him if he were [a] spectator to a fight between a white man and a black man which he would like to see win, and Johnson's black skin will dictate a desire parallel to the one dictated by my white skin.'

There were no shades of black and white for this socialist icon, but the rhetoric began to seesaw. He had to give some credit to Johnson.

'All hail to Johnson!' he wrote. 'His victory was unqualified. It was his fight all through, in spite of published accounts to the contrary, one of which, out of the first six rounds, gives two to Burns, two to Johnson, and two with honours evenly divided. In spite of such mistaken partisanship, it must be acknowledged by every man at ringside that there was never a round that was Burns', and never a round with even honours.'

Modern boxing writers would have given some points to Burns, even if the scorecard was lopsided. But, of course, this did not suit the purposes of Jack London, who was looking for a new cause. A fair match-up would not have allowed him to rally the forces of white supremacy; there had to be a perceived threat. The beating of Burns had to be portrayed as complete — and primeval — for the white race to get aggravated. But at the same time, Burns needed a saving grace and the white race needed hope. There is no cause without hope. So the courage of Burns — courage which in London's mind, no black man could have displayed — became that saving grace and that hope. It was easy for London to take this approach because he could not imagine Burns not being avenged; somewhere there had to be a white hero in the mould of London himself, a hero to face down the savage as he had done in the South Pacific.

'Burns was a little man against a big man, a clever man against a cleverer man, a quick man against a quicker man, and a gritty, gamey man all the way through. But all men are not born equal, and neither are pugilists,' London wrote. 'If grit and gameness should win by the decree of natural law then Burns, I dare to say, would have won on Saturday, and in a thousand additional fights with Johnson he would win. But unfortunately for Burns what did win on Saturday was bigness, coolness, quickness, cleverness, and vast physical superiority.'

This argument, of course, was totally unfair to Johnson. Perhaps the only fight in which he had felt helpless was when he was very young and in against Joe Choynski. London presumed that Johnson, if in the same position as Burns — i.e. totally outclassed — would not have shown the same courage. It was another assumption which allowed him to crusade for a white hope.

Next, London — à la Ernest Hemingway — paused to inform his breathless readers that he didn't mind putting the gloves on himself. That made him and McIntosh both good 'amateurs'. He boasted that he, too, was 'delightfully clever' when he had an opponent about half as strong as himself. He too could smile and swap dialogue with an audience, just like Johnson had. It was as if all the expansive rhetoric about the great skill, brains, and strength of Burns — that impenetrable armour of his head and neck, those advantages in getting inside with his devastating short blows, his sophistication in the infighting — had been instantly forgotten. In order that Johnson could be accorded minimum credit for his win, Burns would only be praised for his courage.

The fight? The word was a misnomer, wrote London.

'No Armenian massacre would compare with the hopeless slaughter that took place in the Stadium. It was not a case of too much Johnson but of all Johnson. A golden smile tells the story, and the golden smile was Johnson's.

'There was no fraction of a second in all the fourteen rounds that could be called Burns's — so far as damage is concerned Burns never landed a blow. He never dazed the black man. It was not Burns's fault. He tried every moment throughout the fight, except when he was groggy. It was hopeless, preposterous, heroic.'

London assessed Burns as being in questionable shape, looking 'pale and sallow as if he had not slept all night, or as if he had just pulled through a bout with fever', while Johnson looked magnificent. It added some credence to Burns' claim that he had lost weight overnight.

'Johnson frivolled with Burns throughout the fight,' he wrote. 'He refused to take Burns seriously, and, with creditable histrionic ability, he played the part of a gentle schoolmaster administering gentle chastisement to a rude and fractious urchin.'

Johnson's mouthful of golden teeth, and his shameless mugging for the cameras were all too much. It was a smile which had to be wiped.

London claimed that the 'mouthfighting' had begun at the opening gong, with Johnson saying, in the exaggerated English accent he had adopted: 'All right Tahmy.' According to every account of the fight there was plenty of talking. But there were many different accounts of when it started and who said what to whom. London seemed to find it of no consequence that Burns had called Johnson 'yellow' before and during the fight. Americans, London opined, were used to taunting in the ring — it was standard-fare.

Burns had plenty to say, but didn't ruffle Johnson. He seemed angry and agitated before the bell sounded for the first round and simply stayed that way. If Burns was trying to make Johnson lose his head, big Jack would just flash that golden smile in his face.

Tactically, Burns stood no chance in the infighting. Johnson was just too strong.

'At times he [Johnson] would hold up his arms to show that he was no party to the clinch,' wrote London. Johnson would simply push Burns away and hit him. Once he smashed Burns with five straight uppercuts as fast as the eye could count.

Johnson seemed to drift in and out of a dream. He would tell Burns to 'hit here', exposing part of his stomach. When Burns obliged he would neither wince nor cover up, just grin and chuckle. It was a portrait of psychological as well as physical destruction.

Why then, did London feel compelled to make his racial rallying call to Jeffries or any other white to whip the nigger?

In 1946, shortly before his death, Johnson, then aged 65, recalled meeting London after the fight. London had told him: 'Well, Jack that was a terrible beating you gave to Tommy. I'm sorry for your sake that you won so readily. The white race won't be satisfied now until they find someone to whip you as badly as you whipped Burns, and that man will have to be Jim Jeffries.'

Johnson said he was bitterly offended by such remarks coming from a great man like London. It took him some time to regain his composure. Then he carefully replied, 'Jack, I won the championship according to the rules of the game. You'll admit I didn't use any foul means to gain it. I'm sorry you feel as you do but I want you to go home with this thought in mind, and write it when you reach New York: I won the championship of the world by defeating Tommy Burns in a square and fair fight and I can whip Jim Jeffries just as easily.

'I feel that I can beat any man in the world and I hope, now that Jeffries has been retired so long, that he won't be foolish and heed the call of those who think he can retake the title. I hope he'll remain retired.'

London, he said, took his hand in farewell and replied, 'I disagree, Jack, and there are thousands in America who are on my side. I shall urge his return to the ring.'

Johnson figured that that meeting was the beginning of the 'Great White Hope' campaign.

After Johnson's victory over Burns it was considered a rare gesture by Charmian to present McIntosh with a London manuscript.

'I have never parted with a single one before,' she said. 'You may not be a collector of curios but keep these 14 sheets of my husband's scrawl as a memento of Saturday's contest.'

History would judge that it should have been burned before it was published.

2

JACK LONDON HAD DISGRACED AMERICA with his racist coverage of the fight, but Australia was not without its own 'distinguished' culprit.

The Melbourne *Herald* had commissioned one of the leading writers of the time, Randolph Bedford, to cover the fight.

Even for a racially paranoid nation, Australia was not prepared for his brand of vitriol.

Johnson was entitled to be bitter at the treatment he received from a so-called 'man's man' in London. And, having spent time in Paris, he would have expected a more enlightened attitude from a man like Bedford, who had been described as one of the great 'bohemians' of Australia in the 1890s.

Bedford may have felt like a bohemian when he was struggling to make a living as a writer at a time when the only magazine paying for freelance work was J.F. Archibald's *The Bulletin*. But now that he was established, his unique brand of bohemianism failed to embrace equality among all men.

Nevertheless, Bedford was enough of an adventurer, knuckleman, and bullshit artist — very much in the London mould — that he should have appreciated both the bravado and the bravery of Johnson's quest.

It was said that he had taken to heart Archibald's advice to his writers: 'Be decisive! Don't lose the prize by fumbling. If you want something grab it before anyone can say "don't!".'

They were words for Bedford, but not Bedford's words for Johnson, who was living them to the letter.

Bedford was yet another remarkable character in this fight story who lived a heady life of chance and challenge. He was, at one time or another, a prospector who made and lost fortunes (he once beat a charge of stealing water for his camels, from Afghans on the West Australian goldfields, by demanding that his accusers 'identify the water'), a pearl-diver, rabbit-trapper, paddlesteamer hand, magazine proprietor, novelist, and even a Queensland parliamentarian.

On his first day in Queensland Parliament, so the legend goes, he strode up to two members, who were whispering in the library, and boomed, 'Gentleman, I am a stranger here. Could you direct me to the bribe department.'

Critics said that in his novel, *True Eyes and the Whirlwind*, he had written an extraordinarily sensitive account of a boy's love for his dying dog. Yet he seemed to have less regard for Johnson than any diggings mongrel.

'The colour line touches the Australian too closely for him to have no skin prejudice. Had Johnson fought in America and played his flashness before an American audience as he did today, some American white might have drawn a gun and been acquitted by a jury on the evidence of the cinemabiographic films,' he wrote. 'But Johnson would not have dared to make such a display in America. He trusted to the fact that Australians carry no guns.'

Bedford was obviously unaware of growing dissatisfaction with the colour line in the American sports media, and the impatience for Johnson to be given his chance. But he ploughed on regardless.

In 1908, this 'flashness' of Johnson irritated many Australians the way many Americans reacted to the 'uppity nigger' Cassius Clay/Muhammad Ali in the 1960s. By all means let the black man fight, and let the best man win. But if the winner happened to be a black man let him keep a tight rein on his lip in front of his betters.

Peter Jackson, a docile man in the Floyd Patterson mould — probably an 'Uncle Tom' to the American black radicals of the 1960s — was revered, the undisputed favourite of most Australian boxing fans. It was ironic that he was the hero of Johnson too, and big Jack even spent some private time at Jackson's grave in Queensland on his first visit. But while most of those same Australians would have publicly abided by the political correctness of the worship of Jackson, and forgiven Johnson his skin colour, they were not prepared to cop what would be described today as his 'attitude'.

Bedford recalled the incident at Manly when Johnson had to flee an angry crowd after Larry Foley failed to show up for a spar. This had reportedly put Johnson in a venomous mood for the 20 000 'mostly good whites' who turned up for the fight. 'Good' meant that they were strongly behind Burns, although a few turncoats chose to glorify the black when the luck turned his way.

Johnson, wrote Bedford, had entered the ring with a 'fine artistic sense of color': purple socks and gold teeth.

'The strongest odds were on Burns — the odds of applause,' he wrote. 'It was brains and brawn against height and hardness.'

Bedford noted how the limp handshake and the 'baleful side glance' from Burns had annoyed Johnson. But, in his mind, the fault lay all with the black man, and there were excuses for Burns.

'The clean-cut face and the stocky strength of Burns, his eye hopeful, young, intrepid, [was] looking at the black as a master at a bad slave. Yet Burns looked ill. He was quiet, but nervous, knowing no fear, but ill at ease from imagination.'

He was not about to daub his portrait of Johnson with the same sense of humanity. The big black was 'impossible of imagination', insolent with his weight advantage, prepared to put on a show, but still frightened that his yellow streak might be revealed.

When Burns rose to have his elbow bandages stripped, wrote Bedford, the hoots for Johnson were for 'all the hatred of twenty thousand whites for all the negroes in the world'.

Burns' indomitable face looked as if its owner must win or die.

'Johnson avoided his steady eyes as a caged brute grows restive under the gaze of a tamer outside the bars,' he wrote.

He must have been watching a different fight to those who saw Burns as the anxious one, and Johnson effulgent with certainty. But after those two first-round knockdowns Johnson's confidence rose and in the clinches he hit Burns in the kidneys with terrible force.

'Yet the white beauty faced the black unloveliness, forcing the fight, bearing the punishment as if it were none. His half-force blows fell without seeming effect on Johnson's iron stomach ... weight and reach were telling against intrepidity, and lightness ...

the black remained waiting for him, set heavily on his great, long feet, plantigrade as a bear's,' he wrote.

The black man as animal again — a fighter completely outclassing his man in every department compared to some kind of plodding grizzly bearing down on a fawn. Bedford, however, was merely warming up.

Johnson, he wrote, was hitting in the clinches. Burns' face was pulped, but still prettier than Johnson's. It was 'clean sunlight' versus 'darkness'.

And now for one of the lowest moments in Australian sportswriting. The writers who covered the fight game for a living saw two men in a lopsided fight. Bedford saw something else.

'Then the black became vainglorious, and proved his yellow streak as conclusively as if defeat had made him craven,' he ranted. 'The white stood up again and again, but without power. The black became more insolent.'

Bedford quoted the Johnson line: 'I thought you was an in-fighter Tahmy.' But he was deaf to any of Burns' 'yellow' dialogue — there was only a quiet smile from Johnson.

'The black posed to the cinematograph, as he held the white on the ropes,' he wrote. 'The black patted the white patronisingly on the head at the close of a round. Johnson himself may have been bruised, but his black skin did not show it, and his gold-filled mouth bled only once ... Burns's beauty was gone in blood, but his eyes looked out still young and hopeful. Yet, with his face cut to pieces he was still the white man.'

He quoted Johnson, after landing a big punch near the end: 'Was that good? Would you want another in the same place?' Not even The Amateur heard that one. Some of the writers seemed to be touching up Jack's dialogue for him.

It was to the credit of many Australians at the fight, wrote Bedford, that they could not, like some 'renegades', bring themselves to support the black.

Bedford foresaw Armageddon.

'Already the insolent black's victory causes skin troubles in Woolloomooloo,' he moaned. 'An hour after, I heard a lascar laying down the law of Queensberry to two whites, and they listened humbly. It is a bad day for Australia, and not a good day for America. The United States has 90 000 citizens of Johnson's color, and would be glad to get rid of them.

'Blessings on the Immigration Restriction Act! I am forced to believe that much is to be said for Simon Legree [the sadistic cotton plantation owner in Harriet Beecher Stowe's *Uncle Tom's Cabin*], and that it is a pity that the churchwardens of Liverpool and Bristol ever went into the slave trade, otherwise Johnson might still be up a tree in Africa.'

Nobody could match that. Bedford's negrophobia was astounding. And while it appealed to some Australians, it made the skins of others crawl with disgust. The ensuing debate would be unprecedented.

Others, however, were not far off Bedford's pace. His old employer, *The Bulletin*, conceded that Johnson had won the fight fairly — and could have finished it at any time — but said that 'flashness' was a miserably inadequate description of his posturing.

Echoing Bedford, one correspondent wrote: 'Had his nods, becks, wreathed smiles etc. occurred in America, a prominent citizen would inevitably have risen impressively somewhere about the close of the fourth round, and, amid encouraging cheers, have drawn a gun upon Johnson and shot that immense mass of black humanity dead.'

Pretty savage. But at least, unlike Bedford, *The Bulletin* was portraying Johnson as *human*.

'In the ensuing murder trial counsel for the defence would have put in the cinematograph film as his sole exhibit and evidence, and on its testimony alone secured a verdict of justifiable homicide,' it added.

To be fair to *The Bulletin*, another correspondent said that, given evidence he had accrued from a photographer and a rubber in a Turkish bath about the Johnson physique, he knew that Johnson was always going to win.

The Sydney *Sportsman* figured that curly-headed coons would now be bashing white folks all over America, their heads swollen like that of Johnson, the 'personification of the flash and triumphant coon'.

It accused a piggish 'Mistah Nabob Johnson' of raging at the young Australian fighter Les O'Donnell, one of Burns' seconds, who had crossed the ring before the fight to examine the hand bandages: 'What the hell do you know abart these things? Git out.' However, it had to concede that Burns did call Johnson a 'yellow cur', but that was no excuse. Nor was his ridiculously thin end of the purse. Peter Jackson had never played the flash nigger; he would never have prolonged the beating.

'Johnson has shown that he has only the instincts of a nigger — pure nigger,' it concluded.

The Amateur liked to portray himself as a reasonable man — a sporting man — and no man in the world, he said, had been a greater supporter of coloured boxers. But the exultation of Johnson over such a clean-living fellow as Tommy Burns led him to believe that there was 'a great deal more than most of us suspected behind America's prejudice against the black'.

He said he never wanted to see another black–white fight. Plainly, Peter Jackson had been 'a prince among the pigmented peoples of the globe'. And the yellow streak? Well, he said, given Johnson's physical advantages nothing could be deduced. Johnson had not proven anything.

The Sydney Mail, in a comparatively restrained editorial, in which it acknowledged that Johnson had been taunted by the biased crowd, still blasted the 'capering, grinning negro': 'He was the superbly-modelled, gloriously-developed son of Ham all through the piece but his place was in the depths of the African forest as the foremost gladiator of an ebony king.'

---------------- 3 ----------------

IN MELBOURNE, WHERE THOUSANDS HAD gathered outside newspaper offices for bulletins on the fight, there was uproar over Bedford's article.

The letters poured in and the Melbourne *Herald* managed to save some face by standing back and letting the citizens of Melbourne fight it out with their pens. In hindsight the bigotry — the public support of Bedford — was not surprising. If the humanity of Aborigines was a puzzling concept to many Australians the confidence and arrogance of Johnson must have been beyond their comprehension.

Yet, just as determined to be heard were those outraged by such racism. Some of this was Christian, some of it was the 'Britishness' of sporting fair play, some of it was the synthesis of both: the Australian 'fair go'.

Australians have not always liked 'Abos', or 'coons', or 'wogs', or 'refos', or 'gooks'. But there have always been Australians — some of them from the ranks of the previously despised — who have called for a fair go. They have rarely been properly represented by their politicians or their press.

Even today it is almost impossible to divorce a debate about immigration from allegations of racism. The debate which raged on the letters page of the Melbourne *Herald* in 1908 was much less self-conscious, and lacked the smugness of American liberalism. It was more 'black and white' in every sense:

HE IS A MAN, THOUGH HE IS BLACK

'Yes, Burns was as plucky as any man in that stadium. Probably pluckier than Bedford if he had to express his thoughts to Jack Johnson face to face, but what Bedford wrote was "an outrage on any civilised community". Johnson had won fairly in the face of 20 000 hostile whites.'

BUT HE WAS YELLOW ANYWAY
'In spite of all his "wariness" Johnson had proved that he was neither "a sport nor a gentleman". Not like the popular black American sprint cyclist Major Taylor. Johnson was unlikely to be recognised as world champion in America and the sooner he was relieved of the title the better.'

BEDFORD WAS INSULTING TO AMERICANS
Wrote 'Not An Aspirant': 'The sentiment [that Johnson might have been shot in America] is neither British nor sportsmanlike. It is a grossly insulting imputation against a great free people — sticklers for fair play — many of whom were recently our guests. [The visit of the American fleet was certainly a public relations triumph.] Randolph Bedford can thank his "stars" that some indignant "Old Glory" boy does not introduce him to the "stripes".'

A (SLIGHTLY MUDDLED) WOMAN'S OPINION
Wrote 'A Victorian Woman': 'It is not Johnson who should be shot but Burns who, for "lucre", prostituted both his race and his color to one of the inferior race. And it wouldn't hurt to shoot Bedford for fanning the flames of racial hatred. I was hoping the black would win for he seemed to have so few well-wishers, and the white man was every shallow-pated man's pet, because he presented a fair front.'

ONE OF 'THEM' OBJECTS TOO
A gentleman calling himself 'A Naturalised Australian' did not reveal his skin colour, but wished to protest Bedford's allusions to white v. black: 'Why should he [Bedford] try to prejudice the public against us for the doings of Jack Johnson? He must not forget that Johnson did not come out willingly, but was brought out by a powerful syndicate. The syndicate is to blame for Johnson being champion. Mr Bedford's mission on earth seems to me nothing but to set the public against us.'

BURNS FIRST
TAUNTED JOHNSON

A man calling himself 'Backer of Squires' — a man for a truly lost cause — saw the politician in Bedford for invoking the Immigration Restriction Act. The anecdote about the lascar may have been 'delicious' but, overall, the bad feeling in the contest was directly caused by Burns publicly taunting Johnson on several occasions with cowardice, or, as he euphemistically called it 'showing the yellow streak'.

In fact, he said, he had searched the American and English sporting papers and found that the 'hard heads' in the sport figured Johnson to be a good bet. But a word for Tommy — he was fair and game.

'But as for Mr Bedford, fie, fie; go to, thou — sportsman.'

IN THE INTERESTS
OF AUSTRALIAN YOUTH

Bedford, wrote Mr J.R.Y. Goldstein, was a cad. There was not a single expression of common manliness in his writing, nothing but 'slavering bitterness and race hatred of a most malevolent type, all of which must be injurious to the formation of a staunch Australian character'.

These, he said, were sentiments utterly opposed to British love of fair play and 'British manliness under defeat'. So incensed was Mr Goldstein that he wished to cry 'faugh' upon Mr Bedford's sentiments.

A WORD AGAINST MR LEGREE

Mr Frederick Fleming Smith could not stomach the Legree reference: 'His [Bedford's] skin prejudice must be strong, indeed, if he can speak with approval of Simon Legree, that infernal scoundrel, typical of the slave trader, who tied down a colored boy and chopped him in little pieces, commencing from his feet upwards, the wretched boy all the while imploring him to "commence at the other end". Dr Johnson said that patriotism was "the last refuge of scoundrels". Mr Bedford shows us a "patriotism" that is put to still baser use.'

BEDFORD NOT SO WEIGHTY

'Fair Play' figured Bedford had no cause to carp about Johnson's weight advantage. Jim Jeffries was nearly 13 kg heavier than Bob Fitzsimmons when he beat him. So was Johnson when he stopped 'Ruby Bob' in two. Bill Lang was 14 kg heavier than his last opponent Griffin. And the decision given to Marvin Hart over Johnson in America was a disgrace — a mere matter of colour.

'Why do the public dislike Johnson as a champion, considering that Joe Gans was a blackfellow, and an American champion boxer? Nothing was said regarding Gans during his career. The black man has proved himself to be a champion, and should get the credit due to him.'

JACK'S TRASH TALK

'One Who Was There' figured he was in a better position to judge than previous correspondents. And he sympathised with Bedford 'when his blood was still at fever heat'.

'White trash' were two words recalled in a stream of insults from the insolent 'mouth fighting' Johnson.

'If Mr Bedford's blood had not boiled, it would have been poor in quality indeed, and indeed, I join with him in invoking blessings on the Immigration Act.'

FORGET JOHNSON — WHAT ABOUT JACKSON?

'South Yarra' opined that Johnson had not been attacked for his colour, size, or weight, but more for his behaviour in the 'roped arena'. Jeffries had named Peter Jackson as the greatest fighter the world had seen. Gans had been named as the greatest technician. Major Taylor, the black American cyclist, was much-loved in Australia.

Burns' two previous wins in Australia had been popular but the same could not be said of Johnson when he beat Lang at Richmond Racecourse and said, 'Gentleman, dis is a cakewalk.' Johnson was just too insolent.

AN UNPARDONABLE OFFENCE

Johnson had mentioned to Burns in the ring that Mrs Burns might not be happy with his looks after his thrashing. This was enough to scandalise 'Observer'. It was 'grossly insulting' to the lady for Johnson to even mention her.

'Men should fight as men. If "Billingsgate" is introduced into prize fights, goodbye to the chances of the sport,' he wrote.

A BLACK MAN CRIES UNCLE

A black man wrote under the nom de plume 'Uncle Tom' — something he might not have done today.

'Reverse the conditions which prevailed at Sydney and place a white boxer in a ring in a southern State of America, with a huge crowd of hostile blacks,' he suggested.

Not a likely scenario. But he presumed that 'it would be pardonable if he replied to their taunts as Johnson did on Saturday'.

'If Jack Johnson's critics are not satisfied with him I might remind them that there are millions of highly cultured colored gentlemen in America and other parts of the world who possess as high an order of intelligence, and certainly more humanity, than Mr Randolph Bedford.'

HE IS NOT ONLY A MAN

'True Sport' of Collingwood — spiritual home of rabidly parochial Australian football supporters — wrote: 'It makes one sick to think that because Johnson happens to be a black man some people are of the opinion that he is not worthy to be classed with a white man. Johnson is not only a man but a thorough sportsman, which is more than can be said of some of our Australians.'

MR BEDFORD'S LIVER

'White or Black' blamed Bedford's reportage on a sluggish liver, which made him vent his spleen. But would Bedford have had the intestinal fortitude to 'stand up to Johnson for one minute'?

'I am an Australian-born white man, and I believe in fair play all round,' he wrote.

A REVERENT VIEW

'How long is civilisation going to tolerate prize fighting?' demanded Rev. J.B. Ronald.

'I say prize fighters are brutes in human form,' he wrote, with a fine sense of tolerance.

BURNED BY TOMMY

'One Law for All' recalled the dreaded 'flashness' of Burns himself. When Tommy was dishing it out to Bill Lang he put his face arrogantly in the face of the beaten man.

'Was this an act compatible with all the yarns of Tommy Burns' manliness that we have had drummed into us?'

TOMMY'S MOUTH

It should not be forgotten that Burns kept calling Johnson a 'black cur', and that Burns grimaced, and refused to act the gentleman at the handshake, even if it was only with a coloured man, wrote another advocate of fair play.

THE NEW WAY

'As to Johnson's taunts while he was fighting, that is a new game here. But so, for that matter, was in-fighting until very lately. Both are now points in the game. When Burns kept Lang waiting before their battle at South Melbourne that was another point. Of Burns's insults to Johnson in public and private I will say not, but I ask fair-minded people whether if Johnson was white enough to be an opponent, why was he too black to receive the credit of winning.'

Here was a sports fan coming to grips with the new professionalism in sport. These days, in Australia, 'mouthfighting' is called 'sledging'; in America, especially among black athletes, it is 'trash talking'. Johnson, it seems, was in many ways a man before his time.

DON'T BE SHELLFISH
'Yank' wrote: 'Had the police not intervened the result would have been in favour of Burns. The correspondent who said Johnson would simply eat Hart, O'Brien, or Jim Jeffries must have had crayfish for supper.'

Unfortunately for Yank, the Australians were not carrying guns to shoot Johnson.

SUPERIOR WEAKNESS
Wrote 'Benecia Boy': 'Burns should have drawn the color line; for this reason — that the superiority of the white should never have been put to the test of physical brute strength. It is a very dangerous object lesson, is utterly opposed to common-sense, and may have far reaching and disastrous results.'

BUT NAMES WILL ALWAYS HURT ME
'The manner in which Johnson laughed and jeered at Burns after clouting him amounted to brutality.'

A LOW BLOW
'Burns was the man who did all the "blow". He is reported to have said that he would take on any man "the bigger the better". Now he says that Johnson was "too big and heavy for him". Why don't Burns and his admirers take their defeat like men?'

LAST WORD FROM WHITE AUSTRALIA
'When I was in 'Frisco I was informed that Johnson once boasted in Coffroth's Saloon that if it had not been for the color line he

would be champion of the world. This remark reached the ears of Jim Jeffries, then champion of the world, and the story goes that he approached Johnson and said, "Look here, you put up $200 and I will put up the same. We will go down into the cellar, and the first up takes the lot. That's what I think of the color line." But Johnson is said to have walked out of the saloon.

'I feel certain Burns never used any unbecoming language as attributed to him by Johnson. Undoubtedly Johnson is a clever boxer, but I agree with the American — draw the color line. As we advocate a White Australia, let us act up to our principles and keep it white.'

4

TWO DAYS AFTER THE FIGHT, *The Sydney Morning Herald* ran an editorial headed 'The Prize Fight' and it started a devil of a row — guerilla warfare on the letters page day after day, with the church leading the wowser do-gooders against the politically incorrect who didn't see a lot of harm in a couple of big fit blokes exercising skill and muscle in the ring.

The editorial began by noting the size of the crowd both inside and outside the stadium and how the cables had been kept busy feeding the description of the battle to England and America.

'We should probably be right in saying, however, that the interest has not had its root exclusively in the love of a prize fight for its own sake,' it wrote.

In America the colour issue — the victory of black over white in any supreme encounter in any 'trying ground' — would have dominated discussion. England would have been more preoccupied with the best man winning. In Australia there would have been a bias towards the white man even though Peter Jackson had fought as an Australian and his adopted country had proved itself 'just and even generous' towards him.

In this case, however, Burns had made himself popular —
enjoying the usual Australian crowd sympathy for the smaller
man — while Johnson, in his two visits, had not.

There was no question, droned the *Herald*, that Johnson
had proved himself the better fighter. It wasn't copping any of
Burns' excuses about the police stopping the fight too soon. But
Johnson, it claimed, had still robbed himself of any acclaim
because of his 'flashness'.

Having put Johnson down, the *Herald* then put the boot
into boxing. It was concerned about the influence which such
spectacles had upon the 'general tone of the community'.

'To say that they are "sport", in any decent meaning of that
term is flatly untrue,' it huffed. 'To claim that they have a tonic
effect upon the "manly" qualities of the race is the sheerest
hypocrisy.'

Given the way Burns had been lauded for his manly and
scientific qualities — having been described as Napoleonic the
moment he and Jewel got off the boat in Fremantle — we are left
to wonder how much hypocrisy was in play here. What might the
Herald have had to say if Burns had given the black a licking? The
Spanish might have blanched at the next statement.

'They [fights] give no more stimulus to "manly" qualities
than do the sanguinary bull-fights of Madrid to the effeminates
who watch them,' it wrote. 'But what they do is to stimulate the
brute not only in those who actually witness them — for a large
proportion of these are animated by nothing more than a
passing curiosity — but upon that unfortunately all too
numerous class at the bottom of society, to whom the mere
"bruiser" is ever the supreme type of hero. The effect is to
glorify brutish practices in quarters where the brutish instinct is
already an anti-social force.'

It was, in short, time for the government to step in.

Meanwhile, men of the cloth had wasted no time in
bringing down their wrath upon the doings at Rushcutters Bay.

At Holy Trinity Anglican Church in the working-class inner-western Sydney suburb of Dulwich Hill, the congregation, after a sermon from Rev. E.A. Colvin, passed a unanimous resolution expressing 'indignation and abhorrence at the degrading and demoralising prizefight' and urged the government to prevent any further brutal exhibitions of pugilism in New South Wales.

Up in the brawling mining city of Newcastle, Bishop Stretch mounted the pulpit and declared the spectators to be worse than the principals, as they lacked the courage to enter the ring themselves. Boxing did not produce courage, he said, but 'blackguardism'.

Outrage echoed up from rural Victoria as well. In Bendigo, Methodist minister Rev. H. Worrall howled about a 'carnival of savagery' in which 'two human brutes fought with all the malice and vindictiveness of Bengal tigers'. The money wasted on the fight, he said, was enough to 'found and maintain a national university, money enough to send forth 400 cultured and inspired missionaries and to maintain them a year in the empires of paganism'.

However, it must have been a peculiar form of Christianity being practiced in Bendigo, because Rev. Worrall claimed that the clock of history had been turned back. There would be racial reprisals.

'God grant,' he shuddered, 'that the defeat of Saturday may not be the sullen and solemn prophecy that Australia is to be outclassed and finally vanquished by these dark-skinned people who everywhere are beginning to realise their immense possibilities.'

Rev. Worrall then got stuck into the Methodist church, in Australia and in England, for trying to make 'merchandise' out of Burns.

And so *The Sydney Morning Herald* letters page battlelines were drawn and the arguments raged:

GOD BLESS PRINCESS ENA

At least in Spain, said 'A.H.N.', a professed lover of sport, Princess Ena had boycotted the bullfights. Here we had seen men, 'with clenched fists and teeth' emulate the bullring. It was a stigma on true lovers of 'manly' sports and the 'ad lib' betting had made a mockery of gambling laws which had outlawed, among other things, shilling sweeps.

LET'S HAVE A MEETING

Not only Sydney, but the Commonwealth had been disgraced, railed a reader. Let the Lord Mayor throw open the Town Hall for a meeting. If Premier Wade continued to hedge let a law be passed so that the Riot Act might be enforced 'where 20 persons or over met to view any sparring or prize fight exhibition'.

A THINKER DOWN FROM QUEENSLAND

'Capricorn' from North Queensland figured it was the fight crowd's privilege to spend their money. The clergy might whinge about wasted money but thanks to 'our splendid supply of national education', folks could do their own thinking. Let not Australia be run from the pulpit but by 'the man who takes off his coat and by the sweat of his brow and muscle, and using his own reasoning powers, produces the wealth which enables the State to exist'.

Unfortunately, such fortitude did not extend to generosity towards the coloured, as Capricorn warned: 'The contest of Saturday shows what a serious matter it would be for Australia to be overrun by the colored races, and many thousands of spectators will go to the uttermost corners of the Commonwealth determined to uphold a white Australia.'

I'M NO MILK SOP, BUT . . .

E.P. Simpson — described as the 'beau ideal of a sportsman' and a 'veritable Chevalier Bayard in sport' — had been to both big

Sydney fights. But it was to be the last time, for such events invoked 'some of the worst passions that are in us'.

He would not ban boxing — men sometimes had to defend themselves — but he would ban prizefights in which the gloves merely extended the brutality of the bareknuckle days. Burns, he was reliably (or so he thought) informed, had a splintered jaw.

'Could anything be more disgusting than the exhibition of the blackfellow spitting words of venom (for they were manifestly intended as such) at his opponent during the whole progress of the fight, preceded and followed up by a handshake which carried with it not a single spark of what should be its true significance ... in other avenues of sport endurance plays a leading part, such as in rowing, running, football, tennis, and in a less degree cricket and golf, but in none of these scientific games do we develop any desire to do personal injury to an opponent,' he wrote.

The very same argument against boxing is produced in Australia today by the Australian Medical Association any time there is death or serious injury in the ring. Defenders of boxing rise up and tell the medicos to look at the results of other sports. Why don't they, for example, ban motor racing, with all its gore, or rugby, with its spinal injuries?

IT COULD BE CONTAGIOUS

A. Keir Murray wrote: 'It is a most depraved and brutal taste that can take pleasure in such sights, and a taste I am ashamed to say, seemingly very deep down in many of our people's hearts.'

ALICE WON'T LIVE HERE ANYMORE?

The Women's Political and Educational League had tried to stop these 'disgraceful events' before the American fleet arrived, wrote Alice Arnold. But it had been unheeded. Now Sydney had been presented to the world as a community of 'brute worshippers'. Her vote would no longer go to the men who had allowed these 'brutal and blood-stained orgies'.

'UNFAIR' SAYS HOSS

W.M. Cartwright wrote: 'Half such treatment shown to a horse as was displayed 'twixt man and man at the Stadium would secure a conviction for cruelty to animals.'

CALL ME AL

W.H.H. Yarrington wrote: '"More than thy flesh, our honour felt the wound," were the words written when Prince Alfred was shot at Clontarf; and the present exhibition of the lowest character is as great a disgrace to us as that untoward event.'

ONLY IF HE HAD TICKETS

Asked 'Christian Endeavourer', who figured his vote had been misused: 'Would Jesus Christ, the fairest and noblest man that ever lived, act as referee or be present at the fight?'

A deputation of Christian men had approached Premier Wade before the fight, but in vain. Now the worst possible damage had been done — forget pubs and barber shops, fight talk had even infiltrated Sunday school, 'showing that the wicked seeds of it had been quickly scattered into their pure and innocent lives'.

BALLS TO THE WOWSERS

'R.E.' spoke for the silent majority when he wrote that the men were not forced to fight; they were merely earning their living, the same as the preachers spouting from the pulpit. The public was not forced to watch, and saw 'no more brutality than they would in a game of football'.

WOULD JESUS LAUNCH A BATTLESHIP?

Indeed, asked 'A Lover of Australia', taking a brutish rhetorical swipe at 'Christian Endeavourer', would Jesus bless an army bent on murder? How about the printing of Bibles at starvation wages?

'Would Christ approve the erection of gorgeous edifices for the worship of God while the sons of God dwell in fever-infected hovels of squalor and filth?' he asked.

An oldie but a goodie.

New South Wales was trying to force religion on the people. A new act made it necessary for any public meeting on a Sunday to have the sanction of the church. And the Anti-Gambling Act was a mere vote-catcher.

'The thousands who witnessed the fistic struggle at the Stadium did no wrong, are not brutes or savages, but simply ungrown souls who later on may approach matters from a different angle ... what we need is a baptism of common-sense, the indwelling of a vigorous national spirit.'

Less religious fuss, less taxation, less law, and more liberty. A man before his time.

BETTER PUNCHES THAN PAUNCHES

Oscar Young proved to be an Armaggedonist of some conviction.

'Europe and Asia are but armed camps, gathering unto themselves ships and trained men for the struggle which, in the near future, must decide the fittest to survive,' he growled. 'Hypocrisy in the guise of diplomacy has been pressing back the war clouds until a more convenient season, but the over-crowding of the East, together with racial hatred, must soon burst them asunder.'

Australia could not rely on England for defence. Australia was a 'rich plum' for the land-hungry foreigner and in the absence of an adequate army and navy it needed men who could shoot: men with muscles and the Anglo-Saxon bulldog spirit. These fights served to stimulate the fighting instinct.

'Let them learn from these contests that the strongest and best prepared must win, and that nature has only a place for the fit,' he wrote. 'Let them wander with their rifles over our mountain ranges, gathering strength and accuracy with the coming years, so that we may face our destiny with a strong heart in a stalwart frame, secure in the knowledge that our bodies are not the atrophied, useless envelopes of an egotistical, self-contained spirit, but as well-developed and alert as our foe; and with nothing less than this let us be content.'

GET THE PICTURE?

Burton Dibbs, in taking a potshot at Simpson for joining with the clerics, prophesised that 'the downfall of the white man before the colored will be told, sung, and cinematographed everywhere where there is a black skin, because they know that the victory of black over white will be preached among every colored race; because they know that the story of the fight will help to promote unrest and sedition; and because they see in the triumph at the Stadium on Saturday last a grinning savage with his foot on the neck of White Australia and exclaiming, "What did I tell yah?"'

But take heart, he advised. And get fit. Remember how the 'Japanese bullies by reason of their superior art, were able to treat the poor Koreans'.

YANKED OUT OF REALITY

'H.P.C.' figured simple-minded Australians (like Simpson) had fallen for a lot of American 'flapdoodle' from the Burns camp, and there would be no such outcry if Burns had won.

'They speak of Mr Johnson "spitting venom" when they know well the insults he himself had to submit to. Did Burns not taunt the despised black man ... a cur with a yellow streak ... have we ever tolerated anything like that in Sydney before we became Americanised?'

Burns, he said, had written about the tactic of making the opponent wild.

'I was at the fight, prepared to cheer the best man irrespective of color or creed, and when I observed the masterful demeanour of that magnificent black man, dominating the whole of that hostile one-eyed crowd, I was lost in admiration ... when Black Peter [Jackson], from here, was at the top of the tree there were no hypocritical tremors for White Australia.'

There had been nothing said before the fight, so the whole ruckus, including the intervention of the churches, could be put down to Australia being sucked in to thinking Burns was 'supernatural', he opined.

PARALYSIS BY ANALYSIS

'J.M.L.' quoted the English expert Harold Furness to the effect that gloved fighting was far more dangerous than bareknuckles — a point made by George Bernard Shaw in *Cashel Byron's Profession*.

This was so, he said, even though fighters these days had comfortable conditions compared to the 'Arctic horror' of the English weather. The gloves prevented hand injuries which once stopped bareknuckle contests. And an American trainer, Donald Cameron, had produced an elaborate chart of the human body showing where any punch could paralyse the nervous system.

A SPLINTERED ARGUMENT

'A Manly Australian' demanded to know how Burns could be so damaged — especially with a splintered jaw — when he tootled off in his motor to the Royal National Park the following day for a picnic, and was later able to work his mouth to the point of demanding another fight.

Fighters were seldom badly hurt, he said, and there were greater evils afoot than two trained men meeting in the ring. And that included the 'feminine, cigarette-smoking weaklings into which many of our young men are degenerating'.

AND WEAK-KNEED WOMEN?

'Another Woman' figured it was her gender which needed a good clout: 'What are women about? They have the much-coveted vote, and at election times they will spout and spout, and make themselves heard for their pet candidates, but when anything vital, such as this fight, occurs they sit down, fold their hands, and moan feebly, and do nothing.'

Suffragism was required in the fight against such greed and brutality. Something had to be done about the 'passions and proclivities' cultivated by 'such scenes as a black and white man fighting'.

DON'T GIVE IT THE BOOT

Stephen McNamee pointed out that Burns attended church the next day. So much for terrible injuries. The uninformed just didn't know how quickly a trained athlete could recover.

'If several of today's critics were to attend football, which is looked upon as the nobler branch of sport, they would witness in almost every match much more brutal attacks made upon players by the use of the boot in place of an opponent's hands. It is not uncommon talk that the last English team brutally ill-treated some of our players ... and what about the treatment meted out to the Australians in the Welsh match, when the large crowd threatened to rush the ground?'

The battlelines were thus comprehensively drawn with the clergy and the 'wowsers' against the 'sportsmen'. It was distinct from the racial debate raging in Melbourne — where one querulous individual had demanded to know how, under the White Australia Policy, Johnson had even been allowed *into* the country.

One clergyman didn't condemn boxing totally — but did call for heavier gloves and cotton helmets and breastplates. One fight fan said the Burns–Johnson embranglement was kid stuff compared with the Joe Goddard–Lut Ryan fight in Johannesburg in which 'both men were butchered'. The same correspondent was pleased with Burns' promise to stay and become an Australian citizen, not knowing that the Canadian seemed to make the same spiel wherever he went.

A Christian 'womanly woman' saw nothing wrong with a clean, fair fight and figured that the ill-feeling between the pugilists was no worse than the 'wretched wrangling' among the churches. She urged exercise for girls so that they could be fit mothers for fighters. But she also called for a white man to rise up and fix Johnson.

Much was made of the attendance of NSW Cabinet Ministers, including the Acting Premier, and Federal Attorney-General Mr Hughes at the stoush. To some it was a disgrace. To others it showed that if it was good enough for such toffs it was good enough for the public.

A person called 'Crocodile' directed the churches to other forms of more insidious brutality which appeared to have escaped their attention: schoolchildren blinded by ill-lit rooms, children sweating on dairy farms and in factories for a shilling a week or even no pay. The Puritans suppressed bear-baiting, he said, not because it hurt the animals but because it pleasured the spectators.

Another anonymous commentator, playing down the brutality, went so far as to compare boxing with golf, which also had degrading aspects, such as the 'sulphurous language used at times in the presence of caddies'.

An 'Anglo-Australian' parson regarded 'the whole business as a special campaign of the devil in Australia', forgetting the English origins of the squared circle.

'A spectacle worthy of Pagan Rome in her most degenerate days,' sighed the joint secretaries of the Evangelical Council, noting that while the fight raised £26000, Hospital Sunday (a fundraising event) had managed only £5000.

'Country Schoolmaster' was having none of the self-defence nonsense. If he was physically attacked, he said, he would defend himself with a club.

But in a long and virulent lecture on the spectre of the Japanese, one 'W.H.S.' railed, 'What are our women crying about?

Don't you know, dear woman, that we stand ready for war for you? In order that you may suckle your babe and ours, we men stand armed to the teeth to keep you in peace and at rest. Then as mothers, wives, sisters, and sweethearts, do you not urge us towards this end? War!'

But there was a strong reaction to any warmongering by 'A Lover of Good Sport'. If in the years that followed there was to be a bitter reaction to the sacrifice of Australian lives at Gallipoli, there already existed a fair measure of rage over the treatment of Boer War veterans.

'There are thousands of mothers, wives, sisters, and children who will curse that war while ever they are alive,' he wrote. 'Young men in the prime of life left sunny Australia never to see it anymore. They were taken to Africa and told to shoot down their fellow white men.

'What is more brutal than after being shot to lie out in the broiling sun, perhaps for six hours, and then to die of thirst? What is more shocking than that? And then those who had the luck not to get shot to come back to Australia to find that they could not get paid their money which was promised to them, which they only got after three years [of] hard fighting and barracking in the law courts; yet you never hear of Canon Boyce preaching about that.'

Another reader bemoaned the demands for legislation to ban boxing saying that legislation was 'killing Australia, cramping our enterprise, bedwarfing our manhood, stifling the best instincts and aspirations of our race'. This writer had been in Germany on a Sunday, where the beer gardens and cafés were in full swing, and hadn't seen a sign of 'rowdyism'. But in Scotland, where drink was banned on the Sabbath, he had seen drunks rolling about everywhere.

One reader cited the Duke of Wellington, Lord Palmerston, and Sir Robert Peel as devotees of the noble art. He then quoted Thackeray, in *Roundabout Papers*, on a famous fight between Sayers and Heenan: 'The one-handed fight of Sayers is one of the most spirit-stirring little stories ever told; and with every love and respect for morality, my spirit says to her, "Do for goodness's sake, my dear madam, keep your true and pure and womanly and gentle remarks for another day. Have the great kindness to stand a leetle aside, and just let us see one or two more rounds between the men."'

Meanwhile, the brutality argument began to run out of steam as Burns and Johnson were making enough public appearances to make it plainly obvious that nobody had been seriously hurt. And some readers were becoming impatient with Tommy's excuses. Why wasn't he taking his beating like the great man he had been made out to be?

A woman reader urged more boxing training, saying that most of the 'straw hat Johnnies' on the street 'can only fight with stones and filthy talk'.

Criticism of Johnson's treatment after the fight was reflected more and more in readers' letters. Let Anglo-Saxons be brave by being just to him, declared 'Dare to be a Daniel'.

The *Herald*, on 2 January 1909, then decided to show its florid hand in a second editorial. It declared that the fight — 'a serious public encounter between two men who were obviously activated by deep personal feeling' — was not an exhibition of skill and could not be described as sport.

Perhaps it was not as brutal as had been first thought, but the question had to be asked whether the fight — with its 'cunning in-blows and kidney slaps' — was necessary to the development of 'manliness' among Australians. There was surely a difference between 'vigorous physicalism' and 'thugism' as understood on the 'Pacific Slope'.

Having made a pile of hay from the great debate, the *Herald* now lectured: 'Without referring to the details of the recent contest, we might very well ask whether it is compatible with the dignity of any civilised community that it should give over-much attention to persons whose business it is to publicly punch or be punched for money, even though they should afterwards whiz through the streets in motor cars and talk largely whenever there is a chance of an audience.

'Very fortunately the Government of this State has come to the conclusion that it is not, and we may be very glad of that.'

The final word was given to one Sylvester Browne, who recommended: 'We shall some day have to fight to maintain our white Australia, and avert the yellow peril, ever present to us. And so do not deprive us of our fighting lessons altogether, although it may offend the delicate non-combative organisations of some people. Give us gloves, police supervision, and orderly crowds, and there will be no brutality with the "human tiger" kept well on the chain.'

Premier Wade, however, in the fine tradition of Australian politics, heeded the press and the pulpit before the punter. In Adelaide he told journalists: 'No-one objects to a boxing contest pure and simple; but when it comes to prizefighting galore it is time for the State to interfere. From the experience gained in the last two fights between Burns and Squires, it seems to me New South Wales is likely to become the convincing ground for many similar contests with their debasing features and unsavoury surroundings. If that is so it must be stopped.'

Meanwhile, *The New York Times* virtually apologised for having covered the fight at all. (It had been one of the few papers to give merit to Johnson, putting his victory down to 'his physical advantages over Burns, his superior knowledge of the fighting game, and his unruffled demeanour while being taunted by the champion'.) It was hay, it editorialised, for critics of newspapers to devote so much space and expense to 'a fight between two inconsequential men, one white and one black'.

There had been no such flood of cables concerning the 'many novel and important experiments, Governmental and sociologic, that have been tried of recent years in that far-away land'. The mails had been good enough for those, but dispatches to practically all the papers in America and Europe had been used for a fight of little significance, 'which all good people unite in condemning as barbarous and demoralizing'.

It was especially puzzling, snorted the *Times*, because both fighters had 'extremely shady records'. However, there was no sign of a diminished interest in fighting — especially in the heavyweight division — even if the sport was banned in New York.

'Australia ought to be ashamed of itself, and doubtless is, for harboring a sport which civilization has condemned, and yet — and yet — well, the only hope of putting an end to prizefights lies in making their brutality widely known.'

On the other side of the world, *The Sydney Mail* said that the crowd had been for Burns because of his skin colour. That was not necessarily the way a 'colored fellow-creature' should be treated. So should Johnson be getting the plaudits would have gone to Burns had he won?

There had been taunting on both sides, and Australia plainly did not understand American ways.

'The American puts all he knows into his games; the Australian is always restrained by quixotic notions of sportsmanship,' wrote the *Mail*. In a lament that we still hear today, it complained that Australia would lose its lily-white ways if it absorbed too much American influence in boxing. Then the *Mail* got in a short, sharp shot to the gut of Johnson and his people.

'There is at once something splendid and heroic in such a fight as that which raised a negro to the company of great boxers of all time,' it commented. 'But it is easy to become absurd over it. The position of the negro in America, and the clamour of the colored races all over the world, give the fight, in the opinion of some critics, a world-wide significance. It is almost laughable that such hysterical views should get into print ... some people fear that the negro in America may rise in the consciousness of pride of race, and become unruly. The organised power of law would settle any such problem.

'Whether a white or black is the holder of the belt matters little. British consuls will remain at a normal level; the German Emperor will send telegrams; the American police will keep the negro in order and the average citizen will get through his business in the same methodical way as in the past whether Jeffries comes from his alfalfa farm and beats Johnson or remains there and gives interviews about his rheumatism.'

The fight, the *Mail* suggested, might actually have reflected well on the black race if Johnson had maintained his decorum. But he was no Peter Jackson.

'Now it is all over, people are asking themselves whether the spectacle of this capering, grinning negro punching a white man was worthy of the city of Sydney.'

In a variation of the *Times* editorial, it went on to dump on Johnson, dump on Sydney, and dump on boxing in general. Having done that it declared that the occasion was worth of only pictorial coverage.

It had been a long and bitter odyssey for Jack Johnson. He had struggled to get his shot at the world title; he had been branded a coward, the worst possible insult, by Burns; he had happily entertained the public; he had trained himself to magnificent condition; and he had won the fight with an overwhelming display of superiority against an opponent who had been declared the favourite. Yet the indiscretion of reacting to taunts from the crowd, and returning the insults of Burns, was blown up by the press into some kind of abomination. Instead of glory the twisted rhetoric of the white press had branded him a disgrace.

Now, as champion, he faced an even more frustrating and demeaning journey. But his struggle was no greater than that of one forgotten group. Nowhere in all of this tumultuous argument about morals, manliness, and munificence among the races did anybody care to discuss the state of Australia's own blacks, the Aborigines. They remained beneath comment.

5

LIKE SO MANY ASPECTS OF the fight itself, Burns–Johnson had its own special irony for Hugh D. McIntosh. Firstly, Huge Deal had not counted on Australian spectators, or the film of the fight, to make his pile when he called for Tommy Burns to come to Australia. Secondly, he made an enormous amount of money out of a fight which was, as Jack London and Larry Foley both declared, a real stinker. But such was the morbid fascination of the world with this sinister turn of events — a smash in the face of white supremacy — that it kept shelling out money.

There are still remnants, some 13 minutes, of that film, shot by one hand-cranked camera from one angle, and new perspectives to be gained from it. Sadly, we don't see the early knockdowns or even the finish, but we do see how much Johnson dominated and just how futile Burns' fight plan really was.

To fully appreciate the reasons why, it is necessary to first take a look at a couple of Burns' earlier fights which were caught on film and a 90-second look at Johnson training at Rushcutters Bay before the big fight. From these few images, one can easily glean what skills Burns had as a champion, but also why they were next to useless against Johnson.

Much of it had to do with the way fighting styles had developed. Totally gone was the old straight-backed bareknuckle style, with the hands held up like a juggler. Hands were now held down by the waist, much like the great modern fighters Sugar Ray Leonard and Tommy Hearns, but without the footwork, or the evasive movement at the waist to go with it. This was what gave a sawn-off fighter like Burns a chance.

It is doubtful that Burns would have succeeded against today's orthodox style of one hand guarding the chin while the other spears out the jab and snaps back to protect.

Against Gunner Moir, Burns was able to launch himself behind a big right, clock Moir on the jaw, and drop him face first. Burns could obviously punch if given a sitting target. He didn't need to set anything up with a jab because the slow fighter with his left down near his pants was an open target.

In his first knockout of Squires it was the same story. Boshter Bill looked slow and wooden, and it was no wonder that the American press declared him to be an impostor. He was so stiff he looked like a puppet controlled by an arthritic.

Burns had perfected a method of stopping punches before they were thrown. If an opponent had both hands low, he would push them down further, affording him a free moment to bring up his own hands and launch an attack.

There was a brief glimpse of Squires at Colma, with chickens running around in the background, skipping rope in training for the fight. He looked in prime shape, and strong in the legs, but not greatly developed in the arms and shoulders. In the fight — hailed in the newsreel as 'The Shortest and Fiercest Contest on Record' — he swayed back and forth, and side to side, awkwardly, with no foot movement, and with his left hand down near his knee. In fact he looked like a rank amateur; it is a mystery how he had built up any kind of record.

Soon enough, he walked smack-bang into a big Burns right and dropped on to his shoulder. He was up without taking advantage of the count, and Burns began to push him around. With this habit of bending back, as if punch-shy, Squires had no forward momentum and, unlike Johnson, no way of laying on Burns and neutralising him.

Squires was determined, however, and did land a left and right which buckled Burns, and had him grabbing Squires around the waist. But Squires walked into another right, with a left following it, and was dumped backwards. He got up again with his arms flailing about like a drunken octopus and was dropped for the third and last time. Squires had no subtlety whatsoever.

His punches were not telegraphed by his shoulders; it was slower than that — more like pony express.

Cut to that short grab at Rushcutters Bay. Johnson is obviously having a great time, with a bunch of admirers standing around. He grins and prances as he goes through a shadow-boxing routine designed to loosen those big arms and keep his hands quick, punching up, down, and straight ahead. Then he has a wrestle with a young, lighter sparring partner who wraps both hands behind Johnson's head and tries to pull him down. Johnson, using only the great strength in his neck and shoulders, keeps lifting the kid. They then have a snappy little spar.

The point is that Johnson was in a buoyant mood and supremely confident in his condition, despite all the rumours about his carousing. He was in the sort of shape to face any man, at any time. He was tremendously muscular in the arms, deltoids and shoulders, and rock-solid in the chest and gut. At 30 years of age, he was probably in the prime condition of his life.

(In fact it is a shock to look at the film of his fight with Jim Jeffries 18 months later. True, Jeffries was a big man and Jack could not have hoped to appear as physically dominant as he did against Burns, but he seemed to have lost much of that muscle development, was plainly carrying a paunch, and was a lot more nervous.)

At Rushcutters Bay most of the men had taken off their straw boaters. McIntosh was duded up in white, with a garish motoring cap, like some kind of posh caddy. And on the film he didn't seem to reef the men apart as the press had made out. They just seemed to part when Johnson got bored.

The difference in size, accentuated by Burns' crouch, was comical. Burns didn't have the massive chest and shoulder development that had been glorified by the swooning writers. Most of his weight seemed to be in his backside and thighs. His upper body just looked weedy next to the magnificent black man.

When he wasn't clamped in Jack's arms, Burns was capering about, dodging and feinting, like Stan Laurel or Charlie Chaplin shaping up to some huge neighbourhood bully.

For all the signals that were coming from his corner he seemed to have only one plan of attack. He jigged around with his hands low and open, like catchers' mitts, trying to snare anything Johnson might throw. He started most of his attacks with looping lefts — he didn't seem to have a conventional jab — which ended up wrapped around the back of Johnson's neck and then got pulled in.

Johnson did none of the low fending that he did against Jeffries. He stood slightly bent with his right forearm across his stomach and his left swinging below it. At times he straightened up and slammed a straight left to Burns' head as if to keep in practice. But he knew that he didn't need any outfighting at all.

Once Burns was in-close he would collapse on to Johnson's chest — the top of his head not even up to Johnson's chin — with his arms around Johnson's waist. Johnson would then pin his arms or hands down so that he couldn't punch. Or drape his long log of a right arm over Burns' left shoulder and bash him in the kidneys. Johnson could then push Burns' shoulders away and have time to ping him, usually with a right uppercut or cross.

At one point, Burns nearly fell when throwing a big right and Johnson pirouetted and whirled him around by the arms the way a father swings a small child in the park.

There is another moment in the disjointed film, however, when Johnson's absolute superiority is startlingly vivid. As if stung by something, Johnson suddenly opens up and starts blazing combinations at Burns who is shot back into the ropes. The punches are swift and savage, like something a big fast 1990s heavyweight like Evander Holyfield might throw. Suddenly Burns is helpless, floundering around with his head down, trying to grab at Johnson's trunks. For a moment the genie was out of the bottle — it could probably have come out at any time.

But it didn't, and that was what made it such a stinker of a fight. It was fought almost entirely in clinches in which Burns was weaponless, a fly thrashing fitfully in a web. When Johnson wanted to engage in any lengthy dialogue with the crowd, or Burns' corner, he stood straight up, embracing Burns like he was waltzing an old lady around at a church social, and smiled and chatted over Burns' shoulder.

Was it flashness? It must have seemed that way to many spectators. They had probably never seen a fight so one-sided or a fighter so relaxed that he could ignore his opposition and enjoy a good argument. And when Johnson smiled it lit up that grey morning like a halogen lamp.

So was Burns badly beaten up? It was hard to tell from the film. At times Burns jogged, pigeon-toed, back to the collapsible chair in his corner, where three men were waiting to flap towels over him. But that seemed more of a show for his sake, a way of convincing himself that there was still a fight on. Most likely — looking at the old celluloid — the fight was degenerating into such bad pantomime the longer Johnson spun it out that the cops were playing critic more than peacekeeper.

Was Tommy's courage heroic? Probably not. Every man who steps into a boxing ring has courage, and every day in small venues around the world overmatched fighters keep punching away as they are pasted by stronger, classier opponents. It is one of the great failings of boxing that the lesser fighter is lionised for spilling his own blood. Fighters with more courage than ability, the so-called 'crowd-pleasers', keep going until they become stumblebums. Burns was not badly hurt. He fought no differently to fighters of any colour who compete to the finish. Burns' pluck was never supernatural. But Australia, and its press, had made him into a hero and wanted to keep it that way.

Did he deserve a rematch? Absolutely not. He was an opportunist who had made the most of his limited abilities. Even he knew that his string was now running out.

6

THE RESULT OF BURNS–JOHNSON was not widely reported immediately in the United States, for there were at most two American correspondents at Rushcutters Bay. However, Jack London's report was seized upon by white America. *The New York Evening Journal*, whose writer and cartoonist Tad Dargan had always been fair to Johnson, ran possibly the largest-ever front-page picture of a black man in a white newspaper.

In Chicago and Galveston, black jubilation was well-reported. *Colored American Magazine* summed up the true reaction in the heart of black America when it wrote, 'Today is the zenith of Negro sport.'

John L. Sullivan tried to spoil the show by claiming that Johnson's win would kill off interest in the sport; he must have known that apart from Jim Jeffries there was no credible white challenger in sight. While Jeffries, for his part, chose to criticise Burns rather than praise Johnson.

Johnson eventually returned to Chicago and opened his Café de Champion club, at which revellers of all colours were welcome. He defended his title only once in 1909, knocking out the undersized Stanley Ketchel in 12 rounds in Los Angeles. However, on 4 July 1910, Jeffries, finally lured out of retirement by Tex Rickard for a purse of $101 000 — McIntosh being one of the underbidders — faced him under a broiling Reno sun.

Jeffries, who had shed 32 kg, looked no bigger or stronger than Johnson and hadn't fought since 1904, yet was made the 10/6 favourite. Blacks all over America, some even wagering their labour, cleaned up as Johnson handled Jeffries with ludicrous ease, toying and taunting him in the first so-called 'Battle of the Century' in front of a crowd of 15 760, which at one point joined in a chorus of the popular song 'All Coons Look Alike to Me'. Johnson, in his element, just grinned and chatted to all around him. The enormous implications of what he was about to do were not lost. And even though he would admit later that he regarded Jeffries as one of the greatest heavyweights, this was going to be done with style. One critic described Johnson as a tiger playing with a stumbling bullock until he tired of the game.

'Now, stop lovin' me like that Mr Jeff,' Johnson sneered at a deflating Jeffries before getting serious in the 15th round and dropping him with a huge arcing right. Jeffries was down for the count, and white pride with him, when referee Rickard declared Johnson the winner.

In the wash-up, *The San Francisco Examiner* ran the headline 'Jeffries Mastered by Grinning Jeering Negro', while *The Los Angeles Times* warned blacks not to get too 'puffed up'. *The New York Times* — at the time when the Hounds of Hell and other white gangs were running wild in Manhattan beating up blacks — penned an editorial expressing the hope that the fight would stimulate 'respect for equality and fairness'.

So much for that. Eight blacks were killed and thousands more injured in white-instigated rioting after the result became known. There were riots in 50 American cities.

Theodore Roosevelt even went so far as to call for an end to boxing. Laws were passed to prevent the fight film being shown or transported across state lines. The fists of Jack Johnson had rattled the white world — even from the farthest outposts of the British Empire came angry reports about bumptious natives.

White America now trembled for its women. White manhood had shrivelled. While a black mistress — especially in the south — was considered a passable fashion accessory for a white man it was unthinkable that white women might begin submitting to the charms of black men.

Johnson had long flaunted his affairs with white women at a time when a black man could be lynched for even the slightest sexual suggestion to one. In fact, during Johnson's reign as champion 354 black men were lynched — 89 for alleged offences against white women.

Johnson figured a white woman to be his right — part of the same philosophy that saw him drink champagne through a straw, change his dandy outfits three times a day, roar around in a fast car, flash $1000 notes, and play his bull fiddle and dance the Grizzly Bear and Bunny Hug at the Café de Champion. If White America couldn't nail him in the ring they would outside it.

In 1912, Johnson's first legitimate wife, the light-skinned Etta Duryea, committed suicide. Soon after a 19-year-old girl named Lucille Cameron travelled from Minnesota to Chicago and attached herself to the champion. Her mother followed, alleging abduction, and Johnson was charged.

Lucille refused to confirm any abduction. Johnson beat the rap, then turned around and married her. However, soon after he was brought down by a high-priced hooker named Belle Schreiber, of Chicago's Everleigh Club, one of the world's most expensive brothels. Johnson had given her $10 000 and had travelled around the entertainment circuit with her.

There was new federal legislation called the Mann Act, which outlawed the transportation of women across state lines for immoral purposes. In Johnson's case the dudgeon against him was so high that in public opinion he had committed sins of the worst bestial nature.

It was a selective prosecution even if the jails were full of white pimps, for the genie of black sexuality was now out of the bottle. Big buck niggers. Big black cocks. Sweet, schooled, porcelain white women grabbing at them with no shame, rutting like baboons. It was just too horrible for the white mind to even contemplate. The white sphincter clenched in panic, the white palm sweated. Johnson was out of control, writing his own rules. He had to be stopped, and this was the perfect opportunity, for not even black support could be guaranteed for a man who had been splurging money on hookers when hiding behind a very public marriage. His obsession with white women was seen as an insult to black women. What was wrong with his own?

Unfortunately for Johnson, Schreiber duly testified against him, and under the terms of the Mann Act he was found guilty and sentenced to 366 days in prison and fined $1000. His disgrace was almost complete. The popular *Police Gazette* went so far as to describe him as 'the vilest, most despicable creature that lives', while conservative black leader Booker T. Washington said he had committed a 'grave injustice to his race'. Even W.W. Naughton wrote: 'The disgust at his alleged misconduct is such that no-one wants to think about him', while Chicago newspapers ambushed him with stories that he had boasted he could get any white woman he wanted.

Laws against mixed marriages were proposed but ultimately rejected: the white man didn't really want to give up his option of a black woman. However, Johnson was still idolised by blacks with no voice — they could always look back and laugh about how that Jack Johnson had whitey steppin' and fetchin' in all directions. But some prominent conservative blacks were relieved that he was no longer a threat to any perceived progress they were making in their struggle for civil rights. Sadly, Johnson's misdemeanour all but instigated the new Jim Crow (segregation) laws, some of which lasted half a century.

For Johnson there was no choice but to flee. He outsmarted the authorities again by smuggling himself into Canada, where he could not be extradited, among a touring black baseball team on a bus. From there he headed to Europe and exile.

Johnson may have been publicly disgraced by whites and disowned by conservative blacks, but he was still the world champion. In 1915, however, he finally lost the title and white promoters drew the heavyweight colour line again.

The next black fighter to breach it was Joe Louis, when he knocked out Jim Braddock in 1937. Louis had been carefully coached not to become the next Jack Johnson — not to give offence — and was managed by the powerful Mike Jacobs, controller of boxing at Madison Square Garden in New York.

The logical contender at the time that Louis got his shot was Max Schmeling. The German won the vacant title, discarded by Gene Tunney, by beating Jack Sharkey in 1930. He defended it once, then lost it back to Sharkey, on a dubious decision, in 1932. From Sharkey the title passed to Primo Carnera, to Max Baer, and then to Braddock.

In 1936 — employing tactics predicted by Jack Johnson — Schmeling knocked out the rising star Louis, inflicting his first defeat. However, Louis got the tilt at Braddock ahead of Schmeling because Jacobs was afraid that Schmeling could beat Braddock — who was signed to Madison Square Garden — and that if Germany went to war the title, and the money that went with it, would end up out of his control.

Thus Joe Louis, a 'tame nigger' compared to the 'flash nigger' Johnson, became the next black man to win the title. When he defended against Schmeling in 1938, and knocked him out in the first round, he suddenly — and somewhat ironically — became the symbol of American democratic superiority over German fascism.

Along with sprinter Jesse Owens, who had embarrassed Hitler at the 1936 Berlin Olympics, Louis was among a pantheon of black athletes who were being accepted into the mainstream for their exceptional deeds and character: Jackie Robinson, Althea Gibson, Wilma Rudolph, Jim Brown, Hank Aaron, and so on. They were the pioneers for the future black stars who would so completely dominate world sport in the latter half of the twentieth century.

The greatest of these stars was boxer Muhammad Ali, the athlete of the century — black or white.

Early in his career, Ali claimed that Johnson was the greatest of all time. And when he made his much-heralded comeback against Jerry Quarry in 1970, his cornerman Drew Bundini Brown was shouting, 'Ghost in the house! Ghost in the house!' It meant that the spirit of Jack Johnson was looking over Ali.

No doubt Ali saw himself as a second coming of Johnson, even though he was more political. Like Johnson, Ali refused to be silenced, refused to go away. After his much-publicised stand against the Vietnam War a whole generation grew to worship him. Johnson was robbed of some of his best years as champion by the colour line. Ali was robbed of three of his prime years when boxing exceeded its authority and banned him. But like Johnson he had a quest and the character to pursue it against the odds.

Ali said that Johnson was the greatest influence on his life before he discovered Islam.

'He came along at a time when black people felt they had nothing to be proud of, and he made them proud,' he once said.

'I grew to love the Jack Johnson image,' he said another time. 'I wanted to be rough, tough, arrogant, the nigger white folks don't like.'

Ali, like Johnson, was accused at first of being an 'uppity nigger'. He, too, taunted his opponents, but times had changed so much that, unlike Johnson, he was ultimately forgiven. In fact he became so popular that late in his career decisions went his way which probably should not have.

In the history of black sport, there hasn't been much room made for Johnson, but there should be. To many blacks at the time, his victory was the next greatest thing to the abolition of slavery, yet he gets little respect from modern-day academics who compile lists of influential blacks of history — even American history at that. In truth, he was a lot closer to the hearts of his people than some who were given laurels for pleading with whites for their rights. Jack just assumed his.

Legendary jazz trumpeter Miles Davis, who released an album titled *A Tribute to Jack Johnson*, said that 'Johnson portrayed Freedom — it rang just as loud as the bell proclaiming the champion.'

Tennis legend and black historian Arthur Ashe believed Johnson had an even larger impact than Muhammad Ali on American society, and was more influential than Frederick Douglass or Booker T. Washington or any other black social leader. Ashe said the fight with Jeffries — after which, he calculated, 19 blacks were killed — had been the most eagerly anticipated event in history for American blacks because they all knew about it and could follow its progress on the telegraph. Even Abraham Lincoln's Emancipation Proclamation took a lot more time to sink into black consciousness than Jack Johnson's great victories.

There is no doubt that Johnson was one of the great heavyweights of history. Boxing historian Nat Fleischer reckoned that the black fighters of the early twentieth century — Joe Jeanette, Sam Langford, Sam McVea, Denver Martin — were vastly superior to the whites and that Johnson was easily the best of them.

Johnson was probably at his fittest for the Burns fight, but added to his reputation with the versatility and lateral movement that he used to beat Jeffries; he was now not only strong, fast, and skilled, but *adaptable*. Fleischer described him as 'one of the most scientific fighters of all times and a stinging, powerful hitter of the first school'.

He classed Johnson's straight left as his best weapon — even though he had little need for it against Burns. He also had a fine left hook, but the right uppercut was a punch which he refined into a work of art. Where most fighters needed to step in to throw this punch, which proved deadly against the new clutching infighters, Johnson could lean in, inside his opponent's left, and throw it short and hard. Then he would follow it with a left to the body or jaw.

Fleischer claimed that Johnson's sway from the hips, which allowed him to throw punches and avoid them, was probably only equalled by Gene Tunney among the pre-World War II heavies. As a boxer, Jack was the equal of great lightweights like Joe Gans and Young Griffo and heavies Peter Jackson and Jim Corbett. Maybe only Jim Jeffries or Joe Louis could dish out more punishment.

Eventually Johnson, Louis, and Muhammad Ali would be bracketed as the greatest of their eras: the best ever.

'Johnson boxed on his toes, could block from almost any angle, was lightning fast on his feet, possessed ring daring, could feint an opponent into knots, and was master of the "kidding" game,' wrote Fleischer in *Black Dynamite*.

Fleischer was also a friend of Johnson for 30 years and painted him not as a loudmouth egotist, but as a soft-spoken, kindly, cheerful, philanthropic man: Li'l Arthur was a big spender and a soft touch. But, said Fleischer, he did brag an awful lot about his white women.

In the 90 years since Burns–Johnson, physical fear among blacks of whites in sport has diminished. In fact, these days 'white America' is accused more of exploiting acknowledged superior black strength, than standing over blacks in head-to-head competition.

Some would even say that in American professional sport, black stars have become so confident, so brash, and in some cases so arrogant that the concept of fear of whites has been rendered laughable. Black power in sport is right in your face, brother, love it or hate it. And much of the youth of the world, including whites, not only love it but ape it.

And it all started at Rushcutters Bay with John Arthur Johnson. The fearlessness of this man in the presence of white fear, hatred and persecution was nothing short of extraordinary. After his momentous victory, the Social Darwinism of the late nineteenth century which dictated that the white man was inherently stronger and smarter could no longer be sustained.

'Stronger' certainly had to go as Johnson beat up one white hope after another. The next twist had to be that in blacks greater physical strength correlated with mental weakness. But that argument was hard to sustain when it became obvious that Johnson had also been outsmarting whites for a long time.

The process that Jack Johnson set in train has come to this. Few sociologists want to acknowledge that blacks have any kind of physical advantages lest they be equated with mental weakness. If any advantages are considered at all they must be moral or psychological. So it is argued that blacks win because they either try harder or believe in themselves more. Johnson could have related to that.

Of course, this argument by 'anti-racists' demeans, for example, all those thousands of white American kids from all social strata who each year set themselves the task of cracking the mega-money worlds of basketball and gridiron only to find that they just don't have the explosive speed or power of their black rivals.

It seems that the argument is gradually being handed over to the geneticists. One of the latest theories is that when DNA is measured blacks and whites probably average out in genes which dictate athletic ability. But among blacks there will be more variety. And that includes less ability at the bottom of the scale, and more ability at the elite level.

The arguments have become contorted and self-conscious. But what a difference this is from 90 years ago. We used to solemnly explain why white people were superior. Now we try to figure polite ways to explain how black people are superior.

7

NATURALLY, BOSHTER BILL OUTLIVED THE lot of them, dying in September 1962 at the age of 83. When he retired from boxing eight years after his fight with Tommy Burns, his record had collapsed completely. A modest man had become a most modest talent. He fought Bill Lang twice in 1909 and was knocked out in the 17th and 20th rounds. He fought Lang again in 1910 and was knocked out in the seventh round. He fought a return bout in 1911 and was knocked out in the fifth round. His next and last fight, at the age of 37, was against Dave Smith in 1916 and he was knocked out in the 10th round.

In the second Lang fight of 1909 Squires had Tommy Burns in his corner. Burns had altered Squires' style to be more like his own. It didn't help. So the great Australian hope — without whom McIntosh could not have lured Jack Johnson to Australia — lost 10 of his last 11 fights by knockout.

Jack London sent his crewman Martin Johnson back to the Solomons to hire a new skipper to bring the *Snark* to Australia. It took 36 days of hard slog to reach Sydney Harbour, where it was sold to a group of Englishmen (for a tenth of the original cost) and returned to the Pacific for blackbirding runs.

Jack and Charmian left Australia in April 1909 on an English tramp steamer bound for South America. They spent a month in Ecuador, crossed the Andes, rode through Panama, and then boarded a ship for New Orleans. When they returned home to California they had been gone 27 months — not quite the seven-year epic that had been envisaged — and were loaded with material for more South Seas adventure books.

London continued his campaign against Johnson in the lead-up to the Jim Jeffries fight the following year. In doing so, he convinced himself that Jeffries would win and bet heavily.

London also resumed his drinking after his recovery in Australia and never stopped. But like a machine, he still cranked out his 1000 words a day. His book *The Cruise of the Snark* confirmed his standing as America's most famous writer of the period, but his heart was broken when he spent $80 000 building a 'perfect' home, called The Wolf House, only to have it destroyed by fire. He moved back to Hawaii, and on 21 November 1916 was found dead from a combination of morphine sulphate and atropine sulphate. He had calculated the dosages and had ritually drunk himself to death.

Hugh D. McIntosh left Australia with the fight film in early January 1909, after rejecting an offer of £10 000 from impresario J.C. Williamson for 50 per cent of the rights. McIntosh had been willing to sell but Williamson, upset by the death of a friend, let the deadline for the deal slip by. Again Huge Deal had been blessed, for he was to make £80 000 out of that strip of film and set himself up for a life of luxury.

He launched himself as a promoter in London and Paris, bringing puggery to the white-tie-and-tails set. In 1911, when he was still just 35, he got out of boxing, sold the Stadium at Rushcutters Bay (which would one day host a Beatles concert) for an enormous sum and went into the theatre business. He bought into the Tivoli circuit for £100 000 and, he said, floated it as a £200 000 company. He became renowned for musical extravaganzas. 'I never count the costs,' he was once quoted.

Too old to fight when World War I broke out he offered to form a Teddy Roosevelt-style cavalry regiment called McIntosh's Rough Riders. The idea was rejected.

He lived extravagantly — taking no less than 26 trips on the *Lusitania* — but did his bit by using his theatres to raise more than a £1 million for the War effort. He was the organiser of Allies Day and had special gold badges struck for Victoria Cross winners which gave them free admission to Tivoli theatres. In 1917 he was named a life member of the New South Wales Legislative Council by his friend Premier W.A. Holman.

His next incarnation was as a newspaperman when he bought the Sydney papers *The Sunday Times* — for, he said, £150 000 — and an old friend, *The Referee*, and brought to both his trademark racy flair. One time, he reportedly offered a murderer, who was about to be hanged, £5000 to return from the dead, and sat in his office with a party of friends waiting, eating caviar and drinking champagne. At the same time that this nonsense was going on he was bringing names like Anna Pavlova and Fritz Kreisler to his theatres.

In the 1920s, now worth £500000, he travelled in the most elegant style in Europe and America. In 1923 he bought Broome Park, the 600-acre estate of the late Lord Kitchener, with its seventeenth-century mansion, sunken gardens, rose walks, Tudor furniture, Renaissance art, and most of the hero of Khartoum's historical collection. During the final details of the sale he tossed Viscount Broome for a grand piano. Then he put in an airstrip and a cricket pitch of Australian soil for visiting Australian teams to play on.

In 1929 he stood as a Labour candidate for an electorate in northern Scotland, but the press turned on him, damning him for his prizefighting promotions and extravagant spending, and as a result he was well and truly beaten at the polls. It was a bad sign, for he had not seen the great economic crash coming, and when he returned to Australia in 1930 he was broke. He kept on spending but in 1932 was declared bankrupt, owing £283000.

He tried his hand fight-promoting, catering, running a guesthouse — all old favourites — but had lost his luck. His one last great fling was to return to England to launch a chain of Australian-style milk bars, which he did with great success. But he expanded the chain too quickly, and found himself broke again three years later. He became ill in 1941 and died shabby and penniless in 1942. Friends had to pay for his funeral and take up a collection for his widow. They raised less than £1000.

Norman Lindsay later commented: 'I consider him one of the most unique and entertaining human beings I ever forgathered with.'

Tommy Burns may not have died broke, but he did suffer the indignity of laying in an unmarked grave in his homeland — an ignominious end for Canada's only world heavyweight champion and one of its most famed sportsmen.

At the age of 74, Burns died from a heart attack in Vancouver on 10 May 1955. His obituary in *The Vancouver Sun* the next day told how he had spent the last years of his life damning boxing as 'vicious and full of hatred'. The year before he had said: 'I've got something better than that — and it is love for my fellow man. My main object in life is to help the sick and the suffering.'

In 1948 he had become an ordained minister and hellfire and brimstone evangelist, spreading the gospel of 'universal love' (in his pockets when he died were neat white cards inscribed: 'Tom Burns, Demonstrator of Universal Love'). One writer who knew Burns said that a well-developed fondness for women partly explained his philosophy.

After losing to Johnson he didn't fight again for four years, and was never again seriously considered in the heavyweight picture. He beat Bill Lang in Australia in 1912 for the Empire title; Bill Rickard at Saskatoon, Canada, the same year; Arthur Felkey in Calgary, Canada, in 1913; and Tex Foster at Prince Rupert, British Columbia, Canada, in 1918. He also spent a year as a physical-training instructor for the Canadian Army during World War I.

In 1920 he attempted a comeback in London and was knocked out by English champion Joe Beckett in seven rounds — the only time in his career that he was counted out. But, typical of Burns, he hired the Albert Hall, promoted the fight himself and made a handsome $20 000 profit. After that he was best known as the owner of a sportsman's pub in Newcastle. Later, during Prohibition, he ran a popular speakeasy in New York, but one day felt the hand of God on his shoulder and instantly found religion.

His lifetime record ran to 58 fights for 45 wins — 36 by knockout and nine by decision. He also had one no-decision, one draw, four losses by decision or intervention, and that KO loss in his last fight. He was credited with 11 successful title defences and in 1996 was inducted into the International Boxing Hall of Fame. It was a highly creditable record for a heavyweight with such physical limitations. The figure put on his total ring earnings was $209 000.

His greatest battle was with arthritis. He was near death from it in 1935 but claimed that he cured himself through faith and meditation. Indeed, until his death, he seemed in remarkably good shape for his age.

Burns' will left his entire estate to Nellie Vanderlip Burns, the widow of a railroad millionaire whom he had married when he was 65. The will mentioned four daughters in England by a previous marriage but they were excluded. There was no mention of the lovely Jewel.

The story of the unmarked grave did not surface until five years later when a Seattle man, Bud Fitzgerald, whose strange hobby was photographing the graves of fighters, discovered that Burns was resting under nothing but weeds at Ocean View Cemetery at Burnaby, in Vancouver. The only witnesses to his burial had been two gravediggers and two passing strangers. There had been no funeral service.

When Fitzgerald wrote to *The Vancouver Sun*, columnist Dick Beddoes revisited Burns' career. The widely held Canadian view was that Burns had done as much foul-mouthed taunting as Johnson at Rushcutters Bay. The bias of Australian writers and Jack London against Johnson had not endeared Tommy to his countrymen.

The discovery of his unmarked grave in turn revealed many secrets. It was said that Jewel died in the 1920s and that Nellie was his third wife. A hockey Hall-of-Famer, Cyclone Taylor, started a fund to get a plaque to mark the grave and a sister named Violet Dempsey, of Hamilton, Ontario, surfaced, claiming that both of Burns' parents were German, not French-Canadian.

In November 1961, 37 people attended a ceremony, complete with 'The Last Post', for the placement of a new bronze marker. All of $300 had been collected in his memory.

After the Belle Schrieber scandal, Jack Johnson ended up in Europe with Lucille Cameron.

Despite the way his country had turned against him, he had lost none of his appetite for a good suit, a fast car, and an intoxicating lifestyle. He still expected to move freely in any kind of exalted company and hold his own in conversation anywhere in the world. Alas, the 'flashness' that had earned him the ire of the good sports of Australia was now almost universally perceived as arrogance.

His expectations of cleaning up on the English stage quickly disappeared when he was jeered by some crowds and had his bull fiddle, clowning and sparring act closed down by influential religious groups.

He went to Paris and, in December 1913, fought a 10-round draw with American fighter Battling Jim Johnson, and broke a bone in his arm. Then he hooked up with a volatile Irish-American promoter named Dan McKetrick to fight an American, Frank Moran, who possessed a huge right-hand punch which he had christened 'Mary Ann'.

On the quiet McKetrick figured that at age 35, Johnson, especially after the broken arm, was finished as a fighter. He tried to sign Moran to a contract, figuring he would be the next champion, but Moran refused. Because of this dispute McKetrick arranged for lawyers to tie up the whole purse as leverage over Moran.

But McKetrick was sadly mistaken about Johnson. Even with restricted use of his left arm, Johnson gave Moran a hiding for 20 rounds, keeping well away from Mary Ann. It did him little good however, as he was told after the fight that police had seized the purse money. The date was 27 June 1914, and the following day, in Sarajevo, Austria's Archduke Franz Ferdinand was assassinated. War broke out, McKetrick's lawyer was killed in action, and neither Johnson or Moran ever got paid.

Johnson took off for Russia, hoping to make some money with his stage act before the war got out of hand. There he had a memorable drinking bout with Rasputin, but was quickly hustled out of the country because of war preparations. He returned to

Paris, found it in turmoil, and ended up back in London. He went back on stage and was quite a remarkable sight strolling in Piccadilly in a silk suit, trilby, and crocodile-skin shoes, or motoring in a big auto with leopard-skin upholstery.

But his popularity ran out when he was accused of making pro-German remarks while drunk. His flat was broken into and papers which Johnson had brought back from St Petersburg — allegedly correspondence between the Tsar and the Kaiser — were stolen.

He was ordered out of England and attacked on the street by thugs. To his 'rescue' came American promoter Jack Curley, who offered him a fight with the new white hope, the 198-cm/ 113-kg American cowboy, Jess Willard, in Cuba.

For the rest of his life Johnson claimed that the fight was a fix: that if he threw it Curley would arrange for him to go home without serving the 366-day jail term. The fight, set to go to a finish, took place in a wooden arena, thrown up McIntosh-style, inside a Havana racetrack on 5 April 1915.

The sun was merciless but Johnson had trained hard and seemed to be handling Willard easily. He claimed that he had agreed to throw the fight in the 10th round if Lucille, placed strategically at ringside, was paid his agreed 'fee' of $50 000.

The fight continued with Johnson, who seemed to like Willard, running a line of friendly chat and looking like he could finish it any moment he pleased. But the 10th came and went with no sign from Lucille that she had received the money. The fight went on, with Johnson beginning to tire and Willard beginning to land blows until, Johnson claimed, at the end of the 25th he got the signal that Lucille had been paid.

'I had specified that it should be $500 notes so that the package should be small and the amount quickly counted ... in the 26th round I let the fight end as it did,' he said.

In the 26th, Johnson was floored and out for the count and a famous photograph flashed around the world with him laying on his back with one arm over his face as if shading it from the sun. That only confused matters because it made it look as if Johnson could easily have got up. But to this day nobody really knows if 37-year-old Jack Johnson, homesick and broke, did end his reign the way he claimed.

Of course, there was no deal for him to get back home. But in a way it was the beginning of Johnson's reclamation. Willard was effusive in his praise for the way the black man had fought.

'I want to say for Johnson that I never fought a cleaner man,' he said. 'He has been the most criticised champion that ever lived, but I certainly found him a white man in the ring.'

An English paper editorialised: 'No single champion in the world's history of the ring ever faced his defeat and the prospect of ruin that accompanied it with either so much good grace or in such a sporting spirit. So, after all, we never knew the real Jack Johnson until today.'

In defeat, Johnson was at last becoming an acceptable human being. But, still, if he set foot on home soil it was straight to jail. He was given word from the British Foreign Office that he could return to London if he promised to behave himself. But soon, in a familiar pattern — like the Alex Maclean punch on the snout — he blackened the eye of a theatre manager in a squabble over money and fled to Spain, where he appeared in one movie and tried his hand, only once, as a bullfighter.

After the war he lived in Mexico where he boxed and wrestled and hung around with generals and mining magnates. But eventually, the homesickness became too much and on 20 July 1920, he surrendered to federal agents in San Diego. He faced the same judge and copped the same 366-day sentence in Leavenworth Prison in Kansas. However, the prison warden was so taken with Johnson that his life was made easy. He boxed exhibitions and was made prison fitness instructor. He began reading the Bible and after 10 months in prison, emerged as a preacher — his vocation for the rest of his life. After his release he received big welcomes in Chicago and New York with no racial problems. In 1924 he even addressed a klavern of the Ku Klux Klan on the subject of sportsmanship.

In 1925 Lucille divorced him. But nothing changed, for he soon married another white woman, divorcee Irene Pineau, who stayed with him until he died. He also kept on fighting small time — two fights in Havana in 1923 for a KO and a no-decision, and two in Mexico and two in America in 1926 for only one win.

He was 48 years old when he beat a promising heavyweight named Pat Lester — said to be a threat to Jack Dempsey — over 15 rounds in the bullring at Nogales in Mexico. Incredibly, he was still going in 1945, at the age of 67. On one night he fought two exhibitions in New York — including one against his perennial black adversary, Joe Jeanette.

He tried a myriad of ways to get rich but never quite made it. At one time or another he was a lecturer, beer salesman, sideshow performer, small-time boxing promoter, writer and commentator, and campaigner for President Franklin D. Roosevelt. He even produced a version of *Othello* with himself in the lead. He failed to make it in movies, but did land a role as a captured Ethiopian slave in a New York Hippodrome production of *Aida*.

His steadiest employment was at Herbert's Museum, a flea circus and sideshow house in New York. He would usually arrive at work in a beret and spats and flourishing a showman's cane. Predictably his love of racy cars — he may have held the world title for speeding tickets — was the end of him. On 10 June 1946, in Raleigh, North Carolina, he ran his car into a power pole while trying to avoid a truck, and died in hospital from internal injuries.

An extract from *Jack Johnson — In The Ring And Out*:

> *The intervals between rounds gave me a chance to scan the*
> *crowd and pick out unusual types of faces, or watch the changing*
> *expressions that flitted across the countenances of the spectators*
> *as they concentrated their attention on us. I even had*

opportunity to examine the outlying landscape and the immediate structure around the ring. As my gaze wandered out into the surrounding territory, I saw a colored man sitting on a fence watching the fight with open mouth and bulging eyes. My glance returned to him again and again. He was one of the very few colored people present, and he became a sort of landmark for me. I became more and more interested in him, and soon discovered that mentally, he was fighting harder than I was. Whenever I unlimbered a blow, he, too, shot one into the air landing it on an imaginary antagonist at about the same spot where I landed on Burns. When I swayed to avert a blow from Burns, the fighter on the fence also swayed in the same direction and at a similar angle. When I ducked he also ducked. But his battle came to an inglorious end when it was necessary for me to make an unusually low duck. He attempted to follow the movement and fell off the fence. This incident so amused me that I laughed heartily, and Burns and the spectators were at a loss to know what had so aroused my mirth. Jack London, the late story writer, and Mrs London were ring-side spectators and I think it was at this time that London got the idea of the golden smile with which he often described me later and which was so frequently mentioned in after years.